Dante Alighieri, 1265-1321
La divina commedia. The divine comedy

DANTE ALIGHIERI

THE DIVINE COMEDY

HELL · PURGATORY · PARADISE

Inferno · Purgatorio · Paradiso

DANTE ALIGHIERI

LA DIVINA COMMEDIA

I

INFERNO

Illustrated by

HARRY BENNETT

WASHINGTON SQUARE PRESS

NEW YORK

DANTE

THE DIVINE COMEDY

I

HELL

Translated into blank verse by

LOUIS BIANCOLLI

WASHINGTON SQUARE PRESS

NEW YORK

*The Italian text is reprinted from
the edition edited by Dr. E. Moore,
published by Oxford University Press
and reprinted with the publisher's permission.*

Library of Congress Catalog Number: 66-10813

*PUBLISHED SIMULTANEOUSLY IN THE UNITED STATES
AND CANADA BY WASHINGTON SQUARE PRESS, INC.*

Printed in the United States of America

The translation is dedicated
with my whole heart and soul to the lady
whose love and faith accompanied me
from the first line of Hell to
the last line of Heaven—
My wife Jeanne

ACKNOWLEDGEMENT

Grateful acknowledgement is hereby made to the Oxford University Press for the use of the Moore-Toynbee text of the original Italian. I chose this rather than the revised Vandelli text of the Dante Society of Italy because I found it a convenient and readable compromise in spelling, punctuation, and other small textual uncertainties, for non-Italian readers of our time. My other reason was personal and symbolic. English literature and scholarship are a passion with me, as are Dante and Italian literature. The Oxford text, a monumental labor of love, appealed to me as one more bridge between the two cultures. Readers who want to go still one more step in the study of Dante are urged to consult the Vandelli text as their next venture. The full archaic flavor is obtainable there, as authentic a flavor as a comparison of the early manuscripts—none, alas, in Dante's hand, and no two of them absolutely alike—can provide. For my purpose, as a promoter of Dante in the English-speaking world, the Oxford text seemed an inevitable choice. I leave it to better Dante scholars and textualists than myself to quarrel over discrepancies.

L. B.

THE DIVINE COMEDY

HELL

I

NEL mezzo del cammin di nostra vita
Mi ritrovai per una selva oscura,
Che la diritta via era smarrita.
Ah quanto a dir qual era è cosa dura
Questa selva selvaggia ed aspra e forte,
Che nel pensier rinnuova la paura!
Tanto è amara, che poco è più morte:
Ma per trattar del ben ch' i' vi trovai,
Dirò dell' altre cose ch' io v' ho scorte.
I' non so ben ridir com' io v' entrai;
Tant' era pien di sonno in su quel punto,
Che la verace via abbandonai.
Ma poi ch' io fui al piè d' un colle giunto,
Là dove terminava quella valle
Che m' avea di paura il cor compunto,
Guardai in alto, e vidi le sue spalle
Vestite già de' raggi del pianeta
Che mena dritto altrui per ogni calle.
Allor fu la paura un poco queta
Che nel lago del cor m' era durata
La notte ch' i' passai con tanta pieta.
E come quei che con lena affannata
Uscito fuor del pelago alla riva,
Si volge all' acqua perigliosa e guata;
Così l' animo mio cher ancor fuggiva,
Si volse indietro a rimirar lo passo,
Che non lasciò giammai persona viva.
Poi ch' ei posato un poco il corpo lasso,
Ripresi via per la piaggia diserta,
Sì che il piè fermo sempre era il più basso;

1

HALFWAY ALONG THE JOURNEY of our life,
Having strayed from the right path and lost it,
I awoke to find myself in a dark wood.
O how hard it is to tell what it was like,
That wild and mighty and unfriendly forest,
The very thought of which renews my fear!
So bitter was it that death could be no worse.
But, to reveal what benefit it brought me,
I shall tell of the other things I found.
How I came to be there, I can scarcely say,
I was so overwhelmed with sleep
When I began to wander off the road.
I soon came to the bottom of a hill
Where the valley that had impaled my heart
With terror came to an end.
I looked high up the hill and could see its back
Already clad in the rays of that star
Which guides other men along the proper way.
And then I felt a lessening of the terror
Which had lingered in the lake of my heart
That entire night, which was so cruelly long.
And just as a man, panting from exhaustion,
Emerges from the sea and feels the shore,
Then turns to glance back at the perilous deep,
So my mind, that had not yet stopped running,
Turned round to contemplate the vale again
That not one person had ever left alive.
My tired body having had some rest,
I resumed my way along that bare incline,
Keeping my lower foot at all times firmer.

Ed ecco, quasi al cominciar dell' erta,
Una lonza leggiera e presta molto,
Che di pel maculato era coperta.
E non mi si partia dinanzi al volto;
Anzi impediva tanto il mio cammino,
Ch' io fui per ritornar più volte volto.
Tempo era dal principio del mattino;
E il sol montava su con quelle stelle
Ch' eran con lui, quando l' amor divino
Mosse da prima quelle cose belle;
Sì che a bene sperar m' era cagione
Di quella fera alla gaietta pelle
L'ora del tempo, e la dolce stagione:
Ma non sì, che paura non mi desse
La vista che mi apparve d' un leone.
Questi parea che contra me venesse
Con la test' alta e con rabbiosa fame,
Sì che parea che l' aer ne temesse:
Ed una lupa, che di tutte brame
Sembiava carca nella sua magrezza,
E molte genti fe' già viver grame.
Questa mi porse tanto di gravezza
Con la paura che uscia di sua vista,
Ch' io perdei la speranza dell' altezza.
E quale è quei che volontieri acquista,
E giugne il tempo che perder lo face,
Che in tutt' i suoi pensier piange e s' attrista:
Tal mi fece la bestia senza pace,
Che venendomi incontro, a poco a poco
Mi ripingeva là, dove il Sol tace.
Mentre ch' io rovinava in basso loco,
Dinanzi agli occhi mi si fu offerto
Chi per lungo silenzio parea fioco.
Quand' io vidi costui nel gran diserto,
'Miserere di me,' gridai a lui,
'Qual che tu sii, od ombra od uomo certo.'
Risposemi: 'Non uomo, uomo già fui,
E li parenti miei furon Lombardi,
Mantovani per patria ambedui.

Suddenly, just where the ground began to rise,
I saw in front of me an agile beast
Whose body was all covered with a dappled fur.
Never moving out of sight, it stood there
And so completely blocked the way
That several times I started to go back.
The time was just about the start of day.
The sun was moving up with all those stars
That were with him when the Love of God
First set in motion all those lovely things.
Both the sweet season and the time of day
Gave me cause to hope that some good still would come
Of having met that beast with the spotted skin.
But that did not make me less terrified
When in a flash a lion sprang into view
Who seemed to be advancing towards me
With his head high and in such a famished rage
That even the air itself appeared to fear him;
And a she-wolf, too, who seemed to have loaded
Every known craving into her leanness
And blighted many lives already:
The terror emanating from her look
Laid on my spirit such a heavy gloom
That I gave up hope of climbing to the top.
As is he who happily amasses wealth,
Until the day comes that he loses it,
And then, each time he thinks, cries and grows sad,
Such was I when that unsatiated beast,
Who step by step was slowly drawing close,
Kept pushing me to where the sun is silent.
While I was hastening down the slope,
There suddenly appeared before my eyes
A man whose voice seemed weak from long disuse.
When I caught sight of him in that bleak place,
I cried out to him: "Have pity on me,
Whatever you are, living man or ghost!"
"No man am I," he said, "though at one time I was.
Both my parents came from Lombardy, and both
Were Mantuans as well.

Nacqui sub Iulio, ancorchè fosse tardi,
E vissi a Roma sotto il buono Augusto,
Al tempo degli Dei falsi e bugiardi.
Poeta fui, e cantai di quel giusto
Figliuol d' Anchise, che venne da Troia,
Poichè il superbo Ilion fu combusto.
Ma tu perchè ritorni a tanta noia?
Perchè non sali il dilettoso monte,
Ch' è principio e cagion di tutta gioia?'
'Or se' tu quel Virgilio, e quella fonte
Che spandi di parlar sì largo fiume?'
Risposi lui con vergognosa fronte.
'O degli altri poeti onore e lume,
Vagliami il lungo studio e il grande amore,
Che m' ha fatto cercar lo tuo volume.
Tu se' lo mio maestro e il mio autore:
Tu se' solo colui, da cui io tolsi
Lo bello stile che m' ha fatto onore.
Vedi la bestia, per cui io mi volsi:
Aiutami da lei, famoso saggio,
Ch' ella mi fa tremar le vene e i polsi.'
'A te convien tenere altro viaggio,'
Rispose, poi che lagrimar mi vide,
'Se vuoi campar d' esto loco selvaggio:
Chè questa bestia, per la qual tu gride,
Non lascia altrui passar per la sua via,
Ma tanto lo impedisce che l' uccide:
Ed ha natura sì malvagia e ria,
Che mai non empie la bramosa voglia,
E dopo il pasto ha più fame che pria.
Molti son gli animali a cui s' ammoglia,
E più saranno ancora, infin che il veltro
Verrà, che la farà morir con doglia.
Questi non ciberà terra nè peltro,
Ma sapienza e amore e virtute,
E sua nazion sarà tra Feltro e Feltro.
Di quell' umile Italia fia salute,
Per cui morì la vergine Cammilla,
Eurialo, e Turno, e Niso di ferute:

I was born while Caesar was alive, though late,
And I lived in Rome while good Augustus ruled
And in a day of false and lying gods.
I was a poet, and sang of that just son
Of Anchises who had come from Troy
When all proud Ilium went up in flames.
But why are you going back to such distress?
Why not climb the delightful mountain, which
Is the reason and beginning of all joy?"
"So you are that Virgil, and that fountain,
Which spreads so broad a river of discourse,"
I answered him with shamed and humble brow.
"O light and honor of all other poets,
May I now profit from the study and great love
I long applied to fathoming your book.
You are my author, and my teacher, too;
You are the only one from whom I took
That style of beauty which has won me praise.
Look there, at that beast who forced me to turn back;
Help me to escape her, O noted sage!
She makes my pulses throb, and all my veins."
"You must take a different direction now,
If you want to get out of this wild place,"
He answered, when he saw that I was crying.
"This animal who makes you scream with fear
Never lets anyone at all get past her.
She blocks his way and finally she slays him.
And she is so evil and malevolent,
She never satisfies her gluttonous wants,
But after a full meal is hungrier still.
Many are the animals with whom she mates,
And there shall be many more, until the day
A greyhound comes to bring her painful death
That nourishes itself on neither land nor wealth,
But feeds instead on wisdom, love, and virtue.
The place of its birth between two Feltros lies.
May he be the Saviour of humble Italy,
For which the maid Camilla gave her life, as did
The wounded Nisus, Turnus, Euryalus.

Questi la caccerà per ogni villa,
Fin che l' avrà rimessa nello inferno,
Là onde invidia prima dipartilla.
Ond' io per lo tuo me' penso e discerno,
Che tu mi segui, ed io sarò tua guida,
E trarrotti di qui per loco eterno,
Ove udirai le disperate strida
Di quegli antichi spiriti dolenti,
Che la seconda morte ciascun grida:
E poi vedrai color che son contenti
Nel fuoco, perchè speran di venire,
Quando che sia, alle beate genti:
Alle qua' poi se tu vorrai salire,
Anima fia a ciò di me più degna;
Con lei ti lascerò nel mio partire:
Chè quello imperador che lassù regna,
Perch' io fui ribellante alla sua legge,
Non vuol che in sua città per me si vegna.
In tutte parti impera, e quivi regge,
Quivi è la sua città e l' alto seggio:
O felice colui cui ivi elegge!'
Ed io a lui: 'Poeta, io ti richieggio
Per quello Dio che tu non conoscesti,
Acciocch' io fugga questo male e peggio
Che tu mi meni là dov' or dicesti,
Sì ch' io vegga la porta di san Pietro,
E color cui tu fai cotanto mesti.'
Allor si mosse, ed io li tenni retro.

The hound shall chase the wolf through every town,
Until at last he puts her back in Hell,
Where jealousy and hate first turned her loose.
For your own welfare, I believe, therefore,
That you should follow me, and I shall guide you
Out of this place into the timeless dwelling
Where you shall hear the cries of desperation
And see the tortured souls of ancient men
Who scream out loud for second death.
Others you will see there who are content
To live in fire, because they hope one day—
Come when it may—to join the blessed ranks.
If you wish to ascend to where those are,
A soul shall come far worthier than I
To whom I shall entrust you when I leave.
The truth is that the Emperor who rules up there,
Because I was a rebel to his law,
Will not admit me into his city.
Everywhere else he commands; there he is King.
That is his city, and that his high throne, too.
Happy the man he chooses to let come!"
And I said to him: "Poet, I implore you,
By that very God whom you did not know,
To help me flee this evil thing and worse,
By conducting me to the place you speak of,
That I may behold St. Peter's gate
And those whom you make out to be so sad."
Then he set off, and I went on behind.

II

LO giorno se n' andava, e l' aer bruno
Toglieva gli animai che sono in terra
Dalle fatiche loro; ed io sol uno
M' apparecchiava a sostener la guerra
Sì del cammino e sì della pietate,
Che ritrarrà la mente, che non erra.
O Muse, o alto ingegno, or m' aiutate:
O mente, che scrivesti ciò ch' io vidi,
Qui si parrà la tua nobilitate.
Io cominciai: 'Poeta che mi guidi,
Guarda la mia virtù, s' ella è possente,
Prima che all' alto passo tu mi fidi.
Tu dici che di Silvio lo parente,
Corruttibile ancora, ad immortale
Secolo andò, e fu sensibilmente.
Però se l' avversario d' ogni male
Cortese i fu, pensando l' alto effetto,
Che uscir dovea di lui, e il chi, e il quale,
Non pare indegno ad uomo d'intelletto:
Ch' ei fu dell' alma Roma e di suo impero
Nell' empireo ciel per padre eletto:
La quale e il quale (a voler dir lo vero)
Fu stabilito per lo loco santo,
U' siede il successor del maggior Piero.
Per questa andata, onde gli dai tu vanto,
Intese cose, che furon cagione
Di sua vittoria e del papale ammanto.
Andovvi poi lo Vas d' elezione,
Per recarne conforto a quella fede
Ch' è principio alla via di salvazione.

2

THE DAY WAS PARTING, and the dusky air
Was drawing from their labors all the living
Who are on earth; and of them only I
Was making preparations to combat
The trials of the journey and the pity,
Which memory, never erring, will evoke.
O Muses, and high skill, come to my help now;
O memory that inscribed what I beheld,
Here your nobility will be revealed.
I then began: "O poet who guide me,
See if my character be strong enough
Before you trust me to this steep descent.
You say Aeneas, Silvius' father,
Though still of tangible and wasting flesh,
Went down into the world that never dies.
But if the adversary of all wrong
Allowed him, mindful of the great effect
And what and who in time would issue from him,
To a man of reason this would seem deserved.
For heaven chose him to be founding father
Of glorious Rome and all her empire,
Which were designed to be the holy place
Where the successor of St. Peter sits.
On that journey, which you celebrated,
He learned the causes of his victory
And heard about the mantle of the Pope.
There later went the Vessel of Election
To render confirmation of that faith
That is the road that opens to salvation.
But who am I to go, and who consents?

Ma io perchè venirvi? o chi 'l concede?
Io non Enea, io non Paolo sono:
Me degno a ciò nè io nè altri 'l crede.
Perchè se del venire io m' abbandono,
Temo che la venuta non sia folle:
Se' savio, intendi me' ch' io non ragiono.'
E quale è quei che disvuol ciò che volle,
E per nuovi pensier cangia proposta,
Sì che dal cominciar tutto si tolle;
Tal mi fec' io in quella oscura costa:
Perchè pensando consumai la impresa,
Che fu nel cominciar cotanto tosta.
'Se io ho ben la tua parola intesa,'
Rispose del magnanimo quell' ombra,
'L' anima tua è da viltate offesa:
La qual molte fiate l' uomo ingombra,
Sì che d' onrata impresa lo rivolve,
Come falso veder bestia, quand' ombra.
Da questa tema acciocchè tu ti solve,
Dirotti perch' io venni, e quel che intesi
Nel primo punto che di te mi dolve.
Io era tra color che son sospesi,
E donna mi chiamò beata e bella,
Tal che di comandare io la richiesi.
Lucevan gli occhi suoi più che la stella:
E cominciommi a dir soave e piana
Con angelica voce in sua favella:
"O anima cortese Mantovana,
Di cui la fama ancor nel mondo dura,
E durerà quanto il moto lontana:
L' amico mio e non della ventura,
Nella diserta piaggia è impedito
Sì nel cammin, che volto è per paura:
E temo che non sia già sì smarrito,
Ch' io mi sia tardi al soccorso levata,
Per quel ch' io ho di lui nel Cielo udito.
Or muovi, e con la tua parola ornata,
E con ciò ch' è mestieri al suo campare,
L'aiuta sì, ch' io ne sia consolata.

I am not Aeneas; I am not St. Paul.
Neither I nor others deem me fit to go.
For that reason, though I utterly submit,
I fear that if I went it might be madness.
You understand me better than I speak."
A man no longer wanting what he wanted,
Who finds new reasons for his change of mind,
Until he abandons what he had begun—
Such a man was I on that dark mountain side.
For in my thoughts I had wholly given up
The adventure I had started with such haste.
"If I have comprehended well your words,"
Replied the shade of that great-hearted man,
"Your soul is stricken with that cowardice
Which so often holds a man back
From the performance of a splendid deed,
The way a shadow makes a beast see falsely.
In order to absolve you of this fear,
I shall tell you why I came and what I heard
In that first moment that I pitied you.
While I was with those souls who wait in Limbo,
A blessed lady summoned me, one so fair
That I implored her to commission me.
Her eyes were shining more than do the stars,
And with an angel's voice, soft and sweet,
In her own mother tongue she told me this:
'O courtly Mantuan spirit,
Whose fame has lasted until now on earth
And will endure as long as time itself,
A friend of mine—but not a friend of fortune, too—
Is at this moment impeded on the
Barren slope, and out of dread is turning back.
I fear that he has gone so far astray,
I may have risen to his help too late—
To judge by what I heard of him in heaven.
Start now, and, with your elevated words
And all that may be needed for his safety,
Help him, that he may be at peace.
I who send you on this mission am Beatrice,

Io son Beatrice, che ti faccio andare:
Vegno di loco, ove tornar disio:
Amor mi mosse, che mi fa parlare.
Quando sarò dinanzi al Signor mio,
Di te mi loderò sovente a lui."
Tacette allora, e poi comincia' io:
"O donna di virtù, sola per cui
L' umana spezie eccede ogni contento
Da quel ciel che ha minor li cerchi sui:
Tanto m' aggrada il tuo comandamento,
Che l' ubbidir, se già fosse, m' è tardi;
Più non t' è uopo aprirmi il tuo talento.
Ma dimmi la cagion che non ti guardi
Dello scender quaggiuso in questo centro
Dall' ampio loco ove tornar tu ardi."
"Da che tu vuoi saper cotanto addentro,
Dirotti brevemente," mi rispose,
"Perch' io non temo di venir qua entro.
Temer si dee di sole quelle cose
Ch' hanno potenza di fare altrui male:
Dell' altre no, che non son paurose.
Io son fatta da Dio, sua mercè, tale,
Che la vostra miseria non mi tange,
Nè fiamma d' esto incendio non m' assale.
Donna è gentil nel ciel, che si compiange
Di questo impedimento ov' io ti mando,
Sì che duro giudizio lassù frange.
Questa chiese Lucìa in suo dimando,
E disse: 'Or ha bisogno il tuo fedele
Di te, ed io a te lo raccomando.'
Lucìa, nimica di ciascun crudele,
Si mosse, e venne al loco dov' io era,
Che mi sedea con l' antica Rachele.
Disse: 'Beatrice, loda di Dio vera,
Chè non soccorri quei che t' amò tanto,
Che uscìo per te della volgare schiera?
Non odi tu la pieta del suo pianto?
Non vedi tu la morte che il combatte
Su la fiumana, ove il mar non ha vanto?'

And have come from where I long so much to be.
Love it was that moved me, and makes me speak.
When once again I stand before my Lord
I shall commend you to him many times.'
She then fell silent, and I thus began:
'O Lady of Virtue, through whom alone
The human race surpasses everything
Within the lesser orbits of the sky,
I am so pleased by your command that, to obey,
Were it already done, would seem too late.
You need reveal no more of your desire.
But tell me why you did not fear to come
Down to this region from that ample place,
Which you so ardently yearn to return to?'
And she replied: 'Because you wish to know
Of this, I shall explain in a few words
Why I am not afraid to be down here.
Those things alone are to be feared
That have the power of doing someone harm;
Other things, lacking that, need rouse no fear.
I am so fashioned by the grace of God
That I cannot be touched by your misery,
Nor can the flames of this great fire burn me.
There is a gracious Lady up in Heaven
Who pities so the plight to which I send you,
That she repealed the judgment made up there.
To carry out her wish she called St. Lucy
And said: "This faithful follower of yours
Now needs you; I commend him to your care."
St. Lucy, enemy of all the cruel,
Stepped forward and came over to the place
Where I was seated at the side of Rachel.
"Beatrice," she said, "O Praise of God, why
Have you not helped that man who loved you so
And left the sordid crowd on your account?
Do you not hear the pity of his plea?
Do you not see the death that battles him
On that river mightier than the sea?"
No one on earth ever acted faster,

Al mondo non fur mai persone ratte
A far lor pro, nè a fuggir lor danno,
Com' io, dopo cotai parole fatte,
Venni quaggiù dal mio beato scanno,
Fidandomi del tuo parlare onesto,
Che onora te e quei che udito l' hanno."
Poscia che m' ebbe ragionato questo,
Gli occhi lucenti lagrimando volse;
Perchè mi fece del venir più presto:
E venni a te così, com' ella volse;
Dinanzi a quella fiera ti levai
Che del bel monte il corto andar ti tolse.
Dunque che è? perchè, perchè ristai?
Perchè tanta viltà nel core allette?
Perchè ardire e franchezza non hai?
Poscia che tai tre donne benedette
Curan di te nella corte del cielo,
E il mio parlar tanto ben t' impromette?'
Quali i fioretti dal notturno gelo
Chinati e chiusi, poi che il Sol gl' imbianca,
Si drizzan tutti aperti in loro stelo;
Tal mi fec' io di mia virtute stanca:
E tanto buono ardire al cor mi corse,
Ch' io cominciai come persona franca:
'O pietosa colei che mi soccorse,
E tu cortese, che ubbidisti tosto
Alle vere parole che ti porse!
Tu m' hai con desiderio il cor disposto
Sì al venir, con le parole tue,
Ch' io son tornato nel primo proposto.
Or va, che un sol volere è d' ambedue:
Tu duca, tu signore, e tu maestro.'
Così gli dissi; e poichè mosso fue,
Entrai per lo cammino alto e silvestro.

For his own gain or to escape great harm,
Than I did, when these words were spoken,
In coming down here from my blessed home
With confidence in your honesty of speech,
Which honors you and everyone who hears it.'
After she had said these things to me,
She turned away her eyes, that shone with tears,
A sight which made me come here all the sooner.
And so I came to you, as she desired;
I snatched you from in front of the wild beast
That blocked the short way to the lovely hill.
Why did you stop? Why? Tell me what it was.
How did this craven fear possess your heart?
Why have you no audacity and daring,
With three such blessed ladies
Anxious for you in the courts of Heaven,
And with my words that promise you such good?"
Like little flowers that from the cold of night
Are bowed and closed, then, brightened by the sun,
Straighten and unfold upon their stems,
So was I with my failing strength of heart.
For such good courage poured into my heart
That I began to feel like one set free:
"O she who out of pity has aided me,
And you who with such gallantry and speed
Obeyed the true words she addressed to you,
You have roused in my heart, with what you say,
Such a great eagerness to go ahead
That I have come back to my first intention.
Let us go; we two have but a single will:
You the guide, you the lord, and you the teacher."
I said this to him and, seeing that he moved,
I entered on the steep and woody way.

III

PER ME SI VA NELLA CITTA' DOLENTE,
Per me si va nell' eterno dolore,
Per me si va tra la perduta gente.
Giustizia mosse il mio alto fattore;
Fecemi la divina potestate,
La somma sapienza e il primo amore.
Dinanzi a me non fur cose create
Se non eterne, ed io eterno duro:
Lasciate ogni speranza voi ch' entrate!
Queste parole di colore oscuro
Vid' io scritte al sommo d' una porta:
Perch' io: 'Maestro, il senso lor m' è duro.'
Ed egli a me, come persona accorta:
'Qui si convien lasciare ogni sospetto;
Ogni viltà convien che qui sia morta.
Noi siam venuti al loco ov' io t' ho detto,
Che tu vedrai le genti dolorose,
Ch' hanno perduto il ben dell'intelletto.'
E poichè la sua mano alla mia pose,
Con lieto volto, ond' io mi confortai,
Mi mise dentro alle segrete cose.
Quivi sospiri, pianti ed alti guai
Risonavan per l' aer senza stelle,
Perch' io al cominciar ne lagrimai.
Diverse lingue, orribili favelle,
Parole di dolore, accenti d' ira,
Voci alte e fioche, e suon di man con elle,
Facevano un tumulto, il qual s' aggira
Sempre in quell' aria senza tempo tinta,
Come la rena quando a turbo spira.

3

THROUGH ME YOU PASS INTO THE WOEFUL CITY:
THROUGH ME YOU PASS INTO ETERNAL PAIN:
THROUGH ME YOU PASS AMONG A PEOPLE LOST.
JUSTICE IT WAS THAT MOVED MY LOFTY MAKER;
DIVINE POWER BROUGHT ME INTO BEING,
THE FIRST LOVE AND THE HIGHEST WISDOM.
BEFORE ME ONLY SUCH THINGS WERE CREATED
THAT WERE ETERNAL, AND I ENDURE FOREVER.
LEAVE ALL HOPE BEHIND, YOU WHO ENTER HERE.
These words, of a dark and somber color,
I saw inscribed above a door; whereupon
I said: "Master, I find their meaning hard."
And he to me, like a discerning man:
"Here all suspicion must be left behind.
Here every kind of cowardice must die.
We have come to the place of which I spoke,
Where you shall see the people doomed to pain,
Who forfeited the good of intellect."
And, having placed his hand on mine,
With a happy look which gave me strength, he then
Admitted me into the secret things.
Here sighs, complaints, and piercing shrieks
Resounded through the air devoid of stars
With such great effect that at first I wept.
Diverse languages and hideous discourse,
Anguished words and accents of great wrath,
Voices high and shrill, and a sound of hands
Together made a tumult which swirled round
And round in that forever blackened air,
Like sand that whirls in spirals in the wind.

LEAVE ALL HOPE BEHIND, YOU WHO ENTER HERE.

Ed io, ch' avea d' orror la testa cinta,
Dissi: 'Maestro, che è quel ch' i' odo?
E che gent' è, che par nel duol sì vinta?'
Ed egli a me: 'Questo misero modo
Tengon l' anime triste di coloro
Che visser senza infamia e senza lodo.
Mischiate sono a quel cattivo coro
Degli angeli che non furon ribelli
Nè fur fedeli a Dio, ma per sè foro.
Cacciarli i Ciel per non esser men belli:
Nè lo profondo inferno gli riceve,
Chè alcuna gloria i rei avrebber d' elli.'
Ed io: 'Maestro, che è tanto greve
A lor, che lamentar gli fa sì forte?'
Rispose: 'Dicerolti molto breve.
Questi non hanno speranza di morte,
E la lor cieca vita è tanto bassa,
Che invidiosi son d' ogni altra sorte.
Fama di loro il mondo esser non lassa,
Misericordia e giustizia gli sdegna:
Non ragioniam di lor, ma guarda e passa.'
Ed io, che riguardai, vidi una insegna,
Che girando correva tanto ratta
Che d' ogni posa mi pareva indegna:
E dietro le venia sì lunga tratta
Di gente, ch' i' non avrei mai creduto,
Che morte tanta n' avesse disfatta.
Poscia ch' io v' ebbi alcun riconosciuto,
Vidi e conobbi l' ombra di colui
Che fece per viltà lo gran rifiuto.
Incontanente intesi, e certo fui,
Che quest' era la setta dei cattivi
A Dio spiacenti ed ai nemici sui.
Questi sciaurati, che mai non fur vivi,
Erano ignudi e stimolati molto
Da mosconi e da vespe ch' erano ivi.
Elle rigavan lor di sangue il volto,
Che, mischiato di lagrime, ai lor piedi,
Da fastidiosi vermi era ricolto.

And I, my head clasped round in horror,
Cried out: "Master, what are these things I hear?
Who are these people who seem crushed by woe?"
And he to me: "This miserable state
Is reserved for the dismal souls of those
Who lived their lives with neither praise nor blame.
They have been mingled with that wicked choir
Of heavenly angels who did not rebel,
Nor were they pledged to God, but to themselves.
Heaven banished them before they marred it,
And even deepest Hell will not accept them
For fear the damned might glory over them."
And I asked: "Master, what bears down so hard
On them that they cry out with such violence?"
And he said: "I shall tell you very briefly.
These people have all lost their hope of death,
And their blind life is so contemptible
That they all envy every other fate.
The world denies them any kind of fame;
Justice and compassion both disdain them.
Let us not talk of them; look, and move on."
And as I gazed and gazed, I saw a banner
Whirling about and running at such speed
That it seemed scornful of the slighest pause.
Behind it followed such a throng of people
That I would never have believed that Death
Could take so great a toll of lives.
When I had recognized a few among them,
I saw and recognized the soul of him
Who made the great refusal out of fear.
I understood at once, and was convinced,
That this was that brand of mean and cringing men
Distasteful to their enemies and God.
These paltry souls that never were alive
Went naked and were bitten constantly
By wasps and large flies that collected there
And lined their faces with great streaks of blood,
Which, mingled with their tears, was then imbibed
By nauseating vermin at their feet.

E poi che a riguardare oltre mi diedi,
Vidi gente alla riva d' un gran fiume:
Perch' io dissi: 'Maestro, or mi concedi,
Ch' io sappia quali sono, e qual costume
Le fa di trapassar parer sì pronte,
Com' io discerno per lo fioco lume.'
Ed egli a me: 'Le cose ti fien conte,
Quando noi fermerem li nostri passi
Sulla trista riviera d' Acheronte.'
Allor con gli occhi vergognosi e bassi,
Temendo no 'l mio dir gli fusse grave,
Infino al fiume di parlar mi trassi.
Ed ecco verso noi venir per nave
Un vecchio bianco per antico pelo,
Gridando: 'Guai a voi anime prave:
Non isperate mai veder lo cielo!
I' vegno per menarvi all' altra riva,
Nelle tenebre eterne, in caldo e in gelo.
E tu che se' costì, anima viva,
Partiti da cotesti che son morti.'
Ma poi ch' ei vide ch' io non mi partiva,
Disse: 'Per altra via, per altri porti
Verrai a piaggia, non qui, per passare:
Più lieve legno convien che ti porti.'
E il duca a lui: 'Caron non ti crucciare:
Vuolsi così colà, dove si puote
Ciò che si vuole, e più non dimandare.'
Quinci fur quete le lanose gote
Al nocchier della livida palude,
Che intorno agli occhi avea di fiamme rote.
Ma quell' anime ch' eran lasse e nude,
Cangiar colore e dibattero i denti,
Ratto che inteser le parole crude.
Bestemmiavano Iddio e lor parenti,
L' umana specie, il luogo, il tempo e il seme
Di lor semenza e di lor nascimenti.
Poi si ritrasser tutte quante insieme,
Forte piangendo, alla riva malvagia
Che attende ciascun uom che Dio non teme.

And then, as I began to look beyond,
I saw people on the bank of a large stream,
And I said: "Master, would you let me know
Who these people are and what is their custom
That makes them seem—as far as I can see
In this dim light—so eager to cross over?"
And he to me: "These things will be told you
When you pause on the shore of Acheron."
Then, lowering my eyes and full of shame,
For fear my talking had molested him,
I held my tongue until we reached the stream.
And, suddenly, there came towards us by boat
An old man white with venerable hair,
Who started shouting: "Woe to you, base spirits!
Abandon hope of ever seeing Heaven!
I come to take you to the other side,
Into eternal darkness, and the ice and fire.
And you, who come here a man of flesh and blood,
Depart from these others: they are dead."
But when he saw I made no move to go,
He said: "By other routes and means of passage
You may cross to the other bank: not here.
You need a lighter boat to ferry you."
And my guide said: "Charon,
This was willed up there where all is willed
And done, and nothing more is asked."
With that, the woolly cheeks were motionless
Of that old steersman of the livid bog,
Whose eyes were circled round by rims of flame.
But those naked and exhausted spirits
Changed color, and their teeth began to chatter
As soon as they had heard those cruel words.
They blasphemed God, and cursed their parents,
The human race, the place, the time, the seed
Of their inheritance and of their birth.
Weeping aloud, they gathered in a crowd
And pressed forward to the pernicious shore
Which waits for every man who fears not God.
With eyes aglow like coals, the demon Charon

Caron dimonio, con occhi di bragia,
Loro accennando, tutte le raccoglie;
Batte col remo qualunque s' adagia.
Come d'autunno si levan le foglie
L' una appresso dell' altra, infin che il ramo
Vede alla terra tutte le sue spoglie,
Similemente il mal seme d' Adamo:
Gittansi di quel lito ad una ad una,
Per cenni, come augel per suo richiamo.
Così sen vanno su per l' onda bruna,
Ed avanti che sian di là discese,
Anche di qua nuova schiera s' aduna.
'Figliuol mio,' disse il Maestro cortese,
'Quelli che muoion nell' ira di Dio
Tutti convegnon qui d' ogni paese:
E pronti sono a trapassar lo rio,
Chè la divina giustizia gli sprona
Sì che la tema si volge in disio.
Quinci non passa mai anima buona;
E però se Caron di te si lagna,
Ben puoi saper omai che il suo dir suona.'
Finito questo, la buia campagna
Tremò sì forte, che dello spavento
La mente di sudore ancor mi bagna.
La terra lagrimosa diede vento,
Che balenò una luce vermiglia,
La qual mi vinse ciascun sentimento:
E caddi, come l' uom cui sonno piglia.

Motioned to them, gathered them together,
And with his oar beat those who fell behind.
As in the autumn the leaves unloose themselves
One after another, until the branch
Sees all its finery upon the ground,
So that bad seed of Adam
Flung headlong from that shore at given signs,
The way the birds do when they hear their call.
And so they go upon the darkened waves,
And long before they step down on that side,
A new crowd has collected over here.
My courteous teacher turned to me and said:
"My son, those dying in the wrath of God
Are brought together here from every land.
And they are eager to embark upon the stream,
Because the justice of the Lord so spurs them
That their anxiety becomes desire.
No good soul ever makes the crossing here.
And so, if Charon speaks complainingly of you,
You now know why he does, and what he means."
When he had finished speaking, the dark ground
Shook so violently that even now
The memory of my fright bathes me in sweat.
The wailing earth erupted in a wind
Flashing vermilion lightning, which won
Complete dominion over all my senses.
And I fell like a man overcome by sleep.

IV

RUPPEMI l' alto sonno nella testa
Un greve tuono, sì ch' io mi riscossi,
Come persona che per forza è desta:
E l' occhio riposato intorno mossi,
Dritto levato, e fiso riguardai
Per conoscer lo loco dov' io fossi.
Vero è che in su la proda mi trovai
Della valle d' abisso dolorosa,
Che tuono accoglie d' infiniti guai.
Oscura, profond' era e nebulosa,
Tanto che, per ficcar lo viso al fondo,
Io non vi discerneva alcuna cosa.
'Or discendiam quaggiù nel cieco mondo,'
Cominciò il poeta tutto smorto:
'Io sarò primo, e tu sarai secondo.'
Ed io, che del color mi fui accorto,
Dissi: 'Come verrò, se tu paventi,
Che suoli al mio dubbiare esser conforto?'
Ed egli a me: 'L' angoscia delle genti
Che son quaggiù, nel viso mi dipigne
Quella pietà che tu per tema senti.
Andiam, chè la via lunga ne sospigne.'
Così si mise, e così me fe' entrare
Nel primo cerchio che l' abisso cigne.
Quivi, secondo che per ascoltare,
Non avea pianto, ma' che di sospiri,
Che l' aura eterna facevan tremare:
Ciò avvenia di duol senza martiri
Ch' avean le turbe, ch' eran molte e grandi,
D' infanti e di femmine e di viri.

4

A LOUD BURST OF THUNDER shattered the sleep
Lodged deep within my head, so that I jumped
Like one who is awakened forcibly;
And, having risen to my feet, I moved
My rested eyes about and looked intently
To learn what place it was that I was in.
The truth is that I found myself on the rim
Of the dolorous valley of the abyss,
Which reaps a thunder of eternal cries.
So dark and clouded was it, and so deep,
That even when I stared into its depths
I was unable to discern a thing.
"Let us go down now into the blind world,"
Began the poet, looking pale as death;
"I shall go first, and you will follow me."
And I , who had perceived his change of color,
Said: "How can I come if you who should
Relieve me of my fear are yourself afraid?"
And he to me: "The anguish of these souls
That dwell down here inscribes upon my face
The pity for them that you take for fear.
Let us proceed; the way is long and urgent."
Thus he went and thus he made me enter
The first ring that encircles the abyss.
There, so far as anyone could hear,
There was no grieving, other than of sighs
That sent a shudder through the timeless air
And came from the sadness without suffering
Of these large and numerous multitudes
Of men, of women, and of children.

Lo buon Maestro a me: 'Tu non dimandi
Che spiriti son questi che tu vedi?
Or vo' che sappi, innanzi che più andi,
Ch' ei non peccaro: e s' elli hanno mercedi,
Non basta, perchè non ebber battesmo,
Ch' è porta della fede che tu credi:
E se furon dinanzi al Cristianesmo,
Non adorar debitamente Dio:
E di questi cotai son io medesmo.
Per tai difetti, non per altro rio,
Semo perduti, e sol di tanto offesi,
Che senza speme vivemo in disio.'
Gran duol mi prese al cor quando lo intesi,
Perocchè gente di molto valore
Conobbi, che in quel limbo eran sospesi.
'Dimmi, Maestro mio, dimmi, Signore,'
Comincia' io, per voler esser certo
Di quella fede che vince ogni errore:
'Uscicci mai alcuno, o per suo merto,
O per altrui, che poi fosse beato?'
E quei, che intese il mio parlar coperto,
Rispose: 'Io era nuovo in questo stato,
Quando ci vidi venire un possente
Con segno di vittoria coronato.
Trasseci l' ombra del primo parente,
D' Abel suo figlio, e quella di Noè,
Di Moisè legista e ubbidiente;
Abraam patriarca, e David re,
Israel con lo padre, e co' suoi nati,
E con Rachele, per cui tanto fe',
Ed altri molti; e fecegli beati:
E vo' che sappi che, dinanzi ad essi,
Spiriti umani non eran salvati.'
Non lasciavam l' andar perch' ei dicessi,
Ma passavam la selva tuttavia,
La selva dico di spiriti spessi.
Non era lunga ancor la nostra via
Di qua dal sonno, quand' io vidi un foco
Ch' emisperio di tenebre vincia.

My good teacher said to me: "Do you not ask
Who all these spirits are that you behold?
Know, then, before you take another step:
None ever sinned, yet their virtue was not
Enough, because they never were baptized—
Which is the only gateway to your faith.
And, since they came before Christianity,
They did not properly believe in God,
And of these spirits I myself am one.
For such defects, and for no other fault,
We are lost souls, but only so far grieved
That we live with desire, though without hope."
Great sorrow filled my heart when I heard that,
Because I knew so many people of high worth
Condemned to a suspended state in Limbo.
"Tell me, my teacher and my master,"
I began, desiring reassurance
Of that faith which vanquishes all error,
"Has anyone left here by his own worth,
Or someone else's, and then acquired grace?"
And he who knew what I was thinking of
Replied: "I had but newly reached this state
When I saw coming towards us a Great Man
Whose head was crowned with the victory sign.
From us He took the shade of our first sire
And of his son Abel, and the shade of Noah,
And Moses the lawmaker who obeyed,
Abraham the patriarch, and King David;
Israel, his father and his children,
And Rachel, too, for whom he strove so hard,
And many more, and all of them He blessed.
You understand, that never once before
Had any human spirit been redeemed."
We never halted while he went on talking,
But passed along the margin of the wood
Which, as I said before, was thick with souls.
The way was not yet long from where I slept
To where we were, when I beheld a flame
That overhung a hemisphere of dark.

Di lungi v' eravamo ancora un poco,
Ma non sì ch' io non discernessi in parte
Che onrevol gente possedea quel loco.
'O tu che onori e scienza ed arte,
Questi chi son, ch' hanno cotanta onranza,
Che dal modo degli altri li diparte?'
E quegli a me: 'L' onrata nominanza,
Che di lor suona su nella tua vita,
Grazia acquista nel ciel che sì gli avanza.'
Intanto voce fu per me udita:
'Onorate l' altissimo poeta;
L' ombra sua torna, ch' era dipartita.'
Poichè la voce fu restata e queta,
Vidi quattro grand' ombre a noi venire;
Sembianza avevan nè trista nè lieta.
Lo buon Maestro cominciò a dire:
'Mira colui con quella spada in mano,
Che vien dinanzi a' tre sì come sire.
Quegli è Omero poeta sovrano,
L'altro è Orazio satiro che viene,
Ovidio è il terzo, e l' ultimo Lucano.
Perocchè ciascun meco si conviene
Nel nome che sonò la voce sola,
Fannomi onore, e di ciò fanno bene.'
Così vidi adunar la bella scuola
Di quei signor dell' altissimo canto,
Che sopra gli altri com' aquila vola.
Da ch' ebber ragionato insieme alquanto,
Volsersi a me con salutevol cenno:
E 'l mio Maestro sorrise di tanto:
E più d' onore ancora assai mi fenno,
Ch' esser mi fecer della loro schiera,
Sì ch' io fui sesto tra cotanto senno.
Così n' andammo infino alla lumiera,
Parlando cose che il tacere è bello,
Sì com' era il parlar colà dov' era.
Venimmo al piè d' un nobile castello,
Sette volte cerchiato d' alte mura,
Difeso intorno d' un bel fiumicello.

Although we were some distance from it yet,
I still could recognize to some degree
The glorious people occupying it.
"O you who honor every art and science,
Who are these souls that possess such worth
That it distinguishes them from the rest?"
And he to me: "The celebrated name
Which echoes their renown up in your world
Finds grace in Heaven and advances them."
Meanwhile, I heard a voice declare:
"All honor to our poet most sublime!
His shade, which had gone from us, has returned."
When the voice fell silent,
I saw four large shadows coming towards us,
Who outwardly were neither sad nor joyous.
The good master then began to speak:
"Behold the man who, with a sword in hand,
Advances like a lord before those three.
That is the sovereign poet Homer;
Horace, the writer of satires, comes next;
Ovid comes third; and last of all is Lucan.
Since each shares the name of poet by which
That solitary voice addressed me,
They do me honor, and thereby do good."
I now saw the splendid school assemble
Of those great masters of exalted song
Who soar like eagles over all the rest.
When they had talked together for a while,
They turned to me and gave a sign of greeting,
Which made my master smile to see.
And they paid me a greater tribute still
By taking me into their company,
Where I was sixth in order of importance.
And so, as we proceeded towards the light,
We spoke of things now well to leave unsaid
As it was well to say them where I was.
We now came to the foot of a noble castle
That seven times was circled by high walls
And guarded by a lovely stream around.

Questo passammo come terra dura:
Per sette porte intrai con questi savi;
Giugnemmo in prato di fresca verdura.
Genti v' eran con occhi tardi e gravi,
Di grande autorità ne' lor sembianti:
Parlavan rado, con voci soavi.
Traemmoci così dall' un de' canti
In loco aperto, luminoso ed alto,
Sì che veder si potean tutti quanti.
Colà diritto sopra il verde smalto
Mi fur mostrati gli spiriti magni,
Che del vederli in me stesso n' esalto.
Io vidi Elettra con molti compagni,
Tra' quai conobbi Ettore ed Enea,
Cesare armato con gli occhi grifagni.
Vidi Cammilla e la Pentesilea
Dall' altra parte, e vidi il re Latino,
Che con Lavinia sua figlia sedea.
Vidi quel Bruto che cacciò Tarquino,
Lucrezia, Julia, Marzia e Corniglia,
E solo in parte vidi il Saladino.
Poi che innalzai un poco più le ciglia,
Vidi il Maestro di color che sanno,
Seder tra filosofica famiglia.
Tutto lo miran, tutti onor gli fanno.
Quivi vid' io Socrate e Platone,
Che innanzi agli altri più presso gli stanno.
Democrito, che il mondo a caso pone,
Diogenes, Anassagora e Tale,
Empedocles, Eraclito e Zenone:
E vidi il buono accoglitor del quale,
Dioscoride dico: e vidi Orfeo,
Tullio e Lino e Seneca morale:
Euclide geometra e Tolommeo,
Ippocrate, Avicenna e Galieno,
Averrois, che il gran comento feo.
Io non posso ritrar di tutti appieno;
Perocchè sì mi caccia il lungo tema,
Che molte volte al fatto il dir vien meno.

We crossed the stream as if it were hard ground.
With these wise men I entered seven doors
And came upon a fresh and verdant field.
People with slow and thoughtful eyes were there,
Who looked like men of great authority.
They rarely spoke, and then with mellow voices.
We then drew off together to one side
Of a place that was so open, luminous,
And high, that everybody could be seen.
And there in front upon the enameled green
The mighty spirits all came into view,
Whom I still pride myself on having seen.
I saw Electra with a group in which
I recognized Hector, and Aeneas,
And armed Caesar with the hawklike eyes.
Elsewhere I saw Penthesilea and
Camilla, and I saw the Latian king,
Who sat beside Lavinia his daughter.
I saw that Brutus who drove out Tarquin,
Lucretia, Julia, Marcia, and Cornelia,
And in one corner, alone, the Saladin.
Then, when I raised my eyes a little more,
I saw the master of all those who know,
Seated with a family of philosophers.
All fixed their eyes on him and did him honor.
And there I saw Socrates and Plato,
Standing closer to him than the others;
Democritus, who traced the world to chance,
Diogenes, Anaxagoras, Thales,
Empedocles, Zeno, Heraclitus;
The good collector of the qualities,
Dioscorides, I saw, and Orpheus,
Tully, and Linus, and moral Seneca;
Euclid the geometer and Ptolemy,
Hippocrates, Galen, Avicenna,
And Averroes of the Great Commentary.
I cannot give a more detailed account,
Because the long theme presses me so hard
That many times my words fall short of need.

La sesta compagnia in due si scema:
Per altra via mi mena il savio duca,
Fuor della queta nell' aura che trema;
E vengo in parte ove non è che luca.

The group of six was now reduced to two.
My good guide led me by another path
Out of the quiet to the trembling air;
And I came to a place where nothing shines.

V

COSI' discesi del cerchio primaio
Giù nel secondo, che men loco cinghia,
E tanto più dolor, che pugne a guaio.
Stavvi Minos orribilmente e ringhia:
Esamina le colpe nell' entrata,
Giudica e manda secondo che avvinghia.
Dico, che quando l' anima mal nata
Li vien dinanzi, tutta si confessa;
E quel conoscitor delle peccata
Vede qual loco d' inferno è da essa:
Cignesi colla coda tante volte
Quantunque gradi vuol che giù sia messa.
Sempre dinanzi a lui ne stanno molte:
Vanno a vicenda ciascuna al giudizio;
Dicono e odono, e poi son giù volte.
'O tu, che vieni al doloroso ospizio.'
Disse Minos a me, quando mi vide,
Lasciando l' atto di cotanto ufizio,
'Guarda com' entri, e di cui tu ti fide:
Non t' inganni l' ampiezza dell' entrare!'
E il duca mio a lui: Perchè pur gride?
Non impedir lo suo fatale andare:
Vuolsi così colà, dove si puote
Ciò che si vuole, e più non dimandare.
Ora incomincian le dolenti note
A farmisi sentire: or son venuto
Là dove molto pianto mi percote.
Io venni in loco d' ogni luce muto,
Che mugghia come fa mar per tempesta,
Se da contrari venti è combattuto.

5

AND SO, FROM THE FIRST CIRCLE, I went down
Into the second, which contains less space
But so much more of pain that stings and shrieks.
There snarling Minos, horrible to see,
Examines every guilt upon admission,
Makes judgments, and commits as he unwinds.
I mean that when a soul of evil birth
Appears before him, it confesses all,
And that authority on sins decides
Which place in Hell is set aside for it.
He winds his tail about him as many times
As the degrees he wants it to descend.
Many stand before him at all times,
Going to their judgment, each in his turn.
They speak and hear, and then are swept below.
"O you who come to this hostel of pain,"
Said Minos to me when he saw me, pausing
In the performance of so large a task,
"Watch how you enter here and whom you trust,
And be not fooled by these spacious portals."
And my guide said to him: "Must you shout, too?
Stand not in this man's destined way.
Thus was it willed up there, where what is willed
Can be fulfilled; beyond that ask no more."
Now I began to hear the doleful notes.
I had at last come to the place
Where a great lamentation beat against me.
I had come to a place where light was mute,
A place that bellows like a stormy sea
When it is battled by contrary winds.

La bufera infernal, che mai non resta,
Mena gli spirti con la sua rapina,
Voltando e percotendo li molesta.
Quando giungon davanti alla ruina,
Quivi le strida, il compianto e il lamento,
Bestemmian quivi la virtù divina.
Intesi che a così fatto tormento
Enno dannati i peccator carnali,
Che la ragion sommettono al talento.
E come gli stornei ne portan l' ali
Nel freddo tempo, a schiera larga e piena,
Così quel fiato gli spiriti mali.
Di qua, di là, di giù, di su gli mena:
Nulla speranza gli conforta mai,
Non che di posa, ma di minor pena.
E come i gru van cantando lor lai,
Facendo in aer di sè lunga riga;
Così vid' io venir traendo guai
Ombre portate dalla detta briga:
Perch' io dissi: 'Maestro, chi son quelle
Genti che l' aura nera sì gastiga?'
'La prima di color, di cui novelle
Tu vuoi saper,' mi disse quegli allotta,
'Fu imperatrice di molte favelle.
A vizio di lussuria fu sì rotta,
Che libito fe' licito in sua legge,
Per torre il biasmo in che era condotta.
Ell' è Semiramis, di cui si legge
Che succedette a Nino, e fu sua sposa:
Tenne la terra che il Soldan corregge.
L' altra è colei che s' ancise amorosa,
E ruppe fede al cener di Sicheo;
Poi è Cleopatras lussuriosa.
Elena vedi, per cui tanto reo
Tempo si volse, e vedi il grande Achille,
Che con amore al fine combatteo.
Vedi Paris, Tristano'; e più di mille
Ombre mostrommi e nominommi a dito,
Che amor di nostra vita dipartille.

This storm of Hell which never is at rest
Drives forward all the spirits in its fury,
Beating, overturning, molesting them.
No sooner are they swept in that abyss
Of screams and moans and lamentations,
Than they begin to curse the power of God.
I learned that to this torment were condemned
The malefactors of the flesh
Who subjugate their reason to desire.
Just as the starlings are carried by their wings
In full and spacious flock when it is cold,
So are those evil souls by that great breath.
Now here, now there, now down, now up it leads them,
Not once consoled by any hope at all,
Not of relief, but only of less pain.
And, like the cranes that, singing their refrains,
Make of themselves a long stripe in the sky,
I saw coming, dragging their laments,
The shadows borne by that same turbulence.
Whereupon I said: "Master, who are
Those people whom the black winds buffet so?"
And he replied to me: "The first of those
Of whom you wish to have some knowledge,
Was empress over many languages.
The vice of lust had so corrupted her,
She legalized all looseness by decree,
In order to absolve herself of blame.
She is Semiramis, of whom one reads
That she succeeded Ninus and was his wife.
Hers was the land the Sultan rules today.
The other one is she who killed herself for love
And broke faith with the ashes of Sichaeus.
Another is licentious Cleopatra.
See Helen, on whose account long years
Of wretchedness unrolled, and see the great
Achilles, who fought up to the end for love;
See Paris, Tristan." Over a thousand souls
He showed me, pointing with his finger,
Souls that forfeited their lives because of love.

Poscia ch' io ebbi il mio dottore udito
Nomar le donne antiche e i cavalieri,
Pietà mi giunse, e fui quasi smarrito.
Io cominciai: 'Poeta, volentieri
Parlerei a que' due che insieme vanno,
E paion sì al vento esser leggieri.'
Ed egli a me: 'Vedrai, quando saranno
Più presso a noi; e tu allor li prega
Per quell' amor che i mena; ed ei verranno.'
Sì tosto come il vento a noi li piega,
Mossi la voce: 'O anime affannate,
Venite a noi parlar, s' altri nol niega.'
Quali colombe dal disio chiamate,
Con l' ali alzate e ferme, al dolce nido
Vegnon per l' aer dal voler portate:
Cotali uscir della schiera ov' è Dido,
A noi venendo per l' aer maligno,
Sì forte fu l' affettuoso grido.
'O animal grazioso e benigno,
Che visitando vai per l' aer perso
Noi che tignemmo il mondo di sanguigno:
Se fosse amico il re dell' universo,
Noi pregheremmo lui della tua pace,
Poichè hai pietà del nostro mal perverso.
Di quel che udire e che parlar vi piace
Noi udiremo e parleremo a vui,
Mentrechè il vento, come fa, ci tace.
Siede la terra dove nata fui,
Sulla marina dove il Po discende
Per aver pace co' seguaci sui.
Amor, che al cor gentil ratto s' apprende,
Prese costui della bella persona
Che mi fu tolta, e il modo ancor m' offende.
Amor, che a nullo amato amar perdona,
Mi prese del costui piacer sì forte,
Che, come vedi, ancor non mi abbandona.
Amor condusse noi ad una morte:
Caino attende chi vita ci spense.'
Queste parole da lor ci fur porte.

No sooner had I heard my teacher name
Those cavaliers and ladies of old times,
Than pity seized me, and I was nearly lost.
Then I began: "Poet, I would gladly
Converse with those two who together go
And seem to be so weightless to the wind."
And he to me: "When they come closer to us,
Entreat them in the name of the love
That moves them, and they will come."
The moment the wind had swept them towards us,
I raised my voice: "O wretched, wretched souls,
If it is not forbidden, come speak to us."
As fly the doves, when beckoned by desire,
To their sweet nest on firm and upraised wings,
Carried by their longing through the air,
So these two left the group where Dido was
And through the evil air came towards us,
So loud and full of feeling was my cry.
"O generous and gracious living man,
Who through this black air
Comes visiting us who stained the world with blood,
If the King of the universe were our friend,
We would be praying to him for your peace,
Because you pity our perverse fate.
Whatever you may wish to say and hear
We shall hear and say to you, so long as
The wind keeps still, as it is doing now.
The land where I was born lies on the coast
Where the river Po, descending to the sea,
Makes peace with all its trailing streams.
Love, which quickly lodges in a tender heart,
Aroused this man's desire for that fair form
So torn from me the manner grieves me still.
Love, that never lets the loved one not love too,
Inflamed me with such pleasure in this man
That, as you see, it has not left me yet.
And love it was that brought us to one death.
The abode of Cain awaits the man who killed us."
Such were the words those two addressed to us.

. . . Poet, I would gladly
Converse with those two who together go
And seem to be so weightless to the wind.

Da che io intesi quelle anime offense,
Chinai 'l viso, e tanto il tenni basso,
Finchè il poeta mi disse: 'Che pense?'
Quando risposi, cominciai: 'O lasso,
Quanti dolci pensier, quanto disio
Menò costoro al doloroso passo!'
Poi mi rivolsi a loro, e parla' io,
E cominciai: 'Francesca, i tuoi martiri
Al lagrimar mi fanno tristo e pio.
Ma dimmi: al tempo de' dolci sospiri,
A che e come concedette amore,
Che conosceste i dubbiosi desiri?'
Ed ella a me: 'Nessun maggior dolore,
Che ricordarsi del tempo felice
Nella miseria; e ciò sa il tuo dottore.
Ma se a conoscer la prima radice
Del nostro amor tu hai cotanto affetto,
Farò come colui che piange e dice.
Noi leggevamo un giorno per diletto
Di Lancelotto, come amor lo strinse:
Soli eravamo e senza alcun sospetto.
Per più fiate gli occhi ci sospinse
Quella lettura, e scolorocci il viso:
Ma solo un punto fu quel che ci vinse.
Quando leggemmo il disiato riso
Esser baciato da cotanto amante,
Questi, che mai da me non fia diviso,
La bocca mi baciò tutto tremante:
Galeotto fu il libro e chi lo scrisse:
Quel giorno più non vi leggemmo avante.'
Mentre che l' uno spirto questo disse,
L' altro piangeva sì, che di pietade
Io venni men così com' io morisse;
E caddi, come corpo morto cade.

And when I understood their tortured souls,
I bowed my head and kept it bowed so long,
The poet said to me, "What are you thinking of?"
When finally I answered him, I said:
"To think that such desire and sweet thoughts
Should bring these two to such a grievous end."
Then I turned to them, beginning with these words:
"Francesca, all these sufferings of yours
Have roused my pity to the point of tears.
But, tell me, how did love contrive that at
The moment of sweet sighs
You should know what your vague desires were?"
And she replied: "There is no greater pain—
Your master knows this—than, in our misery,
To be reminded of a happy time.
But since you want so eagerly to know
The first root of our love for one another,
I shall be like the one who speaks and weeps.
For pleasure we were reading one day of
Lancelot and how love had captivated him.
We were alone and wholly unsuspecting.
Many times that reading drew our eyes together
And drained the color from our faces.
But it was just one place where we succumbed.
When we read how those wanted lips
Were kissed by such a lover,
He, who never will be separate from me,
Kissed me on the mouth, trembling all over.
Galahad was the book and he who wrote it.
We read no more of it that day."
While one spirit went on telling this,
The other wept, till, overcome by pity,
I lost consciousness, as if I had died,
And I fell down as a dead body falls.

VI

AL tornar della mente, che si chiuse
Dinanzi alla pietà de' due cognati,
Che di tristizia tutto mi confuse,
Nuovi tormenti e nuovi tormentati
Mi veggio intorno, come ch' io mi mova,
E ch' io mi volga, e come ch' io mi guati.
Io sono al terzo cerchio della piova
Eterna, maledetta, fredda e greve:
Regola e qualità mai non l' è nuova.
Grandine grossa, e acqua tinta, e neve
Per l' aer tenebroso si riversa:
Pute la terra che questo riceve.
Cerbero, fiera crudele e diversa,
Con tre gole caninamente latra
Sopra la gente che quivi è sommersa.
Gli occhi ha vermigli, la barba unta ed atra,
E il ventre largo, e unghiate le mani;
Graffia gli spiriti, iscuoia, ed isquatra.
Urlar gli fa la pioggia come cani:
Dell' un de' lati fanno all' altro schermo;
Volgonsi spesso i miseri profani.
Quando ci scorse Cerbero, il gran vermo,
Le bocche aperse, e mostrocci le sanne:
Non avea membro che tenesse fermo.
E il duca mio distese le sue spanne;
Prese la terra, e con piene le pugna
La gittò dentro alle bramose canne.
Qual è quel cane che abbaiando agugna,
E si racqueta poi che il pasto morde,
Che solo a divorarlo intende e pugna;

6

WHEN I HAD REGAINED MY SENSES, which I lost
Over the pain of that related pair
Who so bewildered me with sorrow,
New forms of torment, new tormented souls
I saw about me everywhere I went,
And everywhere I turned and fixed my gaze.
I was in the third circle of the rain
That falls eternal, heavy, cold, and damned,
Whose quality and order never change.
Large hailstones, snow, and dirty water,
Poured down through the blackened air, and the ground,
Receiving them, gave off a fetid smell.
Cerberus, strange and ferocious beast,
With his three throats kept barking like a dog
Over the people who were mired there.
With reddened eyes, a greasy and black beard,
A huge belly, and hands with claws on them,
He tore the spirits, skinned, and quartered them.
The downpour made them howl like dogs;
They used one side as shelter for the other,
And thus the godless wretches turned and turned.
When Cerberus, the giant worm, espied us,
He opened his three mouths and showed his fangs,
And not a limb of his was motionless.
And then my guide reached down with both his hands,
Scooped up some earth, and, with full fists,
Flung it into the voracious mouths.
Just like a dog that howls in his hunger,
And grows still only when he starts to eat,
However he may battle over his food,

Cotai si fecer quelle facce lorde
Dello demonio Cerbero che introna
L' anime sì ch' esser vorrebber sorde.
Noi passavam su per l' ombre che adona
La greve pioggia, e ponevam le piante
Sopra lor vanità che par persona.
Elle giacean per terra tutte quante,
Fuor ch' una che a seder si levò, ratto
Ch' ella ci vide passarsi davante.
'O tu, che se' per questo inferno tratto,'
Mi disse, 'riconoscimi, se sai:
Tu fosti, prima ch' io disfatto, fatto.'
Ed io a lei: 'L' angoscia che tu hai
Forse ti tira fuor della mia mente,
Sì che non par ch' io ti vedessi mai.
Ma dimmi, chi tu se', che in sì dolente
Loco se' messa, ed a sì fatta pena
Che, s' altra è maggio, nulla è sì spiacente.'
Ed egli a me: 'La tua città, ch' è piena
D' invidia sì che già trabocca il sacco,
Seco mi tenne in la vita serena.
Voi cittadini mi chiamaste Ciacco:
Per la dannosa colpa della gola,
Come tu vedi, alla pioggia mi fiacco;
Ed io anima trista non son sola,
Chè tutte queste a simil pena stanno
Per simil colpa:' e più non fe' parola.
Io gli risposi: 'Ciacco, il tuo affanno
Mi pesa sì che a lagrimar m' invita:
Ma dimmi, se tu sai, a che verranno
Li cittadin della città partita?
S' alcun v' è giusto: e dimmi la cagione
Perchè l' ha tanta discordia assalita.'
Ed egli a me: 'Dopo lunga tenzone
Verranno al sangue, e la parte selvaggia
Caccerà l' altra con molta offensione.
Poi appresso convien che questa caggia
Infra tre soli, e che l' altra sormonti
Con la forza di tal che testè piaggia.

So were those filthy faces of the fiend
Cerberus, who thundered at the souls
So loudly that they all longed to be deaf.
We walked upon the spirits crushed by the
Heavy rain, and placed our feet
Upon the nothingness that seemed alive.
The spirits were all lying on the ground,
All but one, who raised himself to sit
The moment that he saw us pass before him.
"You who are being guided through this Hell,"
He said, "recognize me if you can;
You were already born before I died."
And I to him: "This agony of yours
May have effaced you from my memory,
For it does not seem to me I ever saw you.
Who are you that you have been put in such
A mournful place at such a torment, that though
There may be greater, none is so revolting?"
And he to me: "Your city, which is
So full of envy it overflows the sack,
Was my home in that other life serene.
You, my fellow citizens, called me Ciacco
For the pernicious vice of gluttony,
And, as you see, I weary in the rain;
And I, sad spirit, I am not by myself;
For all these have been similarly doomed
For the same vice." He spoke no other word.
And I replied: "Ciacco, your suffering
Affects me so, it makes me want to cry;
But tell me, if you know, what will become
Of the citizens of that divided city?
Is there one just man among them? And why
Has such dissension overwhelmed it?"
And he to me: "After considerable strife
Blood will be shed, and the country party
Will drive out its opponents with great force.
Then, within three years' time, this too will fall,
And the other side will win with the support
Of him who so far only temporizes.

Alte terrà lungo tempo le fronti,
Tenendo l' altra sotto gravi pesi,
Come che di ciò pianga, e che ne adonti.
Giusti son due, ma non vi sono intesi:
Superbia, invidia ed avarizia sono
Le tre faville che hanno i cori accesi.'
Qui pose fine al lagrimabil suono.
Ed io a lui: 'Ancor vo' che m' insegni,
E che di più parlar mi facci dono.
Farinata e il Tegghiaio, che fur sì degni,
Jacopo Rusticucci, Arrigo e il Mosca,
E gli altri che a ben far poser gl' ingegni,
Dimmi ove sono, e fa ch' io li conosca;
Chè gran disio mi stringe di sapere,
Se il ciel gli addolcia o lo inferno gli attosca.'
E quegli: 'Ei son tra le anime più nere;
Diversa colpa giù li grava al fondo:
Se tanto scendi, là i potrai vedere.
Ma quando tu sarai nel dolce mondo,
Pregoti che alla mente altrui mi rechi:
Più non ti dico e più non ti rispondo.'
Gli diritti occhi torse allora in biechi:
Guardommi un poco, e poi chinò la testa:
Cadde con essa a par degli altri ciechi.
E il duca disse a me: 'Più non si desta
Di qua dal suon dell' angelica tromba;
Quando verrà la nimica podesta,
Ciascun ritroverà la trista tomba,
Ripiglierà sua carne e sua figura,
Udirà quel che in eterno rimbomba.'
Sì trapassammo per sozza mistura
Dell' ombre e della pioggia a passi lenti,
Toccando un poco la vita futura:
Perch' io dissi: 'Maestro, esti tormenti
Cresceranno ei dopo la gran sentenza,
O fien minori, o saran sì cocenti?'
Ed egli a me: 'Ritorna a tua scienza,
Che vuol, quanto la cosa è più perfetta,
Più senta il bene, e così la doglienza,

Long will it hold its head high, and keep
The other party under harsh restraint,
However it may regret and be ashamed.
The just are two, but no one listens to them.
Arrogance and envy and avarice
Are the three sparks that fire every heart."
Here he put an end to the grieving sound.
And I: "I want to ask you many other things;
Please favor me with more of your discourse.
Worthy Farinata and Tegghiaio,
Rusticucci, Arrigo, and Mosca,
And all who used their talents to do good—
Tell me where they are and how to know them,
For a great desire consumes me to know
If Heaven sweetens or Hell poisons them."
And he: "They are among the blackest souls.
Different vices plunged them to the bottom;
You may see them, if you go that far below.
But when you are again in the sweet world,
I beg of you, remember me to the others.
I tell you no more and answer no further."
With that his staring eyes began to roll;
He looked at me a little, bowed his head,
And thus fell where the other blind ones lay.
And my guide said to me: "He shall not wake
Again until the angel blows the trumpet;
Then shall the opposing power come, and each
Shall find his melancholy tomb again;
Each shall reassume his flesh and shape, and hear
What shall resound through all eternity."
And thus, with slackened steps, we walked across
The intermixing filth of rain and shadows,
And dwelt a little on the future life.
"Master," I said on this subject, "these torments—
Will they increase after the Great Sentence,
Will they be less, or will they burn as much?"
"Refer to your philosophy," he said,
"Which claims that, the more perfect a thing is,
The more perfect its sense of pain and pleasure.

Tuttochè questa gente maledetta
In vera perfezion giammai non vada,
Di là, più che di qua, essere aspetta.'
Noi aggirammo a tondo quella strada,
Parlando più assai ch' io non ridico:
Venimmo al punto dove si digrada:
Quivi trovammo Pluto il gran nimico.

Even though these execrated people
Will never come into a true perfection,
They expect to come closer then than now."
We circled round and round along that road,
Saying far more than I can now repeat,
And came at last to where the slope begins.
There we found Plutus, the great enemy.

VII

'PAPE Satan, pape Satan aleppe,'
Cominciò Pluto colla voce chioccia.
E quel Savio gentil, che tutto seppe
Disse per confortarmi: 'Non ti noccia
La tua paura, chè, poter ch' egli abbia,
Non ci torrà lo scender questa roccia.'
Poi si rivolse a quell' enfiata labbia,
E disse: 'Taci, maledetto lupo:
Consuma dentro te con la tua rabbia.
Non è senza cagion l' andare al cupo:
Vuolsi nell' alto là dove Michele
Fe' la vendetta del superbo strupo.'
Quali dal vento le gonfiate vele
Caggiono avvolte, poichè l' alber fiacca;
Tal cadde a terra la fiera crudele.
Così scendemmo nella quarta lacca,
Pigliando più della dolente ripa,
Che il mal dell' universo tutto insacca.
Ahi giustizia di Dio, tante chi stipa
Nuove travaglie e pene, quante io viddi?
E perchè nostra colpa sì ne scipa?
Come fa l' onda là sovra Cariddi,
Che si frange con quella in cui s' intoppa,
Così convien che qui la gente riddi.
Qui vid' io gente più che altrove troppa,
E d' una parte e d' altra, con grand' urli
Voltando pesi per forza di poppa:
Percotevansi incontro, e poscia pur lì
Si rivolgea ciascun, voltando a retro,
Gridando: 'Perchè tieni,' e 'Perchè burli?'

7

"Pape Satan, pape Satan, aleppe!"[1]
Plutus began, in a clucking voice;
And that gentle wise man, who knew everything,
To reassure me said: "Let not your fear
Retard you, for, no matter what his power is,
He cannot stop our climbing down this rock."
Then, turning to that bloated face, he said:
"Be silent, accursed wolf;
Consume yourself in your own rabid greed.
Not without cause is our descent into
The depths; so was it willed on high, where Michael
Wreaked vengeance for the insolent revolt."
Like sails swelled by the wind that fall
In a tangled heap when the mast breaks,
So fell that cruel beast to the ground.
Thus we descended into the fourth hollow,
Advancing further on that bleak shore, which
Bags all the evil of the universe.
Merciful God, who can encompass
The many new afflictions that I saw,
And why does our guilt consume us so?
Like the waves there above Charybdis
That break against each other when they meet,
So must the people here dance out their round.
Here, on either side, were far more people
Than I ever saw, who with enormous howls
Went rolling weights by pushing with their chests;
They crashed against each other, and at that point
Wheeled about and started to go back,
Shouting: "Why do you hoard?", "Why do you squander?"

Così tornavan per lo cerchio tetro,
Da ogni mano all' opposito punto,
Gridandosi anche loro ontoso metro:
Poi si volgea ciascun, quando era giunto
Per lo suo mezzo cerchio all' altra giostra.
Ed io che avea lo cor quasi compunto,
Dissi: 'Maestro mio, or mi dimostra
Che gente è questa, e se tutti fur cherci
Questi chercuti alla sinistra nostra.'
Ed egli a me: 'Tutti quanti fur guerci
Sì della mente, in la vita primaia,
Che con misura nullo spendio ferci.
Assai la voce lor chiaro l' abbaia,
Quando vengono a' due punti del cerchio,
Ove colpa contraria li dispaia.
Questi fur cherci, che non han coperchio
Piloso al capo, e Papi e Cardinali,
In cui usa avarizia il suo soperchio.'
Ed io: 'Maestro, tra questi cotali
Dovre' io ben riconoscere alcuni
Che furo immondi di cotesti mali.'
Ed egli a me: 'Vano pensiero aduni:
La sconoscente vita che i fe' sozzi,
Ad ogni conoscenza or li fa bruni;
In eterno verranno alli due cozzi;
Questi risurgeranno del sepulcro
Col pugno chiuso, e questi co' crin mozzi.
Mal dare e mal tener lo mondo pulcro
Ha tolto loro, e posti a questa zuffa:
Qual ella sia, parole non ci appulcro.
Or puoi, figliuol, veder la corta buffa
De' ben, che son commessi alla Fortuna,
Perchè l' umana gente si rabbuffa.
Chè tutto l' oro ch' è sotto la luna,
E che già fu, di queste anime stanche
Non poterebbe farne posar una.'
'Maestro,' diss' io lui, 'or mi di' anche:
Questa Fortuna di che tu mi tocche,
Che è, che i ben del mondo ha sì tra branche?'

Thus they drew back, on every hand,
Along the black rim to the other side,
Shouting their rhythmic taunts at one another.
Then, having reached his own half-circle, each
Spun around and moved towards the next joust.
And I, whose heart was nearly pierced with pity,
Said: "Will you explain to me
Who these people are, and if they were all priests,
Those tonsured ones over to our left?"
And he to me: "All of them in their first life
Were so afflicted with a mental squint,
They never in their spending showed restraint.
Loud and clear their voices bark this out
When they come to the two points of the circle
Where their opposite offenses separate them.
These were priests who have no covering of hair
Upon their heads, and Cardinals and Popes,
In whom avarice far exceeds desire."
And I: "Master, among these spirits
I ought easily to recognize a few
Who were polluted by these evils."
And he to me: "You entertain vain thoughts:
The unknowing life that rendered them so vile
Now makes them far too dark for anyone to know.
They shall collide forever with each other.
These will be resurrected from the grave
With their fists closed, the others with cropped hair.
Bad giving and bad keeping have cost them
The fair world, and doomed them to this clash.
What that is like I tell without adornment.
Now you can see, my son, how brief a jest
Fortune makes of all those worldly goods
Over which the human race keeps squabbling.
Take all the gold beneath the moon, and all
The gold that ever was, it could not make
One of these exhausted souls desist and rest."
"Master," I said to him, "tell me now,
This Fortune you have just alluded to,
What is she that she controls all worldly goods?"

Ed egli a me: 'O creature sciocche,
Quanta ignoranza è quella che vi offende!
Or vo' che tu mia sentenza ne imbocche:
Colui lo cui saper tutto trascende,
Fece li cieli, e diè lor chi conduce,
Sì che ogni parte ad ogni parte splende,
Distribuendo egualmente la luce:
Similemente agli splendor mondani
Ordinò general ministra e duce,
Che permutasse a tempo li ben vani,
Di gente in gente e d' uno in altro sangue,
Oltre la difension de' senni umani:
Perchè una gente impera, e l' altra langue,
Seguendo lo giudizio di costei,
Che è occulto, come in erba l' angue.
Vostro saper non ha contrasto a lei:
Questa provvede, giudica e persegue
Suo regno, come il loro gli altri Dei.
Le sue permutazion non hanno triegue:
Necessità la fa esser veloce,
Sì spesso vien chi vicenda consegue.
Quest' è colei ch' è tanto posta in croce
Pur da color che le dovrian dar lode,
Dandole biasmo a torto e mala voce.
Ma ella s' è beata, e ciò non ode:
Con l' altre prime creature lieta
Volve sua spera, e beata si gode.
Or discendiamo omai a maggior pieta:
Già ogni stella cade, che saliva
Quando mi mossi, e il troppo star si vieta.'
Noi ricidemmo il cerchio all' altra riva
Sopra una fonte, che bolle e riversa
Per un fossato che da lei deriva.
L' acqua era buia assai più che persa:
E noi, in compagnia dell' onde bige,
Entrammo giù per una via diversa.
Una palude fa, che ha nome Stige,
Questo tristo ruscel, quando è disceso
Al piè delle malvage piaggie grige.

And he to me: "O witless creatures,
What great stupidity possesses you!
Give heed, now, to my own judgment of her.
He whose wisdom surpasses everything
Made the heavens and gave them overseers,
So that each part would glow on every other,
Thus evenly distributing the light.
So, also, for the splendors of the world
He chose a general minister and guide
Who would from time to time shift vain belongings
From people to people and from kin to kin,
Beyond man's mental powers to prevent:
Thus, one people dominates, another fades,
In consequence of her decisions, which,
Like the serpent in the grass, remain concealed.
Your knowledge is powerless against her;
She provides, judges, and pursues her reign
The way the other gods pursue their own.
The vicissitudes she causes never cease;
Necessity compels her to be swift,
So numerous are those who merit change.
This is she whom even those crucify
Who should be praising her, instead of
Wrongly blaming her with evil voices.
But she is blessed and hears none of this;
Happy among the other first creatures,
She turns her wheel and revels in her blessedness.
Now let us go down into a greater woe;
The stars have set that rose when we began,
And we are not allowed to stay too long."
We crossed the circle to the other bank
Above a spring from which boiling water
Poured into a gully it had made;
The flow was darker than the darkest purple;
And we, accompanied by the murky waves,
Went further down along a different route.
This somber stream, which has the name of Styx,
Forms a morass, when it has settled,
At the foot of the malign and dark incline,

Ed io, che di mirar mi stava inteso,
Vidi genti fangose in quel pantano,
Ignude tutte e con sembiante offeso.
Questi si percotean non pur con mano
Ma con la testa, col petto e co' piedi,
Troncandosi coi denti a brano a brano.
Lo buon Maestro disse: 'Figlio, or vedi
L' anime di color cui vinse l' ira:
Ed anche vo' che tu per certo credi,
Che sotto l' acqua ha gente che sospira,
E fanno pullular quest' acqua al summo,
Come l' occhio ti dice, u' che s' aggira.
Fitti nel limo dicon: "Tristi fummo
Nell' aer dolce che dal sol s' allegra,
Portando dentro accidioso fummo:
Or ci attristiam nella belletta negra."
Quest' inno si gorgoglian nella strozza,
Chè dir nol posson con parola integra.'
Così girammo della lorda pozza
Grand' arco tra la ripa secca e il mezzo,
Con gli occhi volti a chi del fango ingozza:
Venimmo al piè d' una torre al dassezzo.

And I, who fixed my gaze and never moved,
Saw mud-bespattered people in that swamp,
All of them naked and with twisted faces.
These struck each other not only with their hands,
But with their heads, their chests, and with their feet;
And with their teeth they tore themselves to pieces.
My master said: "Observe, my son,
The souls of those whom anger overpowered;
And I want you to accept it as a fact
That beneath the surface there are those who sigh
And make the water bubble up above,
As your own eye tells you everywhere it turns.
Stuck in the slime, they say: 'In the sweet air
That is made happy by the sun, we were
Corrupt, and harbored slothful fumes;
And now we sorrow in this black morass.'
This litany they gurgle in their throats,
Because they cannot speak with complete words."
And so we circled round that squalid bog,
From the dry bank to the wet, in a large arc,
With our eyes fastened on those who swallowed mud.
We came, at last, to the foot of a tower.

VIII

IO dico seguitando, ch' assai prima
Che noi fussimo al piè dell' alta torre,
Gli occhi nostri n' andar suso alla cima,
Per due fiammette che i' vedemmo porre,
E un' altra da lungi render cenno
Tanto ch' a pena il potea l' occhio torre.
Ed io mi volsi al mar di tutto il senno;
Dissi: 'Questo che dice? e che risponde
Quell' altro foco? e chi son quei che il fenno?'
Ed egli a me: 'Su per le sucide onde
Già puoi scorger quello che s' aspetta,
Se il fummo del pantan nol ti nasconde.'
Corda non pinse mai da sè saetta,
Che sì corresse via per l' aere snella,
Com' io vidi una nave piccioletta
Venir per l' acqua verso noi in quella,
Sotto il governo d' un sol galeoto,
Che gridava: 'Or se' giunta, anima fella?'
'Flegiàs, Flegiàs, tu gridi a voto,'
Disse lo mio signore, 'a questa volta:
Più non ci avrai, che sol passando il loto.'
Quale colui, che grande inganno ascolta
Che gli sia fatto, a poi se ne rammarca,
Fecesi Flegiàs nell' ira accolta.
Lo duca mio discese nella barca,
E poi mi fece entrare appresso lui,
E sol quand' io fui dentro parve carca.
Tosto che il duca ed io nel legno fui,
Secando se ne va l' antica prora
Dell' acqua più che non suol con altrui.

8

TO RESUME, let me first say that long before
We came to the foot of that high tower,
Our eyes had traveled to the top because
Of two small flames that flickered there,
As well as one that answered from so far off
That the eye could scarcely make it out.
Turning to that ocean of all wisdom,
I asked: "What does this say, and what does that
Other light reply, and who is doing it?"
And he to me: "There on the muddied waves
You may already see what is to come,
Unless the fumes of the morass conceal it."
No bowstring ever impelled an arrow
That sped so swiftly through the air
As did the little vessel which I saw
Coming through that water towards us
Under the guidance of a single oarsman,
Who shouted: "So you have come at last, vile soul!"
"Phlegyas, Phlegyas," replied my lord,
"This time you shout in vain; you have us only
For so long as it will take to cross the marsh."
Like one who learns of some great treachery
Done to him, and then bitterly resents it,
So was Phlegyas in his gathered wrath.
My guide stepped down into the vessel,
And then he made me board it after him,
And it seemed full only when I was in it.
No sooner were my guide and I aboard,
Than the old prow went sawing through the waves
Faster than was usual with the others.

No sooner were my guide and I aboard,
Than the old prow went sawing through the waves

Mentre noi corravam la morta gora,
Dinanzi mi si fece un pien di fango,
E disse: 'Chi se' tu che vieni anzi ora?'
Ed io a lui: 'S' io vegno, non rimango;
Ma tu chi se,' che sei sì fatto brutto?'
Rispose: 'Vedi che son un che piango.'
Ed io a lui: 'Con piangere e con lutto,
Spirito maledetto, ti rimani:
Ch' io ti conosco, ancor sia lordo tutto.'
Allora stese al legno ambo le mani:
Perchè il Maestro accorto lo sospinse,
Dicendo: 'Via costà con gli altri cani.'
Lo collo poi con le braccia mi cinse,
Baciommi il volto, e disse: 'Alma sdegnosa,
Benedetta colei che in te s' incinse.
Quei fu al mondo persona orgogliosa;
Bontà non è che sua memoria fregi:
Così s' è l' ombra sua qui furiosa.
Quanti si tengon or lassù gran regi,
Che qui staranno come porci in brago,
Di sè lasciando orribili dispregi!'
Ed io: 'Maestro, molto sarei vago
Di vederlo attuffare in questa broda,
Prima che noi uscissimo del lago.'
Ed egli a me: 'Avanti che la proda
Ti si lasci veder, tu sarai sazio:
Di tal disio converrà che tu goda.'
Dopo ciò poco vidi quello strazio
Far di costui alle fangose genti,
Che Dio ancor ne lodo e ne ringrazio.
Tutti gridavano: 'A Filippo Argenti!'
E 'l Fiorentino spirito bizzarro
In sè medesmo si volgea co' denti.
Quivi il lasciammo, chè più non ne narro:
Ma negli orecchi mi percosse un duolo,
Perch' io avanti l' occhio intento sbarro:
Lo buon Maestro disse: 'Omai, figliuolo,
S' appressa la città che ha nome Dite,
Co' gravi cittadin, col grande stuolo.'

While we were racing through the stagnant pond,
A man all full of mud rose up before me
And said: "Who may you be who come before your time?"
And I to him: "I come, but not to stay;
But who are you who have become so foul?"
And he: "You see that I am one who weeps."
And I said to him: "Continue with your
Weeping and your grieving, accursed soul,
For, dirty as you are, I recognize you."
When he stretched his hands out towards our boat,
My ever-watchful master flung him back,
Saying: "Go back there with the other dogs!"
He then entwined his arms about my neck,
Kissed my face, and said: "Indignant man,
Blessed be the woman who gave you birth.
That was an impudent person in the world;
No kindness ornaments his memory,
And so his shadow goes on raging here.
How many take themselves for great kings up there
Who shall one day be mired here like pigs,
Leaving behind them a horrible disgust!"
And I said: "Master, I would be
Overjoyed to watch him sink
In this foul mud before we leave the lake."
And he to me: "Before the other shore
Comes into view, you shall be satisfied.
It is most fitting that you should have your wish."
Presently, I saw the people of the mud
Pounce on and tear that man to pieces,
For which I still thank God and praise Him.
"At Filippo Argenti!" all cried out;
With which that irascible Florentine
Spirit turned on himself with his own teeth.
There we leave him; I say no more about him,
Except that such a shriek assailed my ears,
That I opened wide my eyes and looked ahead.
My good teacher said: "And now, my son,
We approach the city with the name of Dis,
With its somber citizens and great throngs."

Ed io: 'Maestro, già le sue meschite
Là entro certo nella valle cerno
Vermiglie, come se di foco uscite
Fossero.' Ed ei mi disse: 'Il foco eterno
Ch' entro l' affoca, le dimostra rosse,
Come tu vedi in questo basso inferno.'
Noi pur giugnemmo dentro all' alte fosse,
Che vallan quella terra sconsolata:
Le mura mi parean che ferro fosse.
Non senza prima far grande aggirata,
Venimmo in parte dove il nocchier forte
'Usciteci,' gridò, 'qui è l' entrata.'
Io vidi più di mille in sulle porte
Da' ciel piovuti, che stizzosamente
Dicean: 'Chi è costui, che senza morte
Va per lo regno della morta gente?'
E il savio mio Maestro fece segno
Di voler lor parlar segretamente.
Allor chiusero un poco il gran disdegno,
E disser: 'Vien tu solo, e quei sen vada,
Che sì ardito entrò per questo regno.
Sol si ritorni per la folle strada:
Provi se sa; chè tu qui rimarrai
Che gli hai scorta sì buia contrada.'
Pensa, Lettor, se io mi sconfortai
Nel suon delle parole maledette:
Ch' io non credetti ritornarci mai.
'O caro duca mio, che più di sette
Volte m' hai sicurtà renduta, e tratto
D' alto periglio che incontra mi stette,
Non mi lasciar,' diss' io, 'così disfatto:
E se 'l passar più oltre c' è negato,
Ritroviam l' orme nostre insieme ratto.'
E quel signor che lì m' avea menato
Mi disse: 'Non temer, chè il nostro passo
Non ci può torre alcun: da tal n' è dato.
Ma qui m' attendi; e lo spirito lasso
Conforta e ciba di speranza buona,
Ch' io non ti lascerò nel mondo basso.'

And I: "Master, I can already see the mosques
Flashing bright vermilion in the valley,
As if they were rising out of fire."
And he said to me: "The eternal fire
That burns within them makes them seem red
To you who look at them from this low Hell."
And now we came to the deep trenches that
Surround and fortify that joyless place,
The walls of which seemed made of iron to me.
Not without much circling round at first,
We reached a place where our pilot loudly
Shouted to us: "Step out! Here is the entrance."
Above the gates I saw more than a thousand
Of those who had once rained down from Heaven.
"Who is he who, without death," they were saying
Angrily, "goes through the land of the dead?"
And my wise master made a sign that he
Desired to speak to them in secret.
So they held back their great disdain a little,
And said: "You come alone; the other who
So boldly walked into this realm must leave,
And by himself go back his foolish way.
Let him succeed if he can; you, who have
Conducted him to this dark land, stay here."
Judge for yourself, reader, whether the sound
Of those accursed words disheartened me.
I did not think I ever would get back.
"O my dear guide, who more than seven times
Have rescued me from harm, and snatched me
From the great dangers that confronted me,
Do not leave me in this desperate state," said I.
"And if we are forbidden to go on,
Let us retrace our steps at once together."
And that lord who had led me to that place
Said to me: "Have no fear; no one can bar
Our way; thus has it been decreed by Him.
But wait for me here; console and feed
Your tired spirit on good hope.
I shall not leave you in the lower world."

Così sen va, e quivi m' abbandona
Lo dolce padre, ed io rimango in forse;
Che 'l sì e 'l no nel capo mi tenzona.
Udir non pote' quel ch' a lor si porse:
Ma ei non stette là con essi guari,
Che ciascun dentro a prova si ricorse.
Chiuser le porte que' nostri avversari
Nel petto al mio signor che fuor rimase,
E rivolsesi a me con passi rari.
Gli occhi alla terra, e le ciglia avea rase
D' ogni baldanza, e dicea ne' sospiri:
'Chi m' ha negate le dolenti case?'
Ed a me disse: 'Tu, perch' io m' adiri,
Non sbigottir, ch' io vincerò la prova,
Qual ch' alla difension dentro s' aggiri.
Questa lor tracotanza non è nuova,
Chè già l' usaro a men segreta porta,
La qual senza serrame ancor si trova.
Sopr' essa vedestù la scritta morta:
E già di qua da lei discende l' erta,
Passando per li cerchi senza scorta,
Tal che per lui ne fia la terra aperta.'

And so he went, that sweet father,
Leaving me there in a state of wonder,
With "yes" and "no" competing in my head.
I could not hear what he was saying to them;
But he was not with them very long before
They all went rushing back as in a contest.
Those enemies of ours closed the gates
Against my master, who remained outside
And came back to me with unhurried steps.
With his eyes on the ground, and his brow
Shorn of all defiance, he said, sighing:
"Who denied me entrance to the bleak abodes?"
And he said to me: "Be not dismayed
Because I raged; I will surmount the test,
Whatever they devise inside to bar me.
It is not new, this impudence of theirs:
They tried it once at a less secret door,
And from that time it has remained unlocked.
You saw yourself the words of death above it.
Someone is already coming down the slope
And passing through the circles unescorted.
He will open up the city for us."

IX

QUEL color che viltà di fuor mi pinse,
Veggendo il duca mio tornare in volta,
Più tosto dentro il suo nuovo ristrinse.
Attento si fermò com' uom che ascolta;
Chè l' occhio nol potea menare a lunga
Per l' aer nero e per la nebbia folta.
'Pure a noi converrà vincer la punga,'
Cominciò ei: 'se non . . . tal ne s' offerse.
Oh quanto tarda a me ch' altri qui giunga!'
Io vidi ben, sì com' ei ricoperse
Lo cominciar con l' altro che poi venne,
Che fur parole alle prime diverse.
Ma nondimen paura il suo dir dienne,
Perch' io traeva la parola tronca
Forse a peggior sentenza che non tenne.
'In questo fondo della trista conca
Discende mai alcun del primo grado,
Che sol per pena ha la speranza cionca?'
Questa question fec' io; e quei: 'Di rado
Incontra,' mi rispose, 'che di nui
Faccia il cammino alcun per quale io vado.
Ver' è ch' altra fiata quaggiù fui,
Congiurato da quella Eriton cruda
Che richiamava l' ombre a' corpi sui.
Di poco era di me la carne nuda,
Ch' ella mi fece entrar dentro a quel muro,
Per trarne un spirto del cerchio di Giuda.
Quell' è il più basso loco e il più oscuro,
E il più lontan dal ciel che tutto gira:
Ben so il cammin: però ti fa sicuro.

9

THAT COLOR WHICH FEAR IMPARTED to my face
When I beheld my master coming back,
Made him more speedily repress his own.
He stopped, attentive, like a man who listens,
For his eye could not take him very far
In that black air and impenetrable fog.
"This is a battle you and I must win,"
He said; "if not . . . someone else has volunteered.
Oh, how time drags till that other comes!"
I saw clearly how he covered up
The first part of his statement with the second,
The words of which so differed from the other.
None the less, what he said aroused my fear,
Perhaps because I gave the broken phrase
A worse meaning than he had intended.
"Into the depths of the dismal shell
Do any ever come from that first plane
Where the sole punishment is hope denied?"
I asked him this, and he replied: "Only
Rarely does it happen that one of us
Takes the road along which I am going.
The truth is that once before I came
Down here, conjured by that crude Erichtho
Who summoned back the shadows to their bodies.
My flesh had scarcely been denuded of me
When she compelled me to go through that wall
To fetch a spirit from the ring of Judas.
That is the lowest place, the darkest, and
The farthest from the Heaven that encircles
Everything. I know the way well; rest assured.

Questa palude che il gran puzzo spira,
Cinge d' intorno la città dolente,
U' non potemo entrare omai senz' ira.'
Ed altro disse, ma non l' ho a mente;
Perocchè l' occhio m' avea tutto tratto
Ver l' alta torre alla cima rovente,
Dove in un punto furon dritte ratto
Tre furie infernal di sangue tinte,
Che membra femminili aveano ed atto,
E con idre verdissime eran cinte:
Serpentelli e ceraste avean per crine
Onde le fiere tempie eran avvinte.
E quei che ben conobbe le meschine
Della regina dell' eterno pianto:
'Guarda,' mi disse, 'le feroci Erine.
Questa è Megera dal sinistro canto:
Quella che piange dal destro è Aletto:
Tesifone è nel mezzo:' e tacque a tanto.
Con l' unghie si fendea ciascuna il petto;
Batteansi a palme e gridavan sì alto
Ch' io mi strinsi al poeta per sospetto.
'Venga Medusa; sì 'l farem di smalto,'
Dicevan tutte riguardando in giuso:
'Mal non vengiammo in Teseo l'assalto.'
'Volgiti indietro, e tien lo viso chiuso;
Chè se il Gorgon si mostra, e tu il vedessi,
Nulla sarebbe del tornar mai suso.'
Così disse il Maestro; ed egli stessi
Mi volse, e non si tenne alle mie mani,
Che con le sue ancor non mi chiudessi.
O voi che avete gl' intelletti sani,
Mirate la dottrina che s' asconde
Sotto il velame degli versi strani.
E già venia su per le torbid' onde
Un fracasso d' un suon pien di spavento,
Per cui tremavano ambedue le sponde;
Non altrimenti fatto che d' un vento
Impetuoso per gli avversi ardori,
Che fier la selva, e senza alcun rattento

This swamp, which exhales such a stench,
Entirely surrounds the doleful city,
Which we cannot enter without violence."
And he said other things that I cannot recall,
Because my eyes had been completely drawn
To the high tower with the burning top,
Where three infernal blood-stained furies
Bearing limbs and attitudes of women,
Sprang up together unexpectedly.
They were entwined with hydras of deep green;
Instead of hair they had horned snakes and serpents,
Which coiled around their fierce and brazen temples.
And he who was familiar with the handmaids
Of the queen of the perpetual tears,
Said to me: "Behold the wild Erinyes.
This is Megaera, standing on the left;
She on the right who weeps is Alecto;
Tisiphone is in between." He said no more.
Each with her claws was slashing at her breast.
They slapped each other and cried out so loud,
That out of fright I stayed close to the poet.
"Let Medusa come," they all said, looking down,
"That she may turn him into stone!
We did wrong not to avenge the assault of Theseus."
"Turn around and keep your eyes shut tight,
For if the Gorgon comes and you should see her,
You would never get back up there again."
So said the master, and he himself
Turned me round, and, not trusting my own hands,
With both of his he also sealed my eyes.
O you who have good intellects, look closely
At the lesson that lies hidden beneath
This veil of mysterious verses.
And now over the turbid waters
There came a violent and frightening roar,
Which made the two shores tremble, and
Resembled nothing so much as a wind,
Made impetuous by opposing heats,
That batters the forest with unending blows,

Li rami schianta, abbatte, e porta fuori.
Dinanzi polveroso va superbo,
E fa fuggir le fiere e li pastori.
Gli occhi mi sciolse, e disse: 'Or drizza il nerbo
Del viso su per quella schiuma antica,
Per indi ove quel fummo è più acerbo.'
Come le rane innanzi alla nimica
Biscia per l' acqua si dileguan tutte,
Fin che alla terra ciascuna s' abbica;
Vid' io più di mille anime distrutte
Fuggir così dinanzi ad un che al passo
Passava Stige colle piante asciutte.
Dal volto rimovea quell' aer grasso,
Menando la sinistra innanzi spesso;
E sol di quell' angoscia parea lasso.
Ben m' accors' io ch' egli era del ciel messo,
E volsimi al Maestro: e quei fe' segno,
Ch' io stessi cheto, ed inchinassi ad esso.
Ahi quanto mi parea pien di disdegno!
Venne alla porta, e con una verghetta
L' aperse, che non v' ebbe alcun ritegno.
'O cacciati del ciel, gente dispetta,'
Cominciò egli in su l' orribil soglia,
'Ond' esta oltracotanza in voi s' alletta?
Perchè ricalcitrate a quella voglia,
A cui non puote il fin mai esser mozzo,
E che più volte v' ha cresciuta doglia?
Che giova nelle fata dar di cozzo?
Cerbero vostro, se ben vi ricorda,
Ne porta ancor pelato il mento e il gozzo.'
Poi si rivolse per la strada lorda,
E non fe' motto a noi: ma fe' sembiante
D' uomo cui altra cura stringa e morda,
Che quella di colui che gli è davante.
E noi movemmo i piedi in ver la terra,
Sicuri appresso le parole sante.
Dentro v' entrammo senza alcuna guerra:
Ed io, ch' avea di riguardar disio
La condizion che tal fortezza serra,

Snaps off boughs, flings them down, scatters them,
And onward goes, superb in all its dust,
Forcing the wild beasts and shepherds into flight.
Uncovering my eyes, he said: "Now train
Your nerve of vision on that ancient foam,
There where the mist is the most bitter of all."
The way the frogs, before their enemy
The snake, all scatter through the water
Until each of them is crouching on the ground,
So I saw fleeing more than a thousand
Perished souls before someone
Who with dry feet was crossing over the Styx.
He brushed away the foul air from his face,
Moving his left hand frequently before him,
And seemed to tire only of that nuisance.
I knew at once he had been sent from Heaven,
And turned to my master, who made a sign
That I should keep still and bow down before him.
How full of righteous scorn he seemed to me!
Arriving at the gate, he used a wand
And opened it without resistance.
"You contemptible outcasts of heaven!"
He started saying on that fearful threshold.
"Why does this insolence still cling to you?
Why do you stubbornly resist that will
Which can never be divided from its goal
And which has often brought you added pain?
What can you gain from grappling with the Fates?
That Cerberus of yours, if you recall well,
Still bears a skinless chin and throat for trying."
Then he returned along that filthy road,
Said not a word to us, but bore the look
Of one consumed and pressed by other cares
Than those of him who stands in front of him.
Feeling secure after those saintly words,
We started walking towards the city.
We entered without any opposition;
And I, who had a longing to explore
The inside of a fortress of this kind,

Com' io fui dentro, l' occhio intorno invio;
E veggio ad ogni man grande campagna
Piena di duolo e di tormento rio.
Sì come ad Arli, ove Rodano stagna,
Sì com' a Pola presso del Quarnaro,
Che Italia chiude e suoi termini bagna,
Fanno i sepolcri tutto il loco varo:
Così facevan quivi d' ogni parte,
Salvo che il modo v' era più amaro;
Chè tra gli avelli fiamme erano sparte,
Per le quali eran sì del tutto accesi,
Che ferro più non chiede verun' arte.
Tutti gli lor coperchi eran sospesi,
E fuor n' uscivan sì duri lamenti,
Che ben parean di miseri e d' offesi.
Ed io: 'Maestro, quai son quelle genti
Che seppellite dentro da quell' arche
Si fan sentir con gli sospir dolenti?'
Ed egli a me: 'Qui son gli eresiarche
Co' lor seguaci d' ogni setta, e molto
Più che non credi, son le tombe carche.
Simile qui con simile è sepolto,
E i monimenti son più, e men caldi.'
E poi ch' alla man destra si fu volto,
Passammo tra i martiri e gli alti spaldi.

Cast my eyes around the moment I was in;
On every side I saw a great terrain
Crowded with suffering and tormented guilt.
As at Arles, where the river Rhone slows down,
Or at Pola, near the Quarnaro bay,
Which closes Italy and bathes its border,
The tombs make the whole place look uneven,
So was it now on every side of us,
Except that here the purpose was more grim:
For, scattered flames among the sepulchers
Made them glow with such intensity
That not a trade could ask for hotter iron.
The covers of the graves were all removed,
And out of them came bitter howls of pain,
Like those of injured and afflicted men.
And I: "Master, who might those people be
Entombed in those large chests of stone
Who make themselves heard with such sobs of pain?"
And he to me: "Here the arch-heretics are found,
With their followers of every sect;
These graves are far more crowded than you think.
Here like with like has been interred, and
Of the tombs some are more hot than others."
And after turning to the right, we passed
Between the torments and the battlements.

X

ORA sen va per un secreto calle
Tra il muro della terra e li martiri
Lo mio Maestro, ed io dopo le spalle.
'O virtù somma, che per gli empi giri
Mi volvi,' cominciai, 'com' a te piace
Parlami, e satisfammi a' miei desiri.
La gente che per li sepolcri giace
Potrebbesi veder? già son levati
Tutti i coperchi, e nessun guardia face.'
Ed egli a me: 'Tutti saran serrati,
Quando di Josaffàt qui torneranno
Coi corpi che lassù hanno lasciati.
Suo cimitero da questa parte hanno
Con Epicuro tutti i suoi seguaci,
Che l' anima col corpo morta fanno.
Però alla dimanda che mi faci
Quinc' entro satisfatto sarai tosto,
Ed al disio ancor che tu mi taci.'
Ed io: 'Buon Duca, non tegno riposto
A te mio cor, se non per dicer poco;
E tu m' hai non pur mo a ciò disposto.'
'O Tosco, che per la città del foco
Vivo ten vai così parlando onesto,
Piacciati di restare in questo loco.
La tua loquela ti fa manifesto
Di quella nobil patria natio,
Alla qual forse io fui troppo molesto.'
Subitamente questo suono uscìo
D' una dell' arche; però m' accostai,
Temendo, un poco più al duca mio.

10

OUR JOURNEY took us through a secret way
Between the scenes of torture and the city wall,
My master going first and I behind.
"O highest Virtue," I began, "who whirl me
Through these godless circles as you please,
Speak to me and grant me what I wish:
The people who are lying in these tombs,
Can they be seen by anyone? The lids all
Have been lifted, and no one is keeping watch."
And he to me: "They will all be locked in
When they come back from Jehoshaphat
With the bodies they left in the world above.
This is the cemetery which all those
Who followed Epicurus share with him,
Believing that the soul died with the body.
Soon the question that you asked me will be
Answered inside this place, and your wish will be
Granted, too, though you have not expressed it yet."
And I: "My good guide, I have not concealed
My heart from you, but only spoken little,
As you yourself advised me earlier to do."
"O man of Tuscany, so true of speech,
Who in this city of fire walk alive,
May it be your pleasure to pause here.
The language you are speaking proclaims you
A native of that noble fatherland
Which I, perhaps, molested far too much."
Such was the sound that issued suddenly
From one of the stone chests; terrified,
I drew a little closer to my guide.

Ed ei mi disse: 'Volgiti: che fai?
Vedi là Farinata che s' è dritto:
Dalla cintola in su tutto il vedrai.'
I' avea già il mio viso nel suo fitto;
Ed ei s' ergea col petto e colla fronte,
Come avesse lo inferno in gran dispitto:
E l' animose man del duca e pronte
Mi pinser tra le sepolture a lui,
Dicendo: 'Le parole tue sien conte.'
Com' io al piè della sua tomba fui,
Guardommi un poco, e poi quasi sdegnoso
Mi dimandò: 'Chi fur li maggior tui?'
Io, ch' era d' ubbidir desideroso,
Non gliel celai, ma tutto gliel' apersi:
Ond' ei levò le ciglia un poco in soso;
Poi disse: 'Fieramente furo avversi
A me ed a' miei primi ed a mia parte,
Sì che per due fiate gli dispersi.'
'S' ei fur cacciati, ei tornar d' ogni parte,'
Rispos' io lui, 'l' una e l' altra fiata;
Ma i vostri non appreser ben quell' arte.'
Allor surse alla vista scoperchiata
Un' ombra lungo questa infino al mento:
Credo che s' era in ginocchie levata.
D' intorno mi guardò, come talento
Avesse di veder s' altri era meco;
Ma poi che il suspicar fu tutto spento,
Piangendo disse: 'Se per questo cieco
Carcere vai per altezza d' ingegno,
Mio figlio ov' è, e perchè non è teco?'
Ed io a lui: 'Da me stesso non vegno:
Colui, che attende là, per qui mi mena,
Forse cui Guido vostro ebbe a disdegno.'
Le sue parole e il modo della pena
M' avevan di costui già letto il nome:
Però fu la risposta così piena.
Di subito drizzato gridò: 'Come
Dicesti: "egli ebbe?" non viv' egli ancora?
Non fiere gli occhi suoi lo dolce lome?'

And he: "What are you doing? Turn around!
Look at Farinata raising himself up;
You will see all of him above the waist."
My face was already staring into his,
When he straightened up with breast and forehead,
As if he had a great contempt for Hell.
And my guide's ready and intrepid hands
Pushed me towards him between the sepulchers,
Saying: "Let your words be few and to the point."
When I stood at the foot of Farinata's tomb,
He glanced at me a little, and almost
With disdain asked: "Who were your ancestors?"
I, who was only too willing to obey,
Hid nothing from him, but told everything,
On hearing which he raised his brows a little,
And then said: "They were so bitterly opposed
To me, my party, and my ancestors,
That I had to banish them on two occasions."
"If they were banished," I replied to him,
"They came back from all sides on both occasions,
An art which your ancestors never learned."
Close by to him there now loomed into view
A shadow, visible down to the chin,
Which I believe was standing on its knees.
He looked on every side of me as though
He wished to see if someone else were there;
But, once his apprehension was dispelled,
He said to me: "If because of your
Great genius you stride through this blind prison,
Where is my son, and why is he not with you?"
"I am not here of my own volition," I said;
"That one who waits there is guiding me around.
Perhaps your Guido was disdainful of him."
His words and the nature of his torment
Had already spelled his name out for me:
That was why I gave him a full answer.
Suddenly he straightened up and cried:
"What did you say? '*He was?*' Is he not alive?
Does the sweet light no longer pierce his eyes?"

Look at Farinata raising himself up;
You will see all of him above the waist.

Quando s' accorse d' alcuna dimora
Ch' io faceva dinanzi alla risposta,
Supin ricadde, e più non parve fuora.
Ma quell' altro magnanimo, a cui posta
Restato m' era, non mutò aspetto,
Nè mosse collo, nè piegò sua costa.
E, 'Se,' continuando al primo detto,
'S' egli han quell' arte,' disse, 'male appresa,
Ciò mi tormenta più che questo letto.
Ma non cinquanta volte fia raccesa
La faccia della donna che qui regge,
Che tu saprai quanto quell' arte pesa.
E se tu mai nel dolce mondo regge,
Dimmi perchè quel popolo è sì empio
Incontro a' miei in ciascuna sua legge?'
Ond' io a lui: 'Lo strazio e il grande scempio
Che fece l' Arbia colorata in rosso,
Tale orazion fa far nel nostro tempio.'
Poi ch' ebbe sospirando il capo scosso,
'A ciò non fui io sol,' disse, 'nè certo
Senza cagion con gli altri sarei mosso:
Ma fu' io sol colà, dove sofferto
Fu per ciascun di torre via Fiorenza,
Colui che la difesi a viso aperto.'
'Deh, se riposi mai vostra semenza,'
Prega' io lui, 'solvetemi quel nodo,
Che qui ha inviluppata mia sentenza.
E' par che voi veggiate, se ben odo,
Dinanzi quel che il tempo seco adduce,
E nel presente tenete altro modo.'
'Noi veggiam, come quei ch' ha mala luce,
Le cose,' disse, 'che ne son lontano;
Cotanto ancor ne splende il sommo Duce:
Quando s' appressano, o son, tutto è vano
Nostro intelletto; e s' altri non ci apporta,
Nulla sapem di vostro stato umano.
Però comprender puoi che tutta morta
Fia nostra conoscenza da quel punto
Che del futuro fia chiusa la porta.'

When he saw that I delayed a little
Before I gave an answer, he fell back
Once more and did not show himself again.
But that other proud spirit, at whose instance
I had stopped, did not alter his expression,
And neither moved his neck nor turned around.
"And if," he said, resuming our discourse,
"They have so poorly apprehended that art,
That tortures me far more than does this bed.
Not fifty times shall the face of the queen,
Who is ruler here, be reillumined,
Before you learn how heavy an art it is.
And should you ever go back to the sweet world,
Tell me: why are those people, in all their laws,
So merciless towards my descendants?"
To which I said: "The ruin and great massacre,
Which turned the river Arbia to red,
Account for such decrees in our temple."
After he had shaken his head and sighed,
He said: "I was not alone in that, nor
Would I without reason have joined the others:
But I was he, when all the rest agreed
That Florence should be devastated,
Who alone openly defended her."
"That your seed may some day be at peace,
Loosen the knot," I entreated him, "which
Binds my understanding on this point.
If what I hear is true, you can foresee
What lies ahead that time brings with itself,
And yet you view the present differently."
"Things that are distant from us," he said,
"We see the way they do whose sight is poor.
Such light the Supreme Ruler still allows us.
For things that are about to be, or are,
Our minds are blank; if no one brings us news,
We can know nothing of your human state.
You should be able now to understand
Why all our knowledge will be dead
The moment the door closes on the future."

Allor, come di mia colpa compunto,
Dissi: 'Or direte dunque a quel caduto
Che il suo nato è co' vivi ancor congiunto.
E s' io fui innanzi alla risposta muto,
Fat' ei saper che il fei, perchè pensava
Già nell' error che m' avete soluto.'
E già il Maestro mio mi richiamava:
Perch' io pregai lo spirto più avaccio.
Che mi dicesse chi con lui si stava.
Dissemi: 'Qui con più di mille giaccio:
Qua dentro è lo secondo Federico,
E il Cardinale, e degli altri mi taccio.'
Indi s' ascose: ed io in ver l' antico
Poeta volsi i passi, ripensando
A quel parlar che mi parea nimico.
Egli si mosse; e poi così andando,
Mi disse: 'Perchè sei tu sì smarrito?'
Ed io li satisfeci al suo dimando.
'La mente tua conservi quel ch' udito
Hai contra te,' mi comandò quel Saggio,
'Ed ora attendi qui:' e drizzò il dito.
'Quando sarai dinanzi al dolce raggio
Di quella il cui bell' occhio tutto vede,
Da lei saprai di tua vita il viaggio.'
Appresso volse a man sinistra il piede:
Lasciammo il muro, e gimmo in ver lo mezzo
Per un sentier ch' ad una valle fiede,
Che infin lassù facea spiacer suo lezzo.

Then, as if repenting my own folly,
I said: "That being so, tell that fallen soul
That his son is still among the living;
And if I failed to answer him before,
Let him know it was because my mind was still
Caught in that error from which you freed me."
Because the master was already calling
To me to come back, I begged the spirit
To tell me hurriedly who else was with him.
"More than a thousand lie here with me," he said.
"Frederick the Second is in here, as is
The Cardinal; I say nothing of the rest."
With that he disappeared, and I,
Reflecting on those words that seemed unfriendly,
Turned my steps back to the ancient poet.
He started off again, and as we went,
He said to me: "What is it that confuses you?"
I responded to his satisfaction.
"Let your memory preserve what you have heard
Against you," that sage commanded. "And now
Pay close attention"; and he raised a finger.
"When you are standing in the sweet ray
Of her whose lovely eyes see everything,
You will learn from her the voyage of your life."
Whereupon he turned his steps to the left.
Leaving the wall, we went towards the center
Along a path that stopped at an abyss,
From which a disgusting odor reached us.

XI

IN su l' estremità d' un' alta ripa,
Che facevan gran pietre rotte in cerchio,
Venimmo sopra più crudele stipa:
E quivi, per l' orribile soperchio
Del puzzo, che il profondo abisso gitta,
Ci raccostammo dietro ad un coperchio
D' un grande avello, ov' io vidi una scritta
Che diceva: 'Anastasio papa guardo,
Lo qual trasse Fotin della via dritta.'
'Lo nostro scender conviene esser tardo,
Sì che s' ausi un poco prima il senso
Al tristo fiato, e poi non fia riguardo.'
Così il Maestro; ed io: 'Alcun compenso,'
Dissi lui, 'trova, che il tempo non passi
Perduto;' ed egli: 'Vedi che a ciò penso.
Figliuol mio, dentro da cotesti sassi,'
Cominciò poi a dir, 'son tre cerchietti
Di grado in grado, come quei che lassi.
Tutti son pien di spirti maledetti:
Ma perchè poi ti basti pur la vista,
Intendi come e perchè son costretti.
D' ogni malizia ch' odio in cielo acquista,
Ingiuria è il fine, ed ogni fin cotale
O con forza o con frode altrui contrista.
Ma perchè frode è dell' uom proprio male,
Più spiace a Dio; e però stan di sutto
Gli frodolenti, e più dolor gli assale.
De' violenti il primo cerchio è tutto:
Ma perchè si fa forza a tre persone,
In tre gironi è distinto e costrutto.

11

ON THE EXTREMITY of a high cliff,
Shaped like a circle by large broken stones,
We came above a more tormented pack:
And here, because of the insufferable smell,
Which emanated from the deep abyss,
We proceeded behind the cover of a
Large sepulcher, on which I read the words:
"I guard Anastasius the Pope,
He whom Photinus lured from the righteous path."
"We must descend slowly here, so that
We may accustom our sense by degrees
To this foul odor, and then we shall not mind."
Thus spoke the master, and I: "Think of
Some recompense so that the time need not
Be lost." And he: "That was my very thought.
My son," he then began to say to me,
"Within these stones are three little circles
That grow smaller and smaller, like those we left.
All of them are crowded with doomed spirits;
But to make the sight of them alone suffice
Later, learn how and why they are constrained.
Injury is the aim of every malice
Abhorred by Heaven, and every such aim
By force or fraud makes someone suffer.
But since fraud is a wickedness confined
To man, it displeases God the more, and so
The fraudulent are lowest and in more pain.
In the first circle are the violent,
But since violence is done to three,
So it is subdivided in three rings.

A Dio, a sè, al prossimo si puone
Far forza, dico in loro ed in lor cose,
Come udirai con aperta ragione.
Morte per forza e ferute dogliose
Nel prossimo si danno, e nel suo avere
Ruine, incendi e tollette dannose:
Onde omicide e ciascun che mal fiere,
Guastatori e predon, tutti tormenta
Lo giron primo per diverse schiere.
Puote uomo avere in sè man violenta
E ne' suoi beni: e però nel secondo
Giron convien che senza pro si penta
Qualunque priva sè del vostro mondo,
Biscazza e fonde la sua facultade,
E piange là dove esser dee giocondo.
Puossi far forza nella Deitade,
Col cor negando e bestemmiando quella,
E spregiando natura e sua bontade:
E però lo minor giron suggella
Del segno suo e Sodoma e Caorsa,
E chi spregiando Dio col cor favella.
La frode, ond' ogni coscienza è morsa,
Può l' uomo usare in colui che 'n lui fida,
Ed in quei che fidanza non imborsa.
Questo modo di retro par che uccida
Pur lo vinco d' amor che fa natura;
Onde nel cerchio secondo s' annida
Ipocrisia, lusinghe e chi affattura,
Falsità, ladroneccio e simonia,
Ruffian, baratti e simile lordura.
Per l' altro modo quell' amor s' obblia
Che fa natura, e quel ch' è poi aggiunto,
Di che la fede spezial si cria:
Onde nel cerchio minore, ov' è il punto
Dell' universo, in su che Dite siede,
Qualunque trade in eterno è consunto.'
Ed io: 'Maestro, assai chiaro procede
La tua ragione, ed assai ben distingue
Questo baratro e il popol che il possiede.

Violence may be done to God, to oneself,
And to one's neighbors: to both their persons
And possessions, as you shall hear explained.
Death by violence to one's neighbor,
And grievous wounds; and to his property
Ruin, fire, and unlawful tribute:
In short, the murderers and those who injure
Meanly, the pillagers and robbers,
All are tortured separately in the first ring.
A man lays violent hands upon himself
And what he owns; hence, in the second ring,
They must repent in vain who quit your world,
Who gamble and squander fortunes away,
And who weep when they should be rejoicing.
Violence may be done to God,
With the heart denying and blaspheming Him,
And scorning Nature and her plenitude.
And so the seal of Sodom and Cahors,
And of those who in their hearts spurn God,
Is stamped upon the smallest of the rings.
A man may commit fraud, by which
Every conscience is corroded, against
One who trusts him, and another who does not.
The latter of these frauds seems to destroy
Only the ties of love that Nature makes.
So, in the second circle, in one nest together,
Are hypocrisy, flattery, wizardry,
Forgery, thievery, simony,
The procurers, swindlers, and all such filth.
In the other of the frauds, such love as
Nature makes is forgotten, but that love too
Which is added later with a special trust:
Thus, in the smallest circle, in the center
Of the universe where Lucifer sits,
All who have betrayed are forever ravaged."
And I: "Master, your explanation proceeds
Very clearly and gives a vivid picture
Of this chasm and those who occupy it.
But tell me: those of that thick morass

Ma dimmi: Quei della palude pingue,
Che mena il vento, e che batte la pioggia,
E che s' incontran con sì aspre lingue,
Perchè non dentro dalla città roggia
Son ei puniti, se Dio gli ha in ira?
E se non gli ha, perchè sono a tal foggia?'
Ed egli a me: 'Perchè tanto delira,'
Disse, 'lo ingegno tuo da quel che suole?
Ovver la mente dove altrove mira?
Non ti rimembra di quelle parole,
Colle quai la tua Etica pertratta
Le tre disposizion che il ciel non vuole:
Incontinenza, malizia e la matta
Bestialitade? e come incontinenza
Men Dio offende e men biasimo accatta?
Se tu riguardi ben questa sentenza,
E rechiti alla mente chi son quelli
Che su di fuor sostengon penitenza,
Tu vedrai ben perchè da questi felli
Sien dipartiti, e perchè men crucciata
La divina vendetta gli martelli,'
'O Sol che sani ogni vista turbata,
Tu mi contenti sì, quando tu solvi,
Che, non men che saper, dubbiar m' aggrata.
Ancora un poco indietro ti rivolvi,'
Diss' io, 'là dove di che usura offende
La divina bontade, e il groppo solvi.'
'Filosofia,' mi disse, 'a chi la intende,
Nota non pure in una sola parte
Come natura lo suo corso prende
Dal divino intelletto e da sua arte;
E se tu ben la tua Fisica note,
Tu troverai non dopo molte carte
Che l' arte vostra quella, quanto puote,
Segue, come il maestro fa il discente,
Sì che vostr' arte a Dio quasi è nepote.
Da queste due, se tu ti rechi a mente
Lo Genesi dal principio, conviene
Prender sua vita ed avanzar la gente.

Who are driven by the wind, beaten
By the rain and who encounter such sharp tongues,
Why are they not chastised in the red city,
If they have roused the wrath of God;
If they have not, why are they treated thus?"
And he said to me: "Why is your judgment
So much more at fault than usual?
Or perhaps your mind is somewhere else?
Do you not recall those words with which
The 'Ethics' elaborates on those three
Dispositions offensive to heaven:
Incontinence, malice, and insensate
Bestiality? And how incontinence
Offends God least, and is the least condemned?
If you reflect upon this precept well,
And call to mind who those people are who bear
Their punishment up in that place outside,
You will see why they have been separated
From these repugnant souls, and why
Divine justice bludgeons them less fiercely."
"O sun, you who heal all afflicted eyes,
I rejoice so when you enlighten me,
That to doubt becomes as pleasant as to know.
Would you go back a little way," I said;
"To where you said that usury offends
Divine goodness, and untie that knot for me?"
"Philosophy," he said, "to him who heeds
Indicates in more than a single place
How Nature derives the course she follows
From the divine intelligence and skill,
And if you study the 'Physics' carefully,
You will find, after not too many pages,
That your human skill, as far as possible,
Follows her, as pupil follows teacher,
So that your skill is like a grandchild of God.
From these two, if you recollect
The opening part of Genesis, mankind
Must draw its sustenance and move ahead.
And because the usurer pursues another course,

E perchè l' usuriere altra via tiene,
Per sè natura, e per la sua seguace
Dispregia, poichè in altro pon la spene.
Ma seguimi oramai, chè il gir mi piace:
Chè i Pesci guizzan su per l' orizzonta,
E il Carro tutto sopra il Coro giace,
E il balzo via là oltra si dismonta.'

He scorns Nature for herself and for her
Follower, and sets his hopes on something else.
But, now, follow me; I would like to go ahead,
For Pisces flickers on the horizon,
And the Wagon lies wholly over Caurus,
And down that precipice we must descend.

XII

ERA lo loco, ove a scender la riva
Venimmo, alpestro, e per quel ch' ivi er' anco,
Tal ch' ogni vista ne sarebbe schiva.
Qual è quella ruina che nel fianco
Di qua da Trento l' Adice percosse,
O per tremuoto o per sostegno manco,
Chè da cima del monte, onde si mosse,
Al piano è sì la roccia discoscesa,
Ch' alcuna via darebbe a chi su fosse;
Cotal di quel burrato era la scesa:
E in su la punta della rotta lacca
L' infamia di Creti era distesa,
Che fu concetta nella falsa vacca:
E quando vide noi, sè stesso morse
Sì come quei cui l' ira dentro fiacca.
Lo Savio mio inver lui gridò: 'Forse
Tu credi che qui sia il duca d' Atene,
Che su nel mondo la morte ti porse?
Partiti, bestia, chè questi non viene
Ammaestrato dalla tua sorella,
Ma vassi per veder le vostre pene.'
Qual è quel toro che si slaccia in quella
Che ha ricevuto già 'l colpo mortale,
Che gir non sa, ma qua e là saltella,
Vid' io lo Minatauro far cotale.
E quegli accorto gridò: 'Corri al varco;
Mentre ch' è in furia è buon che tu ti cale.'
Così prendemmo via giù per lo scarco
Di quelle pietre, che spesso moviensi
Sotto i miei piedi per lo nuovo carco.

12

THE PLACE TO WHICH WE CAME for climbing down
The bank looked Alpine, and what was there, moreover,
Would have turned every eye away in horror.
Like that avalanche which crashed into the
Adige River on this side of Trent,
From the earthquake or inadequate support,
Leaving the rock, from the mountain top where
It began, down to the plain, so broken
That it made a pass for someone coming down:
Such was the descent into that ravine.
And stretched out on the summit of that
Jagged slope was the infamy of Crete,
Which was conceived in a pretended cow.
He bit himself when he caught sight of us,
Like one who rots away inside from rage.
My wise man turned to him and cried: "Perhaps
You think the Athenian hero is here
Who in the world above put you to death?
Away with you, monster! This man has not
Received instructions from your sister,
But comes to see what punishments are yours."
Just like a bull that wrenches itself free
The moment it receives a mortal thrust,
And cannot walk but throws itself about,
So did the Minotaur behave; and that
Observant man cried out: "Run for the pass!
Now is the time to descend, while he rages."
And so we picked our way down among
Those heaps of stones, which often started moving
Beneath my feet from the unaccustomed weight.

Io gìa pensando; e quei disse: 'Tu pensi
Forse a questa rovina, ch' è guardata
Da quell' ira bestial ch' io ora spensi.
Or vuo' che sappi, che l' altra fiata
Ch' io discesi quaggiù nel basso inferno,
Questa roccia non era ancor cascata.
Ma certo poco pria, se ben discerno,
Che venisse Colui che la gran preda
Levò a Dite del cerchio superno,
Da tutte parti l' alta valle feda
Tremò sì, ch' io pensai che l' universo
Sentisse amor, per lo quale è chi creda
Più volte il mondo in Caos converso:
Ed in quel punto questa vecchia roccia
Qui ed altrove tal fece riverso.
Ma ficca gli occhi a valle; chè s' approccia
La riviera del sangue, in la qual bolle
Qual che per violenza in altrui noccia.'
O cieca cupidigia, e ria e folle,
Che sì ci sproni nella vita corta,
E nell' eterna poi sì mal c' immolle!
Io vidi un' ampia fossa in arco torta,
Come quella che tutto il piano abbraccia,
Secondo ch' avea detto la mia scorta:
E tra il piè della ripa ed essa, in traccia
Correan Centauri armati di saette,
Come solean nel mondo andare a caccia.
Vedendoci calar ciascun ristette,
E della schiera tre si dipartiro
Con archi ed asticciuole prima elette:
E l' un gridò da lungi: 'A qual martiro
Venite voi che scendete la costa?
Ditel costinci, se non, l' arco tiro.'
Lo mio Maestro disse: 'La risposta
Farem noi a Chiron costà di presso:
Mal fu la voglia tua sempre sì tosta.'
Poi mi tentò, e disse: 'Quegli è Nesso,
Che morì per la bella Deianira,
E fe' di sè la vendetta egli stesso:

I walked on, pondering, and he said: "You may
Be thinking of this ruin which is guarded
By that bestial rage I have just silenced.
I wish you now to know that the other time
I descended into these depths of Hell,
This mass of rock had not yet toppled down.
What is certain—as I see it—is that
Shortly before He came who divested Dis
Of the great plunder of the highest circle,
On every side the deep foul valley
Trembled so, that I thought the universe
Was feeling love, through which some believe
The world has many times been turned to chaos.
It was at such a moment that this old rock,
Here and somewhere else, rolled down as it did.
Fix your eyes now on the valley; close by
Is the river of blood in which they boil
Who have hurt others by their violence."
O blind greed and insensate anger,
Which incites us so in this brief life, and then
Cruelly plunges us in the eternal!
I saw a spacious trench shaped like an arc,
As if embracing an entire plane,
Exactly as my guide said it would be.
Between it and the bottom of the cliff
Centaurs, armed with arrows, ran in single file,
As they once did in the world while hunting.
Seeing us coming down, they all stood still,
And from the ranks three of them stepped forward
With carefully selected bows and spears,
And one of them cried from afar: "You who
Descend the slope, to which torment do you come?
Speak from where you are, or else I draw the bow."
My master said: "We shall make our reply
To Chiron, who is standing near you.
You always harmed yourself by being hasty."
Then he touched me, and said: "That is Nessus,
Who died for beautiful Deïanira,
And made himself the means of his revenge;

E quel di mezzo, che al petto si mira,
E il gran Chirone, il qual nudrì Achille:
Quell' altro è Folo, che fu sì pien d' ira.
D' intorno al fosso vanno a mille a mille,
Saettando quale anima si svelle
Del sangue più che sua colpa sortille.'
Noi ci appressammo a quelle fiere snelle:
Chiron prese uno strale, e con la cocca
Fece la barba indietro alle mascelle.
Quando s' ebbe scoperta la gran bocca,
Disse ai compagni: 'Siete voi accorti,
Che quel di retro move ciò ch' ei tocca?
Così non soglion fare i piè de' morti.'
E il mio buon Duca, che già gli era al petto
Dove le duo nature son consorti,
Rispose: 'Ben è vivo, e sì soletto
Mostrarli mi convien la valle buia:
Necessità 'l conduce, e non diletto.
Tal si partì da cantare alleluia
Che mi commise quest' officio nuovo;
Non è ladron, nè io anima fuia.
Ma per quella virtù per cui io movo
Li passi miei per sì selvaggia strada,
Danne un de' tuoi, a cui noi siamo a pruovo,
E che ne mostri là dove si guada,
E che porti costui in su la groppa;
Che non è spirto che per l' aer vada.'
Chiron si volse in sulla destra poppa,
E disse a Nesso: 'Torna, e sì li guida,
E fa cansar, s' altra schiera v' intoppa.'
Or ci movemmo colla scorta fida
Lungo la proda del bollor vermiglio,
Ove i bolliti facean alte strida.
Io vidi gente sotto infino al ciglio;
E il gran Centauro disse: 'Ei son tiranni
Che dier nel sangue e nell' aver di piglio.
Quivi si piangon li spietati danni:
Quivi è Alessandro, e Dionisio fero,
Che fe' Cicilia aver dolorosi anni:

And he between, who gazes at his breast,
Is the great Chiron, who nurtured Achilles;
That other is Pholus, who was so wrathful.
They go around the pit by the thousands,
Firing arrows into any souls that
Rise above the blood more than their guilt allows."
We drew up close to those fleet-footed monsters.
Chiron seized an arrow, and with the notch
Thrust his beard back behind his jaws.
When finally he opened his large mouth,
He said to his companions: "Have you noticed
That the one in back moves what he touches?
The feet of dead men do not act like that."
And my good guide, who was by now abreast
Of him in whom two natures were conjoined,
Replied: "He is very much alive, and
Only to him may I show the dark ravine.
Necessity impels him, not diversion.
A lady came from singing allelujahs,
Who gave me this new errand to fulfil;
He is no thief, nor I a thieving spirit.
But by that power by which I direct
My steps along such a wild path as this,
Assign us one of your band who stand near us,
That he may both conduct us to the ford
And bear this man across upon his back;
For he is not a soul that walks on air."
Chiron turned to his right and spoke to Nessus:
"Go back with them and be their guide,
And shun whatever troop approaches you."
From the shore of that boiling mass of red,
Where those who were being boiled gave piercing screams,
I saw people submerged up to their eyebrows;
And the great Centaur said: "Those are the tyrants
Who gave themselves to blood and depredation.
Here they repent their merciless destruction.
Here is Alexander and proud Dionysius,
Who brought years of suffering to Sicily;
And that brow with such black hair upon it

E quella fronte ch' ha il pel così nero
E' Azzolino; e quell' altro ch' è biondo
E' Opizzo da Esti, il qual per vero
Fu spento dal figliastro su nel mondo.'
Allor mi volsi al Poeta, e quei disse:
'Questi ti sia or primo, ed io secondo.'
Poco più oltre il Centauro s' affisse
Sopra una gente che infino alla gola
Parea che di quel bulicame uscisse.
Mostrocci un' ombra dall' un canto sola,
Dicendo: 'Colui fesse in grembo a Dio
Lo cor che in sul Tamigi ancor si cola.'
Poi vidi gente che di fuor del rio
Tenea la testa ed ancor tutto il casso:
E di costoro assai riconobb' io.
Così a più a più si facea basso
Quel sangue sì che cocea pur li piedi:
E quivi fu del fosso il nostro passo.
'Sì come tu da questa parte vedi
Lo bulicame che sempre si scema,'
Disse il Centauro, 'voglio che tu credi,
Che da quest' altra a più a più giù prema
Lo fondo suo, infin ch' ei si raggiunge
Ove la tirannia convien che gema.
La divina giustizia di qua punge
Quell' Attila che fu flagello in terra,
E Pirro, e Sesto; ed in eterno munge
Le lagrime che col bollor disserra
A Rinier da Corneto, a Rinier Pazzo,
Che fecero alle strade tanta guerra.'
Poi si rivolse, e ripassossi il guazzo.

Is Azzolino; the other who is blond
Is Obizzo da Esti, who in the world
Was actually slain by his own stepson."
I then turned to the poet, and he said:
"Let him be first to you now, and me second."
A little further on, the Centaur stopped
At a place where people appeared to be
Emerging from the froth down to their throats.
Pointing out a lone soul in a corner,
He said to us: "In the bosom of God he stabbed
A heart that is still honored on the Thames."
Then I saw people who held their head high
Above the stream, and even their whole chest,
And a great many of these I recognized.
By degrees that blood sank lower and lower,
Until at last it scalded the feet only;
And there we made our way across the ditch.
"Since you can see, from this side, the boiling foam
Gradually diminishing in depth,"
The Centaur said, "I want you to understand
That from the other side it grows deeper
And deeper, until at last it reappears
Back there where tyranny is castigated.
Divine justice in this place harasses that
Attila who was once a scourge on earth,
And Pyrrhus and Sextus, and eternally
Drains off the tears, which that boiling loosens,
From Rinier da Corneto and Rinier Pazzo,
Who engaged in such warfare on the highways."
Then he turned, and went back across the ford.

XIII

NON era ancor di là Nesso arrivato,
Quando noi ci mettemmo per un bosco
Che da nessun sentiero era segnato.
Non fronde verdi, ma di color fosco;
Non rami schietti, ma nodosi e involti;
Non pomi v' eran, ma stecchi con tosco.
Non han sì aspri sterpi nè sì folti
Quelle fiere selvagge che in odio hanno
Tra Cecina e Corneto i luoghi colti.
Quivi le brutte Arpíe lor nidi fanno,
Che cacciar delle Strofade i Troiani
Con tristo annunzio di futuro danno.
Ali hanno late, e colli e visi umani,
Piè con artigli, e pennuto il gran ventre:
Fanno lamenti in su gli alberi strani.
E 'l buon Maestro: 'Prima che più entre,
Sappi che se' nel secondo girone,'
Mi cominciò a dire, 'e sarai, mentre
Che tu verrai nell' orribil sabbione.
Però riguarda bene, e sì vedrai
Cose che torrien fede al mio sermone.'
Io sentia da ogni parte traer guai,
E non vedea persona che il facesse;
Perch' io tutto smarrito m' arrestai.
Io credo ch' ei credette ch' io credesse
Che tante voci uscisser tra que' bronchi
Da gente che per noi si nascondesse.
Però disse il Maestro: 'Se tu tronchi
Qualche fraschetta d' una d' este piante,
Li pensier ch' hai si faran tutti monchi.'

13

NESSUS HAD NOT YET REACHED the other bank,
When we started moving through a forest
That did not have a single trail to mark it.
The leafage was not green, but almost black;
The branches, not smooth, but gnarled and knotty;
There were no apples; only poisoned thorns.
Even the wild beasts who hate the fertile fields
Between Cecina and Corneto
Are unacquainted with such thorny clumps.
Here the loathsome Harpies make their nests
Who drove the Trojans from the Strophades
With their bleak prophecy of woe to come.
With their wide wings, human necks and faces,
Taloned feet, and large and feathered craws,
They scream laments among the nameless trees.
"Before you go further in," the good master
Began to say to me, "know that you are
In the second ring, and will continue to be,
Until you come to the sands of horror.
Look carefully, and you shall see things you
Never would believe if I spoke of them."
From every side I heard the shrieks of anguish,
Yet could not see whom they were coming from.
This so bewildered me I had to stop.
I believe that he believed that I believed
That all those voices issued from people who
Concealed themselves from us behind the stumps.
The master said, however: "If you snap off
The smallest twig of any of these plants,
Your speculations will all end abruptly."

Allor porsi la mano un poco avante
E colsi un ramicel da un gran pruno:
E il tronco suo gridò: 'Perchè mi schiante?'
Da che fatto fu poi di sangue bruno,
Ricominciò a gridar: 'Perchè mi scerpi?
Non hai tu spirto di pietate alcuno?
Uomini fummo, ed or sem fatti sterpi:
Ben dovrebb' esser la tua man più pia,
Se state fossim' anime di serpi.'
Come d' un stizzo verde, che arso sia
Dall' un de' capi, che dall' altro geme,
E cigola per vento che va via;
Sì della scheggia rotta usciva insieme
Parole e sangue: ond' io lasciai la cima
Cadere, e stetti come l' uom che teme.
'S' egli avesse potuto creder prima,'
Rispose il Savio mio, 'anima lesa,
Ciò ch' ha veduto pur con la mia rima,
Non averebbe in te la man distesa;
Ma la cosa incredible mi fece
Indurlo ad opra che a me stesso pesa.
Ma dilli chi tu fosti, sì che in vece
D' alcuna ammenda tua fama rinfreschi
Nel mondo su, dove tornar gli lece.'
E il tronco: 'Sì con dolce dir m' adeschi
Ch' io non posso tacere; e voi non gravi
Perch' io un poco a ragionar m' inveschi.
Io son colui che tenni ambo le chiavi
Del cor di Federico, e che le volsi
Serrando e disserrando sì soavi,
Che dal secreto suo quasi ogni uom tolsi:
Fede portai al glorioso offizio,
Tanto ch' io ne perdei i sonni e i polsi.
La meretrice che mai dall' ospizio
Di Cesare non torse gli occhi putti,
Morte comune, e delle corti vizio,
Infiammò contra me gli animi tutti,
E gl' infiammati infiammar sì Augusto,
Che i lieti onor tornaro in tristi lutti.

I then put out my hand a little
And broke a twig from a large thorny growth,
And its trunk cried out: "Why do you break me?"
When it had turned dark with blood, it started
To cry out again: "Why do you tear me?
Have you no feeling of compassion at all?
Once we were men, and now we are stumps of trees:
Surely your hand would have shown more pity
If we had been, instead, the souls of snakes."
In much the same way that a green fire-log,
Blazing at one end, whines and whistles
At the other, as the wind blows through it,
So from that splintered limb there issued words
And blood: whereupon I let the tip fall to the
Ground, and stood there like a frightened man.
"If he had been able to believe before
What he had seen only in my poetry,
He would not have put his hand upon you,
O bruised spirit," said my sage in answer;
"But the incredible nature of the thing
Made me urge him to that act, which grieves me, too.
But tell him who you were, that he may make amends
By reanimating your fame in the world,
To which he is permitted to go back."
And the trunk: "You tempt me so with your sweet words
That I cannot keep silent; may it not
Burden you if I succumb and talk a while.
I am he who held both keys to the heart
Of Frederick, and so gently turned them,
Locking and unlocking, that I removed
Almost everybody from his confidence;
Such was my loyalty to that high office
That for it I lost both my sleep and life.
The harlot whose meretricious eyes
Were never turned away from Caesar's house,
That common death and vice of royal courts,
Inflamed every mind against me, and those
Who were inflamed so inflamed Augustus,
That all my happy honors turned to mourning.

L' animo mio per disdegnoso gusto,
  Credendo col morir fuggir disdegno,
  Ingiusto fece me contra me giusto.
Per le nuove radici d' esto legno
  Vi giuro che giammai non ruppi fede
  Al mio signor, che fu d' onor sì degno.
E se di voi alcun nel mondo riede,
  Conforti la memoria mia, che giace
  Ancor del colpo che invidia le diede.'
Un poco attese, e poi: 'Da ch' ei si tace,'
  Disse il Poeta a me, 'non perder l' ora;
  Ma parla e chiedi a lui se più ti piace.'
Ond' io a lui: 'Domandal tu ancora
  Di quel che credi che a me satisfaccia;
  Ch' io non potrei: tanta pietà m' accora.'
Perciò ricominciò: 'Se l' uom ti faccia
  Liberamente ciò che il tuo dir prega,
  Spirito incarcerato, ancor ti piaccia
Di dirne come l' anima si lega
  In questi nocchi; e dinne, se tu puoi,
  S' alcuna mai da tai membra si spiega.'
Allor soffiò lo tronco forte, e poi
  Si convertì quel vento in cotal voce:
  'Brevemente sarà risposto a voi.
Quando si parte l' anima feroce
  Dal corpo, ond' ella stessa s' è disvelta,
  Minos la manda alla settima foce.
Cade in la selva, e non l' è parte scelta;
  Ma là dove fortuna la balestra,
  Quivi germoglia come gran di spelta;
Surge in vermena, ed in pianta silvestra:
  L'Arpíe, pascendo poi delle sue foglie,
  Fanno dolore, ed al dolor finestra.
Come l' altre verrem per nostre spoglie,
  Ma non però ch' alcuna sen rivesta:
  Chè non è giusto aver ciò ch' uom si toglie.
Qui le strascineremo, e per la mesta
  Selva saranno i nostri corpi appesi,
  Ciascuno al prun dell' ombra sua molesta.'

My spirit, in a temper of disdain,
Believing it could flee disdain by dying,
Made me unjust to my own self.
I swear to you, by the new roots of this tree,
That I never violated the trust
Of my master, who merited such honor.
And if one of you returns to the world,
May he revive the memory of me,
Which still lies fallen from the blows of envy."
The poet waited a while, and then said to me:
"Now that he is silent, waste no time;
Speak up and ask him anything you please."
But I replied: "Question him some more yourself
About anything you believe would interest me.
I cannot: my heart is too full of pity."
With that he started once again: "As freely
As that man may do what you have asked,
May it please you, O imprisoned spirit,
To tell us further how the soul is tied up
In these knots; and tell us, if you can,
If any ever frees itself from such limbs."
With that the tree trunk started to blow hard,
And then that wind was changed into a voice:
"The answer shall be given you in brief.
Whenever a wild spirit leaves the body,
From which it has been wrenched by its own hand,
Minos commits it to the seventh gorge.
It falls in the wood, not in a given place,
But wherever Fortune catapults it,
And there it starts to sprout as from a seed.
From a sprig it grows into a woody plant;
The Harpies, then, by biting off the leaves,
Cause pain, and make a window for that pain.
Like the others, we shall come for our bodies,
But not to reassume them; for it is not just
That men should have what they take from themselves.
We shall drag them down here, and all over
This melancholy wood our bodies shall hang,
Each from the tree of its injurious shade."

Noi eravamo ancora al tronco attesi,
Credendo ch' altro ne volesse dire,
Quando noi fummo d'un romor sorpresi,
Similemente a colui che venire
Sente il porco e la caccia alla sua posta,
Ch' ode le bestie e le frasche stormire.
Ed ecco duo dalla sinistra costa,
Nudi e graffiati, fuggendo sì forte,
Che della selva rompièno ogni rosta.
Quel dinanzi: 'Ora accorri, accorri, morte.'
E l' altro, a cui pareva tardar troppo,
Gridava: 'Lano, sì non furo accorte
Le gambe tue alle giostre del Toppo.'
E poichè forse gli fallía la lena,
Di sè e d' un cespuglio fece un groppo.
Diretro a loro era la selva piena
Di nere cagne, bramose e correnti,
Come veltri che uscisser di catena.
In quel che s' appiattò miser li denti,
E quel dilaceraro a brano a brano;
Poi sen portar quelle membra dolenti.
Presemi allor la mia scorta per mano,
E menommi al cespuglio che piangea,
Per le rotture sanguinenti, invano.
'O Jacomo,' dicea, 'da sant' Andrea,
Che t' è giovato di me fare schermo?
Che colpa ho io della tua vita rea?'
Quando il Maestro fu sopr' esso fermo,
Disse: 'Chi fusti, che per tante punte
Soffi con sangue doloroso sermo?'
Ed egli a noi: 'O anime che giunte
Siete a veder lo strazio disonesto
Ch' ha le mie fronde sì da me disgiunte,
Raccoglietele al piè del tristo cesto:
Io fui della città che nel Batista
Mutò 'l primo padrone: ond' ei per questo
Sempre con l' arte sua la farà trista:
E se non fosse che in sul passo d' Arno
Rimane ancor di lui alcuna vista,

We were still listening to the tree trunk,
Thinking that it wanted to say something more
To us, when we were startled by a noise,
The way men are when they sense a boar hunt near
And hear the beasts yelp and the branches rustle.
And, lo, there on our left, two naked and
Lacerated souls were fleeing with such speed
They shivered every sapling in that wood.
The one ahead cried out: "Come quickly, death!"
The other, who seemed to him to be too slow,
Was shouting: "Your legs were not so willing,
Lano, at the jousts of Toppo."
Perhaps because he had run out of breath,
He tried to hide himself behind a bush.
In back of them the wood was overrun
With black bitches, ravenous and swift
As greyhounds that have broken from their chains.
They sank their teeth into the one who crouched there;
They tore him limb from limb, and then
They carried off his pitiful remains.
My escort now took me by the hand and led me
To the bush that was weeping all in vain
Through its bleeding gashes.
"O Giacomo da Sant' Andrea," it said,
"What did it profit you to hide behind me,
Why should I be blamed for your wicked life?"
When the master had stopped in front of him,
He said: "Who were you that through so many wounds
Breathe out such melancholy words with blood?"
And he to us: "O spirits who have come
In time to see the shameful mutilation
That has severed all my leaves from me,
Collect them at the foot of this sad bush!
I was of the city which changed its first patron
For the Baptist, in consequence of which
He will always bring her grief with his arts;
And if some vestige of his image
Did not still remain on the Arno bridge,
Those citizens that later reconstructed her

Quei cittadin, che poi la rifondarno
Sopra il cener che d' Attila rimase,
Avrebber fatto lavorare indarno.
Io fei giubbetto a me delle mie case.'

From the ashes that Attila left behind
Would all have done their work in vain.
I made a gallows for me of my home."

XIV

POICHE' la carità del natio loco
Mi strinse, raunai le fronde sparte,
E rende' le a colui ch' era già fioco.
Indi venimmo al fine, ove si parte
Lo secondo giron dal terzo, e dove
Si vede di giustizia orribil arte.
A ben manifestar le cose nuove,
Dico che arrivammo ad una landa
Che dal suo letto ogni pianta rimove.
La dolorosa selva l' è ghirlanda
Intorno, come il fosso tristo ad essa:
Quivi fermammo i passi a randa a randa.
Lo spazzo era un' arena arida e spessa,
Non d' altra foggia fatta che colei,
Che fu da' piè di Caton già soppressa.
O vendetta di Dio, quanto tu dei
Esser temuta da ciascun che legge
Ciò che fu manifesto agli occhi miei!
D' anime nude vidi molte gregge,
Che piangean tutte assai miseramente,
E parea posta lor diversa legge.
Supin giaceva in terra alcuna gente;
Alcuna si sedea tutta raccolta,
Ed altra andava continuamente.
Quella che giva intorno era più molta,
E quella men che giaceva al tormento,
Ma più al duolo avea la lingua sciolta.
Sopra tutto il sabbion d' un cader lento
Piovean di foco dilatate falde,
Come di neve in alpe senza vento.

14

MOVED BY THE LOVE I bore my native place,
I gathered up the scattered leaves, and gave
Them back to him who had by now grown faint.
We then came to the end that separates
The third ring from the second, and where
A frightful tool of justice may be seen.
To give the new things in their true appearance,
Let me first say that we came to a plane
That from its bed excluded every plant.
Around it the woeful wood formed a garland,
As did the dismal ditch about itself.
There, at the very edge, we halted.
The surface was of dense and arid sand,
No different in quality from the sand
Once trod upon by the feet of Cato.
O vengeance of God, how you should be feared
By everyone who reads about the things
That were made manifest to my eyes!
I saw flocks and flocks of naked souls,
Crying their hearts out in great misery.
Diverse laws seemed to have been imposed on them.
Some of them were lying on their backs;
Some were sitting and all folded up,
And others walked and walked without a stop.
Most numerous were those who went about;
The fewest were the ones who lay in torment,
And they were most vociferous in their pain.
Upon the sandy ground, in a slow fall,
There rained distended flakes of fire,
Like snow falling on a windless Alp.

Quali Alessandro in quelle parti calde
D' India vide sopra lo suo stuolo
Fiamme cadere infino a terra salde;
Perch' ei provvide a scalpitar lo suolo
Con le sue schiere, acciocchè il vapore
Me' si stingeva mentre ch' era solo:
Tale scendeva l' eternale ardore;
Onde l' arena s' accendea, com' esca
Sotto focile, a doppiar lo dolore.
Senza riposo mai era la tresca
Delle misere mani, or quindi or quinci
Iscotendo da sè l' arsura fresca.
Io cominciai: 'Maestro, tu che vinci
Tutte le cose, fuor che i Demon duri
Che all' entrar della porta incontro uscinci,
Chi è quel grande, che non par che curi
L' incendio, e giace dispettoso e torto
Sì che la pioggia non par che il maturi?'
E quel medesmo, che si fue accorto
Ch' io domandava il mio duca di lui,
Gridò: 'Qual io fui vivo, tal son morto.
Se Giove stanchi il suo fabbro, da cui
Crucciato prese la folgore acuta
Onde l' ultimo dì percosso fui;
O s' egli stanchi gli altri a muta a muta
In Mongibello alla fucina negra,
Chiamando: "Buon Vulcano, aiuta aiuta,"
Sì com' ei fece alla pugna di Flegra,
E me saetti con tutta sua forza,
Non ne potrebbe aver vendetta allegra.'
Allora il Duca mio parlò di forza
Tanto, ch' io non l' avea sì forte udito:
'O Capaneo, in ciò che non s' ammorza
La tua superbia, se' tu più punito:
Nullo martirio, fuor che la tua rabbia,
Sarebbe al tuo furor dolor compito.'
Poi si rivolse a me con miglior labbia,
Dicendo: 'Quel fu l' un de' sette regi
Ch' assiser Tebe; ed ebbe e par ch' egli abbia

Much like the flames which Alexander, in those
Warm areas of India, saw fall
Upon his troops and touch the ground unspent,
Causing him to order all his legions
To trample on the earth together, to put
The fire out before another started:
So fell that everlasting fire
From which the sand took flame like tinder
Under flint, in order to give twice the pain.
Without a moment's respite was that dance
Of miserable hands, now here, now there,
All trying to shake off the latest blaze.
"Master," I began, "you who triumph over
Everything except those obdurate fiends
Who issued from the portals to oppose us,
Who is that large one who does not seem to mind
The burning, but lies there gnarled and scornful
As if the rain does not affect him?"
But he himself, having overheard me ask
My guide about him, cried out:
"What I once was, alive, I still am, dead.
Even if Jove should tire out the smith
From whom he angrily seized the thunderbolt
With which I was struck the last day of my life,
And one by one exhausted the other smiths
In the black forge of Mongibello,
Calling out: 'Help me, good Vulcan, help me!'—
As he had done at the battle of Phlegra—
And hurled his bolts at me with all his strength,
He could not have a pleasurable revenge."
My guide then spoke with a vehemence
That I had never heard him use before:
"O Capaneus, to the degree that your pride
Remains unchecked, you are chastised the more;
Other than your own madness, no torture
Would be fit suffering for your violence."
Then he turned to me with a better face
And said: "He was one of the seven kings
Who besieged Thebes. He held, and seems still to hold,

Dio in disdegno, e poco par che il pregi:
Ma, come io dissi a lui, li suoi dispetti
Sono al suo petto assai debiti fregi.
Or mi vien dietro, e guarda che non metti
Ancor li piedi nell' arena arsiccia,
Ma sempre al bosco li ritieni stretti.'
Tacendo divenimmo là ove spiccia
Fuor della selva un picciol fiumicello,
Lo cui rossore ancor mi raccapriccia.
Quale del Bulicame esce ruscello
Che parton poi tra lor le peccatrici,
Tal per l' arena giù sen giva quello.
Lo fondo suo ed ambo le pendici
Fatt' eran pietra, e i margini da lato:
Perch' io m' accorsi che il passo era lici.
'Tra tutto l' altro ch io t' ho dimostrato,
Posciachè noi entrammo per la porta
Lo cui sogliare a nessuno è negato,
Cosa non fu dagli tuoi occhi scorta
Notabil come lo presente rio,
Che sopra sè tutte fiammelle ammorta.'
Queste parole fur del Duca mio:
Perchè il pregai che mi largisse il pasto
Di cui largito m' aveva il disio.
'In mezzo mar siede un paese guasto',
Diss' egli allora, 'che s' appella Creta,
Sotto il cui rege fu già il mondo casto.
Una montagna v' è, che già fu lieta
D' acqua e di fronde, che si chiamò Ida;
Ora è diserta come cosa vieta.
Rea la scelse già per cuna fida
Del suo figliuolo; e per celarlo meglio,
Quando piangea vi facea far le grida.
Dentro dal monte sta dritto un gran veglio,
Che tien volte le spalle inver Damiata,
E Roma guarda sì come suo speglio.
La sua testa è di fin' oro formata,
E puro argento son le braccia e il petto,
Poi è di rame infino alla forcata:

God in disdain, and esteems him little.
But, as I said to him, his defiances
Are appropriate badges for his breast.
Now go behind me, and watch that you
Do not put your feet in the scorching sand,
But always keep them close within the forest."
Without a word we went on, until we came
To where a small stream, whose redness makes me
Shudder even now, gushed out from the wood.
Like the stream that flows from the Bulicame,
Which the sinful women share among themselves,
So through the sand this too went flowing down.
Both the bottom and the overhanging banks
Had become stone, and so had its margins,
From which I knew the place to pass was there.
"Among the other things that I have shown you
Since we first entered through that doorway,
The threshold of which is denied to none,
Your eyes have not beheld anything
So remarkable as this rivulet,
Which extinguishes every flame above it."
These words were spoken by my guide, and I
Implored him to provide the nourishment
For which he had aroused my appetite.
"Far out at sea there is a ruined land,"
He then said, "that has the name of Crete; once,
Under its king, the world was undefiled.
There is a mountain there—Mount Ida, it is called—
That once was gay with leaves and water; today
It is deserted like something long decayed.
At one time Rhea chose it as a safe
Cradle for her son; and ordered loud screams
When he cried, the better to conceal him.
Inside the mountain, his shoulders turned towards
Damiata, an enormous old man stands
And gazes straight at Rome as in a mirror.
His head is fashioned of fine gold;
His arms and breast are of pure silver;
From there, down to his hips, he is of copper,

Da indi in giuso è tutto ferro eletto,
Salvo che il destro piede è terra cotta,
E sta in su quel, più che in sull' altro, eretto.
Ciascuna parte, fuor che l' oro, è rotta
D' una fessura che lagrime goccia,
Le quali accolte foran quella grotta.
Lor corso in questa valle si diroccia:
Fanno Acheronte, Stige e Flegetonta;
Poi sen va giù per questa stretta doccia
Infin là dove più non si dismonta:
Fanno Cocito; e qual sia quello stagno,
Tu il vederai: però qui non si conta.'
Ed io a lui: 'Se il presente rigagno
Si deriva così dal nostro mondo,
Perchè ci appar pure a questo vivagno?'
Ed egli a me: 'Tu sai che il luogo è tondo,
E tutto che tu sii venuto molto
Pur a sinistra giù calando al fondo,
Non se' ancor per tutto il cerchio volto;
Perchè, se cosa n' apparisce nuova,
Non dee addur maraviglia al tuo volto.'
Ed io ancor: 'Maestro, ove si trova
Flegetonta e Letè, chè dell' un taci,
E l' altro di' che si fa d' esta piova?'
'In tutte tue question certo mi piaci,'
Rispose; 'ma il bollor dell' acqua rossa
Dovea ben solver l' una che tu faci.
Letè vedrai, ma fuor di questa fossa,
Là dove vanno l' anime a lavarsi
Quando la colpa pentuta è rimossa.'
Poi disse: 'Omai è tempo da scostarsi
Dal bosco: fa che diretro a me vegne:
Li margini fan via, che non son arsi,
E sopra loro ogni vapor si spegne.'

And then below that, of the finest iron,
Except the right foot, which is terra cotta:
On that he stands more than on the other.
But for the part that is of gold, each part
Is broken by a fissure that sheds tears,
Which collect and break through that mountain wall.
Their course plunges headlong down the valley,
Forming Acheron, the Styx, and Phlegethon;
Then they flow down along this narrow duct,
Until they come where there is no descending,
And form Cocytus; what that pond is like
I need not say; you shall see for yourself."
And I to him: "If this rivulet
Arises in such fashion in the world,
Why does it appear to us only on this bank?"
And he to me: "You know the place is round,
And though you have moved far towards the bottom—
By descending always to the left—
You have not yet completed the full circle.
If, therefore, something new appears, it should not
Bring a look of wonder to your face."
And I again: "Master, where are Phlegethon
And Lethe to be found? Of one you do not speak;
And, of the other, that this rain creates it."
"Your questions always give me pleasure," said he.
"Yet the boiling of that reddened water
Should be answer enough to one of them.
Lethe you shall see, not in this chasm,
But where the souls all go to purge themselves
When the repented misdeeds are absolved."
And he then said: "It is time now to leave
The forest; follow close behind me;
The edges, which are not burning, make a path,
And over them the flames are powerless."

XV

ORA cen porta l' un de' duri margini,
E il fummo del ruscel di sopra aduggia
Sì che dal foco salva l' acqua e gli argini.
Quale i Fiamminghi tra Guizzante e Bruggia,
Temendo il fiotto che ver lor s' avventa,
Fanno lo schermo perchè il mar si fuggia;
E quale i Padovan lungo la Brenta,
Per difender lor ville e lor castelli,
Anzi che Chiarentana il caldo senta;
A tale imagine eran fatti quelli,
Tutto che nè sì alti nè sì grossi,
Qual che si fosse, lo maestro felli.
Già eravam dalla selva rimossi
Tanto, ch' io non avrei visto dov' era,
Perch' io indietro rivolto mi fossi,
Quando incontrammo d' anime una schiera,
Che venia lungo l' argine, e ciascuna
Ci riguardava, come suol da sera
Guardar l' un l' altro sotto nuova luna;
E sì ver noi aguzzavan le ciglia
Come 'l vecchio sartor fa nella cruna.
Così adocchiato da cotal famiglia,
Fui conosciuto da un, che mi prese
Per lo lembo e gridò: 'Qual maraviglia!'
Ed io, quando il suo braccio a me distese,
Ficcai gli occhi per lo cotto aspetto
Sì che il viso abbruciato non difese
La conoscenza sua al mio intelletto;
E chinando la mia alla sua faccia,
Risposi: 'Siete voi qui, ser Brunetto?'

15

WE MOVED ALONG THE BORDER on hard ground,
The vapor of the stream so heavy overhead
Its shade saved the banks and water from the flames.
Just as the Flemings, between Bruges and Wissant,
When they fear the floods advancing towards them,
Set up defenses to throw back the sea;
And as the Paduans do along the Brenta,
To protect their castles and their villages
Before Chiarentana begins to feel the heat;
On the same principle the master workman,
Whoever he might be, constructed these banks,
Though they are neither so high nor so large.
We had already gone so far beyond
The wood that, had I turned about, I would not
Have been able to see where it was,
When we came upon a company of souls
Wending their way along the river bank.
They looked at us as people look at one
Another at nightfall under the new moon.
They wrinkled up their brows and peered at us
Like an old tailor at a needle's eye.
Stared at in this manner by that group,
I was recognized by one, who clasped the hem
Of my garment and cried: "What a miracle!"
And I, when he extended his arm to me,
So fixed my eyes upon his cooked appearance,
That even his scalded face could not
Conceal his true identity from me.
And, bending down my face to his, I answered:
"Are you here, Master Brunetto?" And he:

*E quegli: 'O figliuol mio, non ti dispiaccia
Se Brunetto Latino un poco teco
Ritorna indietro, e lascia andar la traccia.'
Io dissi a lui: 'Quanto posso ven preco;
E se volete che con voi m' asseggia,
Faròl, se piace a costui, chè vo seco.'
'O figliuol,' disse, 'qual di questa greggia
S' arresta punto, giace poi cent' anni
Senza arrostarsi quando il fuoco il feggia.
Però va oltre: io ti verrò a' panni,
E poi rigiugnerò la mia masnada,
Che va piangendo i suoi eterni danni.'
Io non osava scender della strada
Per andar par di lui: ma il capo chino
Tenea, come uom che reverente vada.
Ei cominciò: 'Qual fortuna o destino
Anzi l' ultimo dì quaggiù ti mena?
E chi è questi che mostra il cammino?'
'Là su di sopra in la vita serena,'
Rispos' io lui, 'mi smarri' in una valle,
Avanti che l' età mia fosse piena.
Pure ier mattina le volsi le spalle:
Questi m' apparve, tornand' io in quella,
E riducemi a ca per questo calle.'
Ed egli a me: 'Se tu segui tua stella,
Non puoi fallire al glorioso porto,
Se ben m' accorsi nella vita bella:
E s' io non fossi sì per tempo morto,
Veggendo il cielo a te così benigno,
Dato t' avrei all' opera conforto.
Ma quell' ingrato popolo maligno,
Che discese di Fiesole ab antico,
E tiene ancor del monte e del macigno,
Ti si farà, per tuo ben far, nimico:
Ed è ragion; chè tra li lazzi sorbi
Si disconvien fruttare al dolce fico.
Vecchia fama nel mondo li chiama orbi;
Gente avara, invidiosa e superba,
Da' lor costumi fa che tu ti forbi.*

"O my son, do not be offended if
Brunetto Latini lets the others go ahead
And in your company turns back a little."
I said: "I beg you to with all my heart;
And, should you wish me to sit down with you,
I shall, if it pleases him with whom I go."
"O my son," he said, "if any of this flock
Stops but a moment, he must lie motionless
One hundred years, when the fire smites him.
So you move on, and I will trail beside you
And presently rejoin my company,
Which goes bemoaning its eternal ills."
I dared not step down from the road to be
On the same level with him; instead, I bowed
My head like one who walks in reverence.
He began: "What destiny or fortune,
Before your last mortal day, leads you down here?
And who is he who shows the way?"
"Up there above in the clear, calm life," I said,
"Before I had attained the age of fullness,
I found myself wandering in a valley,
Which only yesterday I put behind me.
As I was turning to go back to it,
He appeared, to lead me home along this path."
And he to me: "By following your star,
You cannot fail to reach the port of glory—
If I judged rightly in that beautiful life.
If I had not died so early, I would have
Given you encouragement in your work,
Seeing that Heaven was so generous to you.
But that malign and thankless populace,
Which in antiquity came down from Fiesole
And savors even now of stone and mountain,
For your good actions will be your enemy.
And that is right; for among sour sorb trees
It is not fitting that sweet figs should ripen.
An old tradition on earth calls them blind,
A greedy people, envious and haughty.
Cleanse yourself of all their practices.

La tua fortuna tanto onor ti serba,
Che l' una parte e l' altra avranno fame
Di te: ma lungi fia dal becco l' erba.
Faccian le bestie Fiesolane strame
Di lor medesme, e non tocchin la pianta,
S' alcuna surge ancor nel lor letame,
In cui riviva la semente santa
Di quei Roman che vi rimaser quando
Fu fatto il nido di malizia tanta.'
'Se fosse tutto pieno il mio dimando,'
Risposi lui, 'voi non sareste ancora
Dell' umana natura posto in bando:
Chè in la mente m' è fitta, ed or mi accora
La cara e buona imagine paterna
Di voi, quando nel mondo ad ora ad ora
M' insegnavate come l' uom s' eterna:
E quant' io l' abbia in grado, mentre io vivo
Convien che nella mia lingua si scerna.
Ciò che narrate di mio corso scrivo,
E serbolo a chiosar con altro testo
A donna che saprà, se a lei arrivo.
Tanto vogl' io che vi sia manifesto,
Pur che mia coscienza non mi garra,
Che alla fortuna, come vuol, son presto.
Non è nuova agli orecchi miei tale arra:
Però giri fortuna la sua rota,
Come le piace, e il villan la sua marra.'
Lo mio Maestro allora in sulla gota
Destra si volse indietro, e riguardommi;
Poi disse: 'Bene ascolta chi la nota.'
Nè per tanto di men parlando vommi
Con ser Brunetto, e domando chi sono
Li suoi compagni più noti e più sommi.
Ed egli a me: 'Saper d' alcuno è buono:
Degli altri fia laudabile tacerci,
Chè il tempo saria corto a tanto suono.
In somma sappi che tutti fur cherci
E letterati grandi, e di gran fama,
D' un peccato medesmo al mondo lerci.

Such honor has destiny in store for you,
That both sides shall be hungry for you.
But the grass shall be out of the goat's reach.
Let the Fiesolan beasts make fodder
Of themselves, and not molest the plant,
If, in all their dung, any blossoms still
In which there might live again the sacred seed
Of those Romans who remained behind
When this malignancy first nested there."
"If my own wishes had been gratified,"
I replied to him, "you would not yet
Have been exiled from humanity.
For that dear and good paternal image
Of you when, from hour to hour, in the world,
You taught me how man gains eternity,
Is fixed in my mind and now desolates me;
And while I am alive it shall be on
My tongue what gratitude I owe to it.
I shall write down what you predict of me,
And keep it with another text to be explained
By a lady who shall know how, if I reach her.
This much I wish to make clear to you:
That, so long as my conscience does not scold me,
I am ready for whatever Fortune wills.
Such prophecy is not new to my ears;
Let Fortune, therefore, turn her wheel as she
Wishes, and the countryman his mattock."
At that point my master turned his head back
To the right, and, looking hard at me, he said:
"He hears well who takes note of what he hears."
I none the less went on conversing with
Master Brunetto, asking him which of his
Companions were the greatest and best known.
And he: "To know about a few is good; of the
Others it is commendable not to speak.
The time would be too short for so much talk.
In sum, know then that all of them were priests
And men of great learning and great fame,
Polluted by the same sin in the world.

Priscian sen va con quella turba grama,
E Francesco d' Accorso; anco vedervi,
S' avessi avuto di tal tigna brama,
Colui potei che dal servo de' servi
Fu trasmutato d' Arno in Bacchiglione,
Dove lasciò li mal protesi nervi.
Di più direi; ma il venir e il sermone
Più lungo esser non può, però ch' io veggio
Là surger nuovo fummo del sabbione.
Gente vien con la quale esser non deggio;
Siati raccomandato il mio Tesoro
Nel quale io vivo ancora; e più non cheggio.'
Poi si rivolse, e parve di coloro
Che corrono a Verona il drappo verde
Per la campagna; e parve di costoro
Quegli che vince e non colui che perde.

Priscian accompanies that dismal throng,
As does Francesco d'Accorso; and if you
Had been inquisitive about such scurf,
You could have seen him whom the servants' servant
Sent from the Arno to the Bacchiglione,
Where he left his evilly twisted sinews.
I would say more; but I cannot go with you,
Or converse any longer; I already
See new vapor ascending from the sand.
People approach with whom I should not be;
Let me recommend my 'Treasure' to you;
In it I still live, and more I do not ask."
Then he spun around, and was like one of those
Who race across the fields at Verona
For the green cloth; and of those he seemed to be
The one that wins and not the one that loses.

XVI

GIA' era in loco ove s' udia il rimbombo
Dell' acqua che cadea nell' altro giro,
Simile a quel che l' arnie fanno rombo;
Quando tre ombre insieme si partiro
Correndo d' una torma che passava
Sotto la pioggia dell' aspro martiro.
Venian ver noi, e ciascuna gridava:
'Sostati tu, che all' abito ne sembri
Essere alcun di nostra terra prava.'
Aimè, che piaghe vidi ne' lor membri
Recenti e vecchie dalle fiamme incese!
Ancor men duol, pur ch' io me ne rimembri.
Alle lor grida il mio Dottor s' attese,
Volse, il viso ver me, ed: 'Ora aspetta,'
Disse; 'a costor si vuole esser cortese:
E se non fosse il foco che saetta
La natura del loco, io dicerei
Che meglio stesse a te, che a lor, la fretta.'
Ricominciar, come noi ristemmo, ei
L' antico verso; e quando a noi fur giunti,
Fenno una rota di sè tutti e trei,
Qual soleno i campion far nudi ed unti,
Avvisando lor presa e lor vantaggio,
Prima che sien tra lor battuti e punti:
E sì rotando, ciascuno il visaggio
Drizzava a me, sì che in contrario il collo
Faceva a' piè continuo viaggio.
E 'se miseria d' esto loco sollo
Rende in dispetto noi e nostri preghi,'
Cominciò l' uno, 'e il tinto aspetto e brollo;

16

I NOW WAS WHERE A ROARING could be heard
Of water falling to the circle underneath,
A roaring like the buzzing sound of beehives:
When three running shadows broke away together
From a company that was passing by
Under the torment of that cruel rain.
As they drew closer to us, they all cried out:
"Halt there, you whose clothes proclaim you
To be someone from our corrupted land!"
Alas, what scars I saw upon their bodies—
New and old ones, inflicted by those flames!
It pains me still whenever I recall them.
After listening to their cries, my teacher
Turned his face to me and said: "Wait for them!
To such as these you should be courteous.
But for the fire darting from the very
Nature of the place, I would say that it is
Better for you to hasten than for them."
As we waited, they started once again
Their ancient chant, and then, as they reached us,
They made a wheel out of themselves, all three.
As greased and naked wrestlers used to do,
When studying their holds and their advantages,
Before they started pounding one another:
Thus, each of these, as he went wheeling round,
Turned his face to me, so that the neck kept
Going one way and the feet another.
"If the misery of this place of sand,"
One began, "and our charred and tainted look
Bring scorn upon ourselves and our prayers,

La fama nostra il tuo animo pieghi
A dirne chi tu se', che i vivi piedi
Così sicuro per lo inferno freghi.
Questi, l' orme di cui pestar mi vedi,
Tutto che nudo e dipelato vada,
Fu di grado maggior che tu non credi.
Nepote fu della buona Gualdrada:
Guido Guerra ebbe nome, ed in sua vita
Fece col senno assai e con la spada.
L' altro che appresso me l' arena trita,
E' Tegghiaio Aldobrandi, la cui voce
Nel mondo su dovria esser gradita.
Ed io, che posto son con loro in croce,
Jacopo Rusticucci fui: e certo
La fiera moglie più ch' altro mi nuoce.'
S' io fussi stato dal foco coperto,
Gittato mi sarei tra lor disotto,
E credo che il Dottor l' avria sofferto.
Ma perch' io mi sarei bruciato e cotto,
Vinse paura la mia buona voglia,
Che di loro abbracciar mi facea ghiotto.
Poi cominciai: 'Non dispetto, ma doglia
La vostra condizion dentro mi fisse
Tanta che tardi tutta si dispoglia,
Tosto che questo mio Signor mi disse
Parole, per le quali io mi pensai
Che qual voi siete, tal gente venisse.
Di vostra terra sono; e sempre mai
L' opre di voi e gli onorati nomi
Con affezion ritrassi ed ascoltai.
Lascio lo fele, e vo per dolci pomi
Promessi a me per lo verace Duca;
Ma fino al centro pria convien ch' io tomi.'
'Se lungamente l' anima conduca
Le membra tue,' rispose quegli ancora,
'E se la fama tua dopo te luca,
Cortesia e valor di' se dimora
Nella nostra città sì come suole,
O se del tutto se n' è gita fuora?

May our fame at least incline your mind
To tell us who you are, who with living feet
Go wandering unharmed through Hell.
This one, whose tracks you see me following,
For all that he goes skinless and unclad,
Was once of higher rank than you suppose.
He was a grandson of the good Gualdrada.
Guido Guerra was his name; in his life
He accomplished much with his good sense and sword.
The other who behind me grinds the sand
Is Tegghiaio Aldobrandi,
Whose reputation should be good on earth.
And I who share this punishment with them
Was Jacopo Rusticucci; and more
Than any other my proud wife ruined me."
If I had been protected from the fire,
I would have flung myself among those souls below,
And I believe my teacher would have let me.
But since I would have been all cooked and sizzling,
Fear overcame my worthy inclinations,
Which made me hunger to take them in my arms.
Then I began: "It was not scorn, but pain—
So great it will be long before it ceases—
That your condition planted deep inside me,
From the moment that my master here spoke
Words to me that gave me cause to think
That people like yourselves might be approaching.
I come from the same land as you do
And always with affection heard proclaimed
Your accomplishments and estimable names.
Soon I shall leave this gall and go for the
Sweet apples promised by my honest guide;
But first I must go down into the center."
"Long may the soul accompany all parts
Of you," that one answered further. "And, that your
Fame may continue shining after you,
Tell me if courtesy and valor still
Dwell within your city, as they once did;
Or if they have moved away completely.

Chè Guglielmo Borsiere, il qual si duole
Con noi per poco, e va là coi compagni,
Assai ne cruccia con le sue parole.'
'La gente nuova, e i subiti guadagni,
Orgoglio e dismisura han generata,
Fiorenza, in te, sì che tu già ten piagni.'
Così gridai colla faccia levata:
E i tre, che ciò inteser per risposta,
Guardar l' un l' altro, come al ver si guata.
'Se l' altre volte sì poco ti costa,'
Risposer tutti, 'il satisfare altrui,
Felice te, se sì parli a tua posta.
Però se campi d' esti lochi bui
E torni a riveder le belle stelle,
Quando ti gioverà dicere "Io fui,"
Fa che di noi alla gente favelle.'
Indi rupper la rota, ed a fuggirsi
Ali sembiar le gambe loro snelle.
Un ammen non saria potuto dirsi
Tosto così, com' ei furo spariti:
Perchè al Maestro parve di partirsi.
Io lo seguiva, e poco eravam iti,
Che il suon dell' acqua n' era sì vicino
Che per parlar saremmo appena uditi.
Come quel fiume ch' ha proprio cammino
Prima da monte Veso in ver levante
Dalla sinistra costa d' Apennino,
Che si chiama Acquaqueta suso, avante
Che si divalli giù nel basso letto,
Ed a Forlì di quel nome è vacante,
Rimbomba là sopra san Benedetto
Dell' Alpe, per cadere ad una scesa,
Ove dovea per mille esser ricetto;
Così, giù d' una ripa discoscesa,
Trovammo risonar quell' acqua tinta,
Sì che in poc' ora avria l' orecchia offesa.
Io aveva una corda intorno cinta,
E con essa pensai alcuna volta
Prender la lonza alla pelle dipinta.

Guglielmo Borsiere, who recently
Arrived to share our pain, and goes there with our
Companions, distresses us with his reports."
"New people and sudden prosperity,
O Florence, have generated such pride
And such excess that you already rue them."
Thus I declaimed with my face upraised,
And the three who took this as an answer
Stared at each other as one stares at the truth.
"If it always costs you so little,"
They all answered, "to respond to others' needs,
Happy indeed are you to speak at will!
If, therefore, you survive these dark domains,
And go back to see the lovely stars again,
When it shall serve you to announce, 'I was,'
Do not fail to speak of us to people."
With that they broke the wheel,
And as they fled their swift legs were like wings.
An "Amen" could not have been pronounced
As rapidly as they vanished. After that,
It seemed time to my master to depart.
I followed him. We had not proceeded
Very far when the sound of water was so near,
We barely would have heard each other's words.
Like that river which follows its own course,
First down Monte Veso to the east,
On the left slope of the Apennines,
And is called the Acquacheta, up there,
Before it flows down into its low bed,
To be divested of that name, at Forli,
And which roars above San Benedetto
Dell'Alpe, and falls below in one descent
Where there should be a thousand to receive it:
So down a precipitous incline
We found that stained water echoing so loud,
Our ears would soon have suffered from it.
I had a cord around my waist, which once
Or twice I had thought earlier of using
To catch the panther with the dappled skin.

Poscia che l' ebbi tutta da me sciolta,
Sì come il Duca m' avea comandato,
Porsila a lui aggroppata e ravvolta.
Ond' ei si volse inver lo destro lato,
Ed alquanto di lungi dalla sponda
La gittò giuso in quell' alto burrato.
'E' pur convien che novità risponda,'
Dicea fra me medesmo, 'al nuovo cenno
Che il Maestro con l' occhio sì seconda.'
Ahi quanto cauti gli uomini esser denno
Presso a color che non veggon pur l' opra,
Ma per entro i pensier miran col senno!
Ei disse a me: 'Tosto verrà di sopra
Ciò ch' io attendo, e che il tuo pensier sogna
Tosto convien ch' al tuo viso si scopra.'
Sempre a quel ver ch' ha faccia di menzogna
De' l' uom chiuder le labbra finch' ei puote,
Però che senza colpa fa vergogna;
Ma qui tacer nol posso: e per le note
Di questa commedia, lettor, ti giuro,
S' elle non sien di lunga grazia vote,
Ch' io vidi per quell' aer grosso e scuro
Venir notando una figura in suso,
Maravigliosa ad ogni cor sicuro,
Sì come torna colui che va giuso
Talora a solver l' ancora ch' aggrappa
O scoglio od altro che nel mare è chiuso,
Che in su si stende, e da piè si rattrappa.

When I had loosened it completely from me,
Just as my guide had ordered me to do,
I handed it to him rolled up in a coil.
He thereupon swung back with his right side,
And threw it—a little distance from the brink—
Deep down into that bottomless abyss.
"Some strange new thing must certainly respond,"
I said to myself, "to this new signal which
The master's eye is following so closely."
How cautious men should be in the company
Of those who not only observe their actions
But with the mind can look into their thoughts!
He said to me: "What I am expecting
Will soon ascend, and what you have been dreaming
Will soon materialize before your eyes."
To that truth which has the face of falsehood
A man should always try to seal his lips,
For guiltless though he be, it brings him shame;
But here I cannot be silent, reader.
I swear to you, by the notes of this "Comedy"—
If they are not denied a long esteem—
That through the dark and heavy air I saw
Approaching a figure swimming upwards—
A thing of awe for even the bravest heart.
He looked like a man who, having gone down
To free an anchor clinging to a rock
Or something else beneath the sea, returns
With arms extended up and legs contracted.

XVII

'ECCO la fiera con la coda aguzza,
Che passa i monti, e rompe i muri e l' armi;
Ecco colei che tutto il mondo appuzza.'
Sì cominciò lo mio Duca a parlarmi,
Ed accennolle che venisse a proda,
Vicino al fin de' passeggiati marmi:
E quella sozza imagine di froda
Sen venne, ed arrivò la testa e il busto;
Ma in sulla riva non trasse la coda.
La faccia sua era faccia d' uom giusto;
Tanto benigna avea di fuor la pelle,
E d' un serpente tutto l' altro fusto.
Due branche avea pilose infin l' ascelle:
Lo dosso e il petto ed ambedue le coste
Dipinte avea di nodi e di rotelle.
Con più color, sommesse e soprapposte,
Non fer mai drappo Tartari nè Turchi,
Nè fur tai tele per Aragne imposte.
Come tal volta stanno a riva i burchi,
Che parte sono in acqua e parte in terra,
E come là tra li Tedeschi lurchi
Lo bevero s' assetta a far sua guerra;
Così la fiera pessima si stava
Sull' orlo che, di pietra, il sabbion serra.
Nel vano tutta sua coda guizzava,
Torcendo in su la venenosa forca,
Che a guisa di scorpion la punta armava.
Lo Duca disse: 'Or convien che si torca
La nostra via un poco infino a quella
Bestia malvagia che colà si corca.'

17

"BEHOLD THE WILD BEAST with the sharp tail,
That scales mountains and crushes walls and weapons;
Behold the one that makes the whole world stink!"
With these words my guide began to speak to me,
And beckoned to it to come ashore
Close to the edge of our stony road;
And that foul incarnation of Deceit
Approached, and put ashore its head and chest,
But did not drag its tail out of the sea.
The beast's face was the face of a just man,
So thoroughly benign was its expression;
But the remainder was a serpent's trunk.
It had two taloned arms, hairy to the pit.
Depicted on its back, and on its breast
And both its sides, were knots and little wheels.
Neither Turk nor Tartar ever fashioned cloth
With more colors, in embroidery or base;
Nor had Arachne ever woven such a web.
Like little boats that sometimes, when ashore,
Lie partly on the sand and partly in the sea,
And like the beaver sitting down to battle
For his food, there among the gluttonous Germans:
In such manner lay that worst of monsters
Upon the ledge that rings the sand with stone.
He lashed the empty space with his whole tail,
Twisting upwards its envenomed sting,
Which had a weaponed point, as scorpions' do.
My guide said to me: "We must alter
Our course a little, and proceed towards the
Malevolent beast that is reclining there."

Però scendemmo alla destra mammella,
E dieci passi femmo in sullo stremo,
Per ben cessar la rena e la fiammella.
E quando noi a lei venuti semo,
Poco più oltre veggio in sulla rena
Gente seder propinqua al loco scemo.
Quivi il Maestro: 'Acciocchè tutta piena
Esperienza d' esto giron porti,'
Mi disse, 'va, e vedi la lor mena.
Li tuoi ragionamenti sian là corti:
Mentre che torni parlerò con questa,
Che ne conceda i suoi omeri forti.'
Così ancor su per la strema testa
Di quel settimo cerchio tutto solo
Andai, ove sedea la gente mesta.
Per gli occhi fuori scoppiava lor duolo:
Di qua, di là soccorrien con le mani,
Quando a' vapori, e quando al caldo suolo.
Non altrimenti fan di state i cani,
Or col ceffo or col piè, quando son morsi
O da pulci o da mosche o da tafani.
Poi che nel viso a certi gli occhi porsi,
Ne' quali il doloroso foco casca,
Non ne conobbi alcun; ma io m' accorsi
Che dal collo a ciascun pendea una tasca,
Che avea certo colore e certo segno,
E quindi par che il loro occhio si pasca.
E com' io riguardando tra lor vegno,
In una borsa gialla vidi azzurro,
Che d' un leone avea faccia e contegno.
Poi procedendo di mio sguardo il curro
Vidine un' altra come sangue rossa
Mostrare un' oca bianca più che burro.
Ed un, che d' una scrofa azzurra e grossa
Segnato avea lo suo sacchetto bianco,
Mi disse: 'Che fai tu in questa fossa?
Or te ne va: e perchè se' vivo anco,
Sappi che il mio vicin Vitaliano
Sederà qui dal mio sinistro fianco.

We accordingly descended to the right
And walked ten paces forward to the brink,
In order to avoid the sand and flames.
And, when we had come close to it, I saw,
A little further on, people who were
Sitting on the sand near the abyss.
There the master said to me: "So that
You may have full experience of this ring,
Go and observe the condition they are in.
Keep your conversation with them short; while
You are gone I shall talk with this creature
And ask if we may use its sturdy back."
Thus I proceeded all alone along
That seventh circle's outermost extreme,
To where those melancholy souls were seated.
Their suffering was bursting from their eyes;
They moved their hands from one place to another
To shield themselves from the hot ground and the steam.
Not otherwise do dogs behave in summer,
With snout and paw, when they are bitten
By fleas and flies and stinging horseflies.
When my eyes settled on the faces
Of some on whom the painful fire fell,
I did not recognize a single one.
But I saw hanging from each neck a small bag
Of a particular device and color.
Upon it their eyes seemed to be feeding.
And as I went among them peering,
On a yellow pouch I saw in azure
The visage and the outlines of a lion.
Continuing my examination,
I saw another bag as red as blood
Showing a goose that was whiter than butter.
One soul, who had a bulky azure sow
Engraved upon his miniature white sack, 68
Said to me: "What are you doing in this hole?
Go now; and, since you are still alive,
Know that my neighbor Vitaliano
Shall be sitting here at my left side.

Con questi Fiorentin son Padovano;
Spesse fiate m' intronan gli orecchi,
Gridando: "Vegna il cavalier soprano,
Che recherà la tasca con tre becchi." '
Qui distorse la bocca, e di fuor trasse
La lingua, come 'l bue che il naso lecchi.
Ed io, temendo nol più star crucciasse
Lui che di poco star m' avea monito,
Torna' mi indietro dall' anime lasse.
Trovai lo Duca mio ch' era salito
Già in sulla groppa del fiero animale,
E disse a me: 'Or sii forte ed ardito.
Omai si scende per sì fatte scale:
Monta dinanzi, ch' io voglio esser mezzo,
Sì che la coda non possa far male.'
Qual è colui, ch' ha sì presso il riprezzo
Della quartana, ch' ha già l' unghie smorte,
E trema tutto pur guardando il rezzo,
Tal divenn' io alle parole porte;
Ma vergogna mi fer le sue minacce,
Che innanzi a buon signor fa servo forte.
Io m' assettai in su quelle spallacce:
'Sì' (volli dir, ma la voce non venne
Com' io credetti) 'fa che tu m' abbracce.'
Ma esso che altra volta mi sovvenne
Ad altro forse, tosto ch' io montai,
Con le braccia m' avvinse e mi sostenne:
E disse: 'Gerion, moviti omai:
Le rote larghe, e lo scender sia poco:
Pensa la nuova soma che tu hai.'
Come la navicella esce del loco
In dietro, in dietro, sì quindi si tolse;
E poi ch' al tutto si sentì a giuoco,
Là ov' era il petto, la coda rivolse,
E quella tesa, come anguilla, mosse,
E con le branche l' aria a sè raccolse.
Maggior paura non credo che fosse,
Quando Fetòn abbandonò li freni,
Per che il ciel, come pare ancor, si cosse:

I am a Paduan among these Florentines.
Time and again they shout into my ears:
'Let come the sovereign cavalier who will
Bring with him the bag with three goats on it.'"
Here he twisted his mouth and stuck out his tongue,
The way an ox does when he licks his nose.
And I, fearing that if I stayed longer I might
Displease him who had warned me not to linger,
Now turned away from those exhausted souls.
I found my guide, who was already mounted
Upon the back of the ferocious beast.
"Be strong and daring!" he said to me.
"On such a staircase must we now descend;
You get on in front; I want to be between
So that the tail can do no injury."
Like him who feels the cold chill of the ague
Drawing near, whose nails are already pale,
And who shivers when he sees a shady place,
Such I became when those words were spoken.
But his warning made me feel ashamed—which makes
A servant brave in front of a good master.
I sat down on those gigantic shoulders.
I wanted to say: "Throw your arms about me!"
But my voice did not come out as I thought.
Now he who had once helped me in another
State of doubt, as soon as I was mounted,
Clasped me in his arms and thus steadied me;
And he said: "Start moving now, Geryon!
Go down slowly and in large circles;
Be mindful of the kind of load you have."
Like a vessel backing slowly out of
Its landing place, the monster moved away.
The moment it felt completely at large,
It swung its tail around to where its breast was
And, having stretched it like an eel, shook it,
And with its giant paws embraced the air.
I doubt if there was any greater fear
When Phaëton relinquished the reins
And scorched the heavens, as is still apparent—

Nè quando Icaro misero le reni
Sentì spennar per la scaldata cera,
Gridando il padre a lui: 'Mala via tieni,'
Che fu la mia, quando vidi ch' i' era
Nell' aer d' ogni parte, e vidi spenta
Ogni veduta fuor che della fiera.
Ella sen va nuotando lenta lenta;
Rota e discende, ma non me n' accorgo,
Se non ch' al viso e disotto mi venta.
Io sentia già dalla man destra il gorgo
Far sotto noi un orribile stroscio;
Per che con gli occhi in giù la testa sporgo.
Allor fu' io più timido allo scoscio:
Perocch' io vidi fochi, e sentii pianti;
Ond' io tremando tutto mi raccoscio.
E vidi poi, chè nol vedea davanti,
Lo scendere e il girar, per li gran mali
Che s' appressavan da diversi canti.
Come il falcon ch' è stato assai sull' ali,
Che senza veder logoro o uccello,
Fa dire al falconiere: 'Oimè tu cali:'
Discende lasso onde si move snello,
Per cento rote, e da lungi si pone
Dal suo maestro, disdegnoso e fello:
Così ne pose al fondo Gerione
A piè a piè della stagliata rocca,
E discarcate le nostre persone,
Si dileguò, come da corda cocca.

Nor when luckless Icarus felt his wings
Unloosened from him by the scalded wax,
While his father screamed: "You went the wrong way!"—
Than my own fear when I found myself
Suspended in mid-air, and realized
That nothing could be seen except the monster.
Very, very slowly he swam on, wheeling
And descending, though I would not have known
But for the wind that struck me from below.
On my right I could already hear
The whirlpool roaring fearfully beneath us;
Whereupon I thrust my head out and looked down
And became even more afraid of falling.
For I saw fires and heard lamentations
That made me crouch and shake from head to foot.
And then I saw what I had not yet seen:
The revolving and descending among
The torments that closed in from every side.
Like a falcon that has long been on the wing,
Without catching sight of lure or bird, making
The falconer say: "Must you come down? Too bad!"
And then comes down wearied, in a hundred circles,
Where it went up fast, and stands—contemptuous
And mean—a great distance from his master:
So Geryon deposited us below,
Close to the foot of that precipitous rock,
And, having been unburdened of our persons,
He shot off like an arrow from a bow.

. . . I found myself
Suspended in mid-air, and realized
That nothing could be seen except the monster.

XVIII

LOCO è in inferno detto Malebolge,
Tutto di pietra e di color ferrigno,
Come la cerchia che d' intorno il volge.
Nel dritto mezzo del campo maligno
Vaneggia un pozzo assai largo e profondo,
Di cui suo loco *dicerò l' ordigno.*
Quel cinghio che rimane adunque è tondo,
Tra il pozzo e il piè dell' alta ripa dura,
Ed ha distinto in dieci valli il fondo.
Quale, dove per guardia delle mura,
Più e più fossi cingon li castelli,
La parte dov' ei son rende figura:
Tale imagine quivi facean quelli:
E come a tai fortezze dai lor sogli
Alla ripa di fuor son ponticelli,
Così da imo della roccia scogli
Movien, che recidean gli argini e fossi
Infino al pozzo, che i tronca e raccogli.
In questo loco, dalla schiena scossi
Di Gerion, trovammoci: e il Poeta
Tenne a sinistra, ed io retro mi mossi.
Alla man destra vidi nuova pieta;
Nuovi tormenti e nuovi frustatori,
Di che la prima bolgia era repleta.
Nel fondo erano ignudi i peccatori:
Dal mezzo in qua ci venian verso il volto,
Di là con noi, ma con passi maggiori:
Come i Roman, per l' esercito molto,
L'anno del Giubbileo, su per lo ponte
Hanno a passar la gente modo colto:

18

IN HELL THERE IS A PLACE called Malebolge,
Made, like the cliff that circles it around,
Entirely of stone, and iron-colored.
Right in the center of this evil field
There gapes a very deep and spacious well,
Whose form I shall describe in its due place.
The remaining area is therefore round
Between the hard high precipice and well,
And ten separate grooves divide its depth.
Like the appearance of the ground where
Trenches in a row surround a castle—
The better to protect its walls—
Such was the picture of those ditches here.
And just as there are little bridges from the
Thresholds of such castles to the farthest banks,
So from the bottom of the cliff, ridges
Cut across the ditches and embankment
Up to the well, where all of them converged.
Here, after dismounting from the back of
Geryon, we found ourselves; and the poet
Proceeded to the left, and I behind him.
To my right I saw new cause for pity:
Unfamiliar torments and tormentors,
With which the first ditch was completely filled.
The sinners of the lowest depths were nude;
They were coming towards us on the nearer side,
And with us on the other, but much faster:
Like the Romans, who, because of the great host
Of the Jubilee year, took measures
To circumvent the crowding on the bridge,

Che dall' un lato tutti hanno la fronte
Verso il castello, e vanno a santo Pietro;
Dall' altra sponda vanno verso il monte.
Di qua, di là, su per lo sasso tetro
Vidi Demon cornuti con gran ferze,
Che li battean crudelmente di retro.
Ahi come facean lor levar le berze
Alle prime percosse! già nessuno
Le seconde aspettava nè le terze.
Mentr' io andava, gli occhi miei in uno
Furo scontrati; ed io sì tosto dissi:
'Di già veder costui non son digiuno.'
Perciò a figurarlo i piedi affissi:
E il dolce Duca meco si ristette,
Ed assentì ch' alquanto indietro gissi:
E quel frustato celar si credette
Bassando il viso, ma poco gli valse:
Ch' io dissi: 'Tu che l' occhio a terra gette,
Se le fazion che porti non son false,
Venedico se' tu Caccianimico;
Ma che ti mena a sì pungenti Salse?'
Ed egli a me: 'Mal volentier lo dico;
Ma sforzami la tua chiara favella,
Che mi fa sovvenir del mondo antico.
Io fui colui, che la Ghisolabella
Condussi a far la voglia del Marchese,
Come che suoni la sconcia novella.
E non pur io qui piango Bolognese:
Anzi n' è questo loco tanto pieno,
Che tante lingue non son ora apprese
A dicer sipa *tra Savena e Reno:*
E se di ciò vuoi fede o testimonio,
Recati a mente il nostro avaro seno.'
Così parlando il percosse un demonio
Della sua scuriada, e disse: 'Via,
Ruffian, qui non son femmine da conio.'
Io mi raggiunsi con la scorta mia:
Poscia con pochi passi divenimmo
Là dove un scoglio della ripa uscia.

By having all on one side looking towards
The Castle and going to St. Peter's
And, on the other, going towards the Mount.
Here, there, everywhere, along that gloomy rock,
I saw horned demons carrying great whips,
Who struck the spirits cruelly from behind.
Ah, how they made them kick up their heels
When the first blows fell, and you may be sure
No one waited for the second or the third.
While I was walking, my eyes fell on
One of them, and I said immediately:
"I have already seen this one before."
I therefore stopped and tried to remember
Who he was, and my sweet guide stopped with me
And agreed to let me go back a little.
If that whipped soul, by lowering his face,
Thought to conceal himself, it was no help;
For I said: "You whose eyes are on the ground,
If the features that you bear are not false,
You are Venedico Caccianemico.
But what thrust you into such a pungent sauce?"
And he: "I answer most reluctantly;
But I am compelled to speak by your plain talk,
Which makes me recollect the world of old.
However the unsavory story is told,
I was the one who brought Ghisolabella
To do the bidding of the Marquis.
Nor am I the sole Bolognese who pines here:
Indeed, this place so overflows with us
That, between the Reno and Savena rivers,
Not as many tongues are saying *sipa*[2] now.
And, if you want proof and confirmation of it,
Remember our avaricious nature."
While he was speaking, a demon struck him
With his scourge and said: "Go away, you pimp!
There are no women here to turn to cash."
I then rejoined my escort, and, after
Taking a few steps, we arrived at a place
Where a precipice rose from the bank.

I saw horned demons carrying great whips,
Who struck the spirits cruelly from behind.

Assai leggieramente quel salimmo,
E volti a destra su per la sua scheggia,
Da quelle cerchie eterne ci partimmo.
Quando noi fummo là dov' ei vaneggia
Di sotto, per dar passo agli sferzati,
Lo Duca disse: 'Attienti, e fa che feggia
Lo viso in te di questi altri mal nati,
A' quali ancor non vedesti la faccia,
Perocchè son con noi insieme andati.'
Dal vecchio ponte guardavam la traccia
Che venia verso noi dall' altra banda,
E che la ferza similmente scaccia.
Il buon Maestro, senza mia domanda,
Mi disse: 'Guarda quel grande che viene,
E per dolor non par lagrima spanda:
Quanto aspetto reale ancor ritiene!
Quelli è Jason, che por core e per senno
Li Colchi del monton privati fene.
Egli passò per l' isola di Lenno,
Poi che le ardite femmine spietate
Tutti li maschi loro a morte dienno
Ivi con senno e con parole ornate
Isifile ingannò, la giovinetta,
Che prima avea tutte l' altre ingannate.
Lasciolla quivi gravida e soletta:
Tal colpa a tal martiro lui condanna;
Ed anco di Medea si fa vendetta.
Con lui sen va chi da tal parte inganna:
E questo basti della prima valle
Sapere, e di color che in sè assanna.'
Già eravam là 've lo stretto calle
Con l' argine secondo s' incrocicchia,
E fa di quello ad un altro arco spalle.
Quindi sentimmo gente che si nicchia
Nell' altra bolgia, e che col muso isbuffa,
E sè medesma con le palme picchia.
Le ripe eran grommate d' una muffa
Per l' alito di giù che vi si appasta,
Che con gli occhi e col naso facea zuffa.

We ascended it very easily
And, once upon its ridge, we turned to our right
And took our leave of those eternal circles.
When we were where the ridge was open underneath
To let those being flagellated through,
My guide said: "Hold on, and let the sight of
These other misbegotten souls assail you,
Whose faces until now you have not seen,
Because they have been going our way."
From the old bridge we looked at the procession
That was approaching from the other side
And which was also fleeing from the whip.
Without my asking him, the good master
Said to me: "See that tall figure coming,
Who does not seem to weep because of pain.
What a majestic look he still retains!
That is Jason, who through artfulness and pluck
Left the Colchians plundered of their sheep.
On his way he visited the isle of Lemnos,
After those rash and merciless women
Had annihilated all their males.
There it was, with words and testimonials,
That he deceived Hypsipyle, the maiden
Who had earlier tricked all the others.
There he abandoned her, lonely and with child.
To such torment such misdeed condemns him;
And even Medea is being avenged.
With him goes everyone who so deceives.
Let it suffice to know this of the first vale
And of all those it holds between its jaws."
We had now come to where the narrow path
Intersected with the second bank, and made
A shoulder of it for another arch.
From there we could hear people whimpering
In the adjoining chasm, sniffling,
And belaboring themselves with their own palms.
The banks were thickly coated with a paste
Formed of the exhalations from below,
Which quarreled with both the eyes and nose.

Lo fondo è cupo sì, che non ci basta
Loco a veder senza montare al dosso
Dell' arco, ove lo scoglio più soprasta.
Quivi venimmo, e quindi giù nel fosso
Vidi gente attuffata in uno sterco,
Che dagli uman privati parea mosso:
E mentre ch' io là giù con l' occhio cerco,
Vidi un col capo sì di merda lordo,
Che non parea s' era laico o cherco.
Quei mi sgridò: 'Perchè se' tu sì ingordo
Di riguardar più me, che gli altri brutti?'
Ed io a lui: 'Perchè, se ben ricordo,
Già t' ho veduto coi capelli asciutti,
E sei Alessio Interminei da Lucca:
Però t' adocchio più che gli altri tutti.'
Ed egli allor, battendosi la zucca:
'Quaggiù m' hanno sommerso le lusinghe,
Ond' io non ebbi mai la lingua stucca.'
Appresso ciò lo Duca: 'Fa che pinghe,'
Mi disse, 'il viso un poco più avante,
Sì che la faccia ben con gli occhi attinghe
Di quella sozza e scapigliata fante,
Che là si graffia con l' unghie merdose,
Ed or s' accoscia, ed ora è in piede stante.
Taide è, la puttana, che rispose
Al drudo suo, quando disse: "Ho io grazie
Grandi appo te?" "Anzi meravigliose."
E quinci sien le nostre viste sazie.'

The bottom was so deep and dark, there was
No place to see it from, except the summit
Of the arch, where the precipice was highest.
We climbed up to it and looked down below
Into a pit where people were immersed in dung
That seemed to come from all the world's latrines.
And while my eyes were scouring below,
I saw one with his head so smeared with shit,
I could not tell if he were priest or layman.
"Why are you more greedy to look at me,"
He shrieked, "than at these other loathsome creatures?"
And I: "Because, if I recall correctly,
I saw you once before, when your hair was dry.
You are Alessio Interminei da Lucca;
Hence, I look at you more than all the others."
Beating himself on the head, he then said:
"Flattery, with which my tongue was never
Surfeited, was the cause of my submersion."
After which my guide said to me:
"Thrust your face forward a little more,
In order that you may the better see
That slovenly and sluttish creature there,
Scratching herself with shit-encrusted nails,
Who stands up at times and squats at others.
This is Thaïs the prostitute, who, when
Her lover asked: 'Are you very grateful
To me?' replied, 'Enormously grateful!'
And with that let our eyes be satisfied."

XIX

O Simon mago, o miseri seguaci,
Chè le cose di Dio, che di bontate
Deono essere spose, e voi rapaci
Per oro e per argento adulterate;
Or convien che per voi suoni la tromba,
Perocchè nella terza bolgia state.
Già eravamo alla seguente tomba
Montati dello scoglio in quella parte.
Che appunto sopra mezzo il fosso piomba.
O somma Sapienza, quanta è l' arte
Che mostri in cielo, in terra e nel mal mondo,
E quanto giusto tua virtù comparte!
Io vidi per le coste e per lo fondo
Piena la pietra livida di fori
D' un largo tutti, e ciascuno era tondo.
Non mi parean meno ampi nè maggiori,
Che quei che son nel mio bel San Giovanni
Fatti per loco de' battezzatori;
L' un delli quali, ancor non è molt' anni,
Rupp' io per un che dentro vi annegava:
E questo sia suggel ch' ogni uomo sganni.
Fuor della bocca a ciascun soperchiava
D' un peccator li piedi, e delle gambe
Infino al grosso, e l' altro dentro stava.
Le piante erano a tutti accese intrambe;
Per che sì forte guizzavan le giunte,
Che spezzate averian ritorte e strambe.
Qual suole il fiammeggiar delle cose unte
Moversi pur su per l' estrema buccia;
Tal era lì da' calcagni alle punte.

19

O SIMON THE MAGICIAN, you and your
Miserable followers, and all you
Rapacious rogues who, for gold and silver,
Adulterate the things of God that should be pure:
Now is the time, since you are gathered in
The third chasm, to blow the trumpet for you!
We had climbed up to the adjoining tomb
Along the precipice, at that place where
It overhangs the center of the pit.
O highest Wisdom, what skill you reveal
In Heaven, on earth, and in the world below,
And how rightly you apportion justice!
I saw along the slopes and on the bottom
A livid stone full of openings
Of the same size, each one of which was round.
They seemed neither larger nor smaller than those
Provided for the use of the baptizers
In my beautiful church of San Giovanni,
One of which, not too many years ago,
I broke, because a child was drowning in it.
And may this serve as proof to disabuse all men.
The feet of every sinner, and his legs
Up to the calves, protruded from the mouth
Of every hole; the rest was wedged inside.
The soles of both feet blazed, on all of them,
Making the joints twitch so violently,
They would have broken any rope that bound them.
The way that flames invariably move
Only on the surface of oily things,
So was it there, from every heel to toe.

'Chi è colui, Maestro, che si cruccia,
Guizzando più che gli altri suoi consorti,'
Diss' io, 'e cui più rozza fiamma succia?'
Ed egli a me: 'Se tu vuoi ch' io ti porti
Laggiù per quella ripa che più giace,
Da lui saprai di sè e de' suoi torti.'
Ed io: 'Tanto m' è bel, quanto a te piace:
Tu sei signore, e sai ch' io non mi parto
Dal tuo volere, e sai quel che si tace.'
Allor venimmo in su 'l argine quarto;
Volgemmo, e discendemmo a mano stanca
Laggiù nel fondo foracchiato ed arto.
Lo buon Maestro ancor della sua anca
Non mi dipose, sì mi giunse al rotto
Di quel che sì piangeva con la zanca.
'O qual che se', che 'l di su tien di sotto,
Anima trista, come pal commessa,'
Comincia' io a dir, 'se puoi, fa motto.'
Io stava come il frate che confessa
Lo perfido assassin, che poi ch' è fitto,
Richiama lui, perchè la morte cessa:
Ed ei gridò: 'Sei tu già costì ritto,
Sei tu già costì ritto, Bonifazio?
Di parecchi anni mi mentì lo scritto.
Se' tu sì tosto di quell' aver sazio,
Per lo qual non temesti torre a inganno
La bella Donna, e poi di farne strazio?'
Tal mi fec' io quai son color che stanno,
Per non intender ciò ch' è lor risposto,
Quasi scornati, e risponder non sanno.
Allor Virgilio disse: 'Digli tosto,
Non son colui, non son colui che credi:'
Ed io risposi come a me fu imposto.
Per che lo spirto tutti storse i piedi:
Poi sospirando, e con voce di pianto,
Mi disse: 'Dunque che a me richiedi?
Se di saper chi io sia ti cal cotanto
Che tu abbi però la ripa corsa,
Sappi ch' io fui vestito del gran manto:

"Who is that, Master, in such agony
That he quivers more than his companions,"
I said, "and whom a redder fire licks?"
And he replied to me: "If you want me
To take you down along that lower bank,
You will find out from him about his crimes."
And I: "Whatever pleases you suits me;
You are the master; you know I never go
Against your will; and you know what is not said."
We had by now arrived at the fourth ridge.
We turned to our left and then descended
Into the narrow, perforated bottom.
The good master did not leave my side
Until he brought me to the opening
Of that one who was weeping with his legs.
"You who have the upper part of you below,
Stuck in the ground—unhappy spirit—like a pole,"
I began to say, "say something, if you can."
I stood there like a priest who has confessed
A wily murderer, who, head in earth,
Calls him back and thus puts off his death.
And he cried: "Is it you who stands up there?
You, Boniface—are you already here?
The script has lied to me by many years.
Were you so quickly glutted with possessions,
For which you did not scruple to abduct
The Beautiful Lady and then ruin her?"
Whereupon he became like one of those
Who, not understanding what is said to them,
Feel ridiculed and cannot make reply.
Then Virgil said: "Tell him immediately:
'I am not the one you think I am.'"
And I answered exactly as I was told.
This made the spirit twist and turn his feet;
After which he sighed and, with a plaintive voice,
Said to me: "Well, then, what do you wish of me?
If it means so much to you to know
Who I am that you have climbed across the bank,
Know that at one time I wore the Great Mantle;

E veramente fui figliuol dell' orsa,
  Cupido sì per avanzar gli orsatti,
  Che su l' avere, e qui me misi in borsa.
Di sotto al capo mio son gli altri tratti
  Che precedetter me simoneggiando,
  Per le fessure della pietra piatti.
Laggiù cascherò io altresì, quando
  Verrà colui ch' io credea che tu fossi,
  Allor ch' io feci il subito domando.
Ma più è il tempo già che i piè mi cossi,
  E ch' io son stato così sottosopra,
  Ch' ei non starà piantato coi piè rossi:
Chè dopo lui verrà, di più laid' opra,
  Di ver ponente un pastor senza legge,
  Tal che convien che lui e me ricopra.
Nuovo Iason sarà, di cui si legge
  Ne' Maccabei: e come a quel fu molle
  Suo re, così fia a lui chi Francia regge.'
Io non so s' io mi fui qui troppo folle,
  Ch' io pur risposi lui a questo metro:
  'Deh or mi di', quanto tesoro volle
Nostro Signore in prima da san Pietro,
  Che ponesse le chiavi in sua balìa?
  Certo non chiese se non: "Viemmi retro."
Nè Pier nè gli altri tolsero a Mattia
  Oro od argento, quando fu sortito
  Al loco che perdè l' anima ria.
Però ti sta, che tu se' ben punito;
  E guarda ben la mal tolta moneta,
  Ch' esser ti fece contra Carlo ardito.
E se non fosse, che ancor lo mi vieta
  La riverenza delle somme chiavi,
  Che tu tenesti nella vita lieta,
I' userei parole ancor più gravi;
  Chè la vostra avarizia il mondo attrista,
  Calcando i buoni e sollevando i pravi.
Di voi pastor s' accorse il Vangelista,
  Quando colei, che siede sopra l' acque,
  Puttaneggiar co' regi a lui fu vista:

And, truthfully, I was born of the Bear,
So greedy to advance the little Bears,
That, there, I pocketed wealth and, here, myself.
Below my head are wedged the others who
Committed simony before me and now
Lie hidden in the fissures of this stone.
I too will sink to where they are, as soon as
That one comes whom I believed you to be
When I questioned you so hurriedly.
But my feet have cooked a longer time,
And I have been standing longer upside down
Than he shall be planted here with red feet.
For, after him, from the west, there shall come
An outlaw pastor of still fouler deeds,
Who is destined to cover him and me.
Such a one will be a new Jason, of whom
One reads in Maccabees that he swayed his king,
Just as this other will the King of France."
I do not know if I was too audacious,
But I responded to him in this measure:
"Tell me, if you will, how much recompense
Our Lord wanted from St. Peter at the time
He placed the keys in his authority?
Indeed, all he asked of him was, 'Follow me.'
Neither Peter nor the others asked Matthia
For gold or silver, when he was selected
To fill the place lost by that guilty soul.
Stay where you are, for you are justly punished,
And guard carefully that ill-gotten money
Which made you so courageous against Charles.
Let me add that, if I were not restrained
By the reverence I bear the Highest Keys
Which you once held in the joyful life,
I would be using even graver words.
For your avarice has saddened the whole world,
Trampling the good and raising the depraved.
The Evangelist first learned of pastors
Like yourself when he saw her who sits
Upon the waters whoring with the kings;

Quella che con le sette teste nacque,
E dalle dieci corna ebbe argomento,
Fin che virtute al suo marito piacque.
Fatto v' avete Dio d' oro e d' argento:
E che altro è da voi all' idolatre,
Se non ch' egli uno, e voi n' orate cento?
Ahi, Constantin, di quanto mal fu matre,
Non la tua conversion, ma quella dote
Che da te prese il primo ricco patre!'
E mentre io gli cantava cotai note,
O ira o coscienza che il mordesse,
Forte spingava con ambo le piote.
Io credo ben che al mio Duca piacesse,
Con sì contenta labbia sempre attese
Lo suon delle parole vere espresse.
Però con ambo le braccia mi prese,
E poi che tutto su mi s' ebbe al petto,
Rimontò per la via onde discese;
Nè si stancò d' avermi a sè distretto,
Sì mi portò sopra il colmo dell' arco,
Che dal quarto al quinto argine è tragetto.
Quivi soavemente spose il carco,
Soave per lo scoglio sconcio ed erto,
Che sarebbe alle capre duro varco:
Indi un altro vallon mi fu scoperto.

She who was born with seven heads, and had
Ten horns to testify for her, so long
As to be virtuous pleased her husband.
You have made yourself a god of gold and silver.
How else do you differ from idolators
Than that they worship one and you a hundred?
Ah, Constantine, what wickedness was mothered,
Not by your conversion, but by that dowry
Received from you by the first rich Father!"
While I descanted to him in this fashion,
He kicked vigorously with both his feet,
As if his conscience stung him, or his rage.
I do believe my guide was pleased with me,
For he listened to the true words I had
Spoken with a look of satisfaction.
Whereupon he seized me with both arms
And, when he had me fast upon his breast,
He climbed back up the way he had descended,
And held on to me untiringly.
Thus he bore me to the summit of the arch
That serves as passage from the fourth to the fifth bank.
There he gently deposited his burden:
Gently, because the cliff was so steep and rough
That even goats would find it hard to climb.
From there another valley lay before me.

DI nuova pena mi convien far versi,
E dar materia al ventesimo canto
Della prima canzon, ch' è de' sommersi.
Io era già disposto tutto quanto
A riguardar nello scoperto fondo,
Che si bagnava d' angoscioso pianto:
E vidi gente per lo vallon tondo
Venir tacendo e lagrimando, al passo
Che fan le letaníe in questo mondo.
Come il viso mi scese in lor più basso,
Mirabilmente apparve esser travolto
Ciascun tral mento e 'l principio del casso:
Chè dalle reni era tornato il volto,
Ed indietro venir gli convenia,
Perchè il veder dinanzi era lor tolto.
Forse per forza già di parlasìa
Si travolse così alcun del tutto;
Ma io nol vidi, nè credo che sia.
Se Dio ti lasci, Lettor, prender frutto
Di tua lezione, or pensa per te stesso,
Com' io potea tener lo viso asciutto,
Quando la nostra imagine da presso
Vidi sì torta, che il pianto degli occhi
Le natiche bagnava per lo fesso.
Certo i' piangea, poggiato ad un de' rocchi
Del duro scoglio, sì che la mia scorta
Mi disse: 'Ancor sei tu degli altri sciocchi?
Qui vive la pietà quando è ben morta.
Chi è più scellerato che colui
Che al giudizio divin passion porta?

20

OF NEW AFFLICTIONS I must now make verses
And furnish matter for the twentieth Canto
Of this first Canticle of the submerged.
I was thoroughly prepared by now
To gaze into those depths disclosed to me
That were flooded by an anguished weeping;
And I saw people coming through that round
Ravine, silent and in tears, walking
At the pace used in the litanies of this world.
As my glance settled lower on them,
Each seemed to have been monstrously reversed
Between the chin and where the chest begins.
Their faces now were turned to look behind,
And when they walked they had to do so backwards,
For to look forward had been taken from them.
It may be that once, because of palsy,
Someone was thus contorted; but I never
Saw it, nor do I think it possible.
If God lets you, reader, enjoy the fruits
Of your reading, imagine to yourself
How I could possibly have kept my eyes dry,
When close to me I saw a human face
So distorted that the tears falling from
Its eyes bathed the buttocks where they parted.
Leaning on a boulder of that jagged cliff,
I wept so violently that my guide
Said to me: "Are you another of those fools?
Whatever pity lives here is better dead.
Who is more blasphemous than he who feels
Compassion where God's justice has prevailed?

Drizza la testa, drizza, e vedi a cui
S' aperse agli occhi de' Teban la terra,
Per ch' ei gridavan tutti: "Dove rui,
Anfiarao? perchè lasci la guerra?"
E non restò di ruinare a valle
Fino a Minòs, che ciascheduno afferra.
Mira che ha fatto petto delle spalle:
Perchè volle veder troppo davante,
Diretro guarda, e fa retroso calle.
Vedi Tiresia, che mutò sembiante,
Quando di maschio femmina divenne,
Cangiandosi le membra tutte quante;
E prima poi ribatter gli convenne
Li due serpenti avvolti con la verga,
Che riavesse le maschili penne.
Aronta è quel che al ventre gli s' atterga,
Che nei monti di Luni, dove ronca
Lo Carrarese che di sotto alberga,
Ebbe tra bianchi marmi la spelonca
Per sua dimora; onde a guardar le stelle
E il mar non gli era la veduta tronca.
E quella che ricopre le mammelle,
Che tu non vedi, con le trecce sciolte,
E ha di là ogni pilosa pelle,
Manto fu, che cercò per terre molte,
Poscia si pose là dove nacqu' io;
Onde un poco mi piace che m' ascolte.
Poscia che il padre suo di vita uscìo,
E venne serva la città di Baco,
Questa gran tempo per lo mondo gìo.
Suso in Italia bella giace un laco
Appiè dell' alpe, che serra Lamagna
Sopra Tiralli, ch' ha nome Benaco.
Per mille fonti, credo, e più si bagna,
Tra Garda e Val Camonica, Apennino
Dell' acqua che nel detto lago stagna.
Loco è nel mezzo là, dove il Trentino
Pastore, e quel di Brescia, e il Veronese
Segnar potria, se fesse quel cammino.

Raise your head, raise it high, and behold him
For whom, under Theban eyes, the earth opened,
At which all shouted: 'Where have you fallen,
Amphiaraüs? why have you fled the battle?
And he did not stop plunging until he came
To Minos, who catches every one of them.
Look how he makes a breast of his shoulders.
Because he wished to see too far ahead,
He gazes backward, and advances backward.
Notice Tiresias, who changed his features,
When from a man he made himself a woman
By transforming his entire body,
And had to beat the intertwining snakes
With his stick a second time before
He could repossess his manly plumage.
Walking backwards towards his belly is Aruns,
Who in the mountains of Luni—where the
Carrarese, who lives below, tills the soil—
Made his home in a cavern among the
White marbles, from which he could contemplate
The stars and the sea without obstruction.
And she who, with her disheveled locks
Covers up her breasts—which you cannot see—
And has all her hair growing on that side,
Was Manto, who searched everywhere before
She settled where I was born—concerning which
I should like you to listen to me a little.
After her father departed this life,
And the city of Bacchus was enslaved,
This one went about the world for a long time.
Up in fair Italy there lies a lake
Among the Alps that close off Germany
Above the Tyrol, whose name is Benaco.
By a thousand springs, and more, is Mount Pennino,
Between Garda and the Val Camonica,
Bathed by the waters collecting in that lake.
In the center is a place where the pastors
Of Brescia, of Verona, and of Trento
Could all make signs of blessing if they passed it.

Siede Peschiera, bello e forte arnese
Da fronteggiar Bresciani e Bergamaschi,
Ove la riva intorno più discese.
Ivi convien che tutto quanto caschi
Ciò che in grembo a Benaco star non può,
E fassi fiume giù per verdi paschi.
Tosto che l' acqua a correr mette co,
Non più Benaco, ma Mencio si chiama
Fino a Governo, dove cade in Po.
Non molto ha corso, che trova una lama,
Nella qual si distende e la impaluda,
E suol di state talora esser grama.
Quindi passando la vergine cruda
Vide terra nel mezzo del pantano,
Senza cultura, e d' abitanti nuda.
Lì, per fuggire ogni consorzio umano,
Ristette co' suoi servi a far sue arti,
E visse, e vi lasciò suo corpo vano.
Gli uomini poi che intorno erano sparti
S' accolsero a quel loco, ch' era forte
Per lo pantan che avea da tutte parti.
Fer la città sopra quell' ossa morte;
E per colei che il loco prima elesse,
Mantova l' appellar senz' altra sorte.
Già fur le genti sue dentro più spesse,
Prima che la mattìa di Casalodi
Da Pinamonte inganno ricevesse.
Però t' assenno, che se tu mai odi
Originar la mia terra altrimenti,
La verità nulla menzogna frodi.'
Ed io: 'Maestro, i tuoi ragionamenti
Mi son sì certi, e prendon sì mia fede,
Che gli altri mi sarian carboni spenti.
Ma dimmi della gente che procede,
Se tu ne vedi alcun degno di nota;
Chè solo a ciò la mia mente rifiede.'
Allor mi disse: 'Quel che dalla gota
Porge la barba in sulle spalle brune,
Fu, quando Grecia fu di maschi vota

A beautiful and mighty stronghold
To face the Brescians and the Bergamese,
Peschiera lies where its shore is lowest.
There, all the water that cannot linger
In the lap of Lake Benaco descends,
To become a river in the green fields below.
Once the water starts to flow, it is
No longer called Benaco, but Mincio,
Up to Governo, where it falls into the Po.
Before it has run far, it finds a plane,
In which it widens and creates a swamp
That sometimes is injurious in summer.
While passing by that place, the cruel virgin
Saw in the middle of the marsh some land
That was untilled and bare of inhabitants.
There, to escape all human company,
She settled with her slaves to work her spells,
And lived, and there she left behind her body.
Men who lived scattered thereabout began
To congregate in that place, which was strong
Because of the marshes that surrounded it.
They made a city on top of those dead bones,
And for her who first chose the place, they called it,
Without further auguries, Mantua.
The people were already crowding it
When Casalodi's dereliction
Was thwarted by the fraud of Pinamonte.
But, I caution you, lest you should ever hear
That my city had a different origin,
Let no such lie make pretense of the truth."
And I: "Master, your explanation is so
Convincing to me, and so invites belief,
That any other would seem a burned-out coal.
But tell me something of the people passing:
If there be one deserving of attention.
My mind keeps coming back to that alone."
He then said to me: "That one who from the cheeks
Arrays his beard upon his swarthy shoulders,
Was augur when Greece was so deprived of males,

Sì che appena rimaser per le cune,
Augure, e diede il punto con Calcanta
In Aulide a tagliar la prima fune.
Euripilo ebbe nome, e così il canta
L' alta mia Tragedia in alcun loco:
Ben lo sai tu, che la sai tutta quanta.
Quell' altro che ne' fianchi è così poco,
Michele Scotto fu, che veramente
Delle magiche frode seppe il gioco.
Vedi Guido Bonatti, vedi Asdente,
Che avere inteso al cuoio ed allo spago
Ora vorrebbe, ma tardi si pente.
Vedi le triste che lasciaron l' ago,
La spuola e il fuso, e fecersi indivine;
Fecer malìe con erbe e con imago.
Ma vienne omai, chè già tiene il confine
D' ambedue gli emisperi, e tocca l' onda
Sotto Sibilia, Caino e le spine,
E già iernotte fu la luna tonda:
Ben ten dee ricordar, chè non ti nocque
Alcuna volta per la selva fonda,'
Sì mi parlava, ed andavamo introcque.

There were scarcely any even in the cradle;
And he with Calchas divined the moment
For cutting the first cable in Aulis.
Eurypilus was his name, and thus, in one
Passage, my high tragedy sings of him:
Well do you know it, who knows the whole of it.
That one who is so slender in the hips
Was Michael Scott, a man who was truly
A master at playing magic tricks.
Look at Guido Bonatti, and Asdente,
Who wishes now he had confined himself
To thread and leather, but repents too late.
Look at those cheerless women who gave up
The needle, spool, and spindle to divine,
And worked their spells with herbs and effigies.
But, come now, for Cain and his thorns already
Dominate the boundary of the hemispheres
And touch the ocean there below Seville.
Last night the moon was full; remember that
Carefully, for at no time did she cause
You any harm through that deep forest."
Thus he spoke to me, and we walked on meanwhile.

COSI' di ponte in ponte, altro parlando
Che la mia commedia cantar non cura,
Venimmo, e tenevamo il colmo, quando
Ristemmo per veder l' altra fessura
Di Malebolge, e gli altri pianti vani;
E vidila mirabilmente oscura.
Quale nell' Arzanà de' Viniziani
Bolle l' inverno la tenace pece
A rimpalmar li legni lor non sani,
Chè navicar non ponno, e in quella vece
Chi fa suo legno nuovo, e chi ristoppa
Le coste a quel che più viaggi fece;
Chi ribatte da proda, e chi da poppa;
Altri fa remi, ed altri volge sarte;
Chi terzeruolo ed artimon rintoppa:
Tal, non per foco ma per divina arte
Bollia laggiuso una pegola spessa
Che inviscava la ripa da ogni parte.
Io vedea lei, ma non vedeva in essa
Ma' che le bolle che il bollor levava,
E gonfiar tutta, e riseder compressa,
Mentr' io laggiù fisamente mirava,
Lo Duca mio, dicendo: 'Guarda, guarda,'
Mi trasse a sè del loco dov' io stava.
Allor mi volsi come l' uom cui tarda
Di vedèr quel che gli convien fuggire,
E cui paura subita sgagliarda,
Che per veder non indugia il partire:
E vidi dietro a noi un diavol nero
Correndo su per lo scoglio venire.

21

AND SO, FROM BRIDGE TO BRIDGE, while saying things
With which my "Comedy" is not concerned,
We reached the summit; and once there, we paused
To contemplate the adjoining crevice
Of Malebolge and hear its hopeless cries.
And I noticed then how strangely dark it was.
Like the tenacious pitch that boils
In winter in the docks of the Venetians
To retar disabled ships that cannot
Navigate; when, instead of sailing,
One makes his ship new, while another recaulks
The sides of one that made so many trips;
Who hammers the prow, and who the stern;
Others making oars, and still others cordage;
Who patches foresails, and who the main;
Such, not by fire but by divine intent,
Was the thick pitch that was boiling there below,
Making the embankment sticky all around.
I looked at it but saw nothing in it
Except the bubbles that the boiling raised,
And the swelling and contracting of it all.
As I was still gazing down at it,
My guide said to me: "Watch out! Watch out!",
And pulled me towards him from where I stood.
I turned about like a man who lingers
To see what he knows he must escape from—
And whom a sudden fright unnerves, so that
He no longer delays his going to see more—
And I saw in back of us a black devil,
Who came bounding up the precipice.

Ahi quanto egli era nell' aspetto fiero!
E quanto mi parea nell' atto acerbo,
Con l' ali aperte, e sopra il piè leggiero!
L' omero suo, ch' era acuto e superbo,
Carcava un peccator con ambo l'anche,
E quei tenea de' piè ghermito il nerbo.
Del nostro ponte disse, 'O Malebranche,
Ecco un degli anzian di santa Zita:
Mettetel sotto, ch' io torno per anche
A quella terra ch' i' n' ho ben fornita:
Ognun v' è barattier, fuor che Bonturo:
Del no, *per li denar, vi si fa* ita.'
Laggiù il buttò, e per lo scoglio duro
Si volse, e mai non fu mastino sciolto
Con tanta fretta a seguitar lo furo.
Quei s' attuffò, e tornò su convolto;
Ma i demon, che del ponte avean coperchio,
Gridar: 'Qui non ha loco il santo volto;
Qui si nuota altrimenti che nel Serchio;
Però se tu non vuoi de' nostri graffi,
Non far sopra la pegola soperchio.'
Poi l' addentar con più di cento raffi;
Disser: 'Coperto convien che qui balli,
Sì che, se puoi, nascosamente accaffi.'
Non altrimenti i cuochi ai lor vassalli
Fanno attuffare in mezzo la caldaia
La carne cogli uncin, perchè non galli.
Lo buon Maestro: 'Acciocchè non si paia
Che tu ci sii,' mi disse, 'giù t' acquatta
Dopo uno scheggio che alcun schermo t' haia;
E per nulla offension che mi sia fatta,
Non temer tu, ch' io ho le cose conte,
Perchè altra volta fui a tal baratta.'
Poscia passò di là dal co del ponte,
E com' ei giunse in su la ripa sesta,
Mestier gli fu d' aver sicura fronte.
Con quel furor e con quella tempesta
Ch' escono i cani addosso al poverello,
Che di subito chiede ove s' arresta;

What a ferocious look was on his face!
And how sinister his pose seemed to me,
With his wide-open wings and restless feet!
His back, which was very high and pointed,
Was carrying a sinner on both hips
Whom he was holding tightly by the heels.
"O Malebranche," he said from our bridge,
"Behold one of the elders of Saint Zita!
Put him below while I go back for more
To that land that I have crowded with them.
All are embezzlers there, except Bonturo.
For money, there, they make a 'yes' of 'no.'"
He flung him below, and then whirled down
Along the jagged cliff; and never was
A hound let loose so fast to chase a thief.
That other plunged and re-emerged hunched up,
But the demons, who used the bridge as cover,
Shouted: "There is no 'Holy Visage' here!
The swimming here is different from the Serchio's!
Unless, therefore, you want our hooks in you,
Stay well below the surface of the pitch!"
They poked him with over a hundred prongs,
And said: "Here you must dance under cover,
And plunder, if you can, without detection."
Exactly so do cooks make their scullions
Stop the meat from floating, by pushing it
Deep down into the kettle with their hooks.
The good master said to me: "Lest someone
Become aware that you are here, squat down
Behind a boulder and remain concealed;
And however I may be harassed by them,
Have no fear; these things are familiar to me,
From having once engaged in such a brawl."
He crossed beyond the summit of the bridge,
And when he came to the sixth embankment,
He assumed a needed air of confidence.
With all the storm and fury with which dogs
Rush out and leap upon a poor man
When he stops and suddenly starts begging,

Usciron quei di sotto al ponticello,
E volser contra lui tutti i roncigli;
Ma ei gridò: 'Nessun di voi sia fello.
Innanzi che l' uncin vostro mi pigli,
Traggasi avanti l' un di voi che m' oda,
E poi d' arroncigliarmi si consigli.'
Tutti gridaron: 'Vada Malacoda;'
Perchè un si mosse, e gli altri stetter fermi;
E venne a lui dicendo: 'Che gli approda?'
'Credi tu, Malacoda, qui vedermi
Esser venuto,' disse il mio Maestro,
'Sicuro già da tutti vostri schermi,
Senza voler divino e fato destro?
Lasciane andar, chè nel cielo è voluto
Ch' io mostri altrui questo cammin silvestro.'
Allor gli fu l' orgoglio sì caduto,
Che si lasciò cascar l' uncino ai piedi,
E disse agli altri: 'Omai non sia feruto.'
E il Duca mio a me: 'O tu, che siedi
Tra gli scheggion del ponte quatto quatto,
Sicuramente omai a me tu riedi.'
Perch' io mi mossi, ed a lui venni ratto;
E i diavoli si fecer tutti avanti,
Sì ch' io temetti ch' ei tenesser patto.
E così vid' io già temer li fanti
Ch' uscivan patteggiati di Caprona,
Veggendo sè tra nimici cotanti.
Io m' accostai con tutta la persona
Lungo il mio Duca, e non torceva gli occhi
Dalla sembianza lor ch' era non buona.
Ei chinavan gli raffi, e, 'Vuoi che 'l tocchi,'
Diceva l'un con l' altro, 'in sul groppone?'
E rispondean: 'Sì, fa che gliele accocchi.'
Ma quel demonio che tenea sermone
Col Duca mio, si volse tutto presto
E disse: 'Posa, posa, Scarmiglione.'
Poi disse a noi: 'Più oltre andar per questo
Iscoglio non si può, perocchè giace
Tutto spezzato al fondo l' arco sesto:

Those fiends issued from beneath the little bridge
And directed all their pitchforks at him.
But he cried out: "None of your viciousness!
Before you dig your pitchforks into me,
Let one of you step out to listen to me,
And then you may consult about impaling me."
All cried out: "Let Malacoda go!"
While the others hung back, one stepped forward,
And he came, saying: "What good will it do him?"
"Do you think, Malacoda," said my master,
"That you would have seen me here at all,
No matter how secure against your weapons,
Without the will of God and a friendly fate?
Let us pass, for Heaven has desired
That I show this savage path to another."
With that his arrogance so far subsided,
That he let fall the pitchfork at his feet,
And to the others said: "See that he is not hurt."
And my guide said to me: "O you who sit there
Cowering among the rubble of the bridge,
You may now return to me with confidence."
At which I got up and hurried to him;
And the devils all advanced together,
Which made me fear they would not keep their word.
I once saw soldiers frightened that way,
As they came out of Caprona by agreement
And saw themselves among so many foes.
With my whole body I drew up alongside
Of my guide, yet could not tear my eyes from the
Expression on their faces, which was not good.
Lowering their hooks, they asked each other:
"Would you like me to poke him in the rump?"
And they answered: "Yes; let him have it!"
But that demon, who was conversing with
My guide, turned about suddenly and said:
"Not so fast, Scarmiglione; not so fast!"
Then he said to us: "It is not possible
To advance any further along this cliff,
For the sixth arch lies shattered at the bottom.

E se l' andare avanti pur vi piace,
Andatevene su per questa grotta;
Presso è un altro scoglio che via face.
Ier, più oltre cinqu' ore che quest' otta,
Mille dugento con sessanta sei
Anni compiè, che qui la via fu rotta.
Io mando verso là di questi miei
A riguardar s' alcun se ne sciorina:
Gite con lor, ch' ei non saranno rei.'
'Tratti avanti, Alichino e Calcabrina,'
Cominciò egli a dire, 'e tu, Cagnazzo,
E Barbariccia guidi la decina.
Libicocco vegna oltre, e Draghignazzo,
Ciriatto sannuto, e Graffiacane,
E Farfarello, e Rubicante pazzo.
Cercate intorno le boglienti pane;
Costor sien salvi insino all' altro scheggio
Che tutto intero va sopra le tane.'
'O me! Maestro, che è quel che io veggio?'
Diss' io: 'deh! senza scorta andiamci soli,
Se tu sai ir, ch'io per me non la chieggio.
Se tu sei sì accorto come suoli,
Non vedi tu ch' ei digrignan li denti,
E colle ciglia ne minaccian duoli?'
Ed egli a me: 'Non vo' che tu paventi:
Lasciali digrignar pure a lor senno,
Ch' ei fanno ciò per li lessi dolenti.'
Per l' argine sinistro volta dienno;
Ma prima avea ciascun la lingua stretta
Coi denti, verso lor duca per cenno,
Ed egli avea del cul fatto trombetta.

But if you still wish to proceed this way,
Take the road that goes up along the grotto.
Close by, another cliff provides a path.
It was one thousand two hundred sixty-six
Years ago, five hours later than this,
Yesterday, that this road was demolished.
I have sent some of my men ahead to see
If anyone is coming up for air.
Go with them; they will not do you any harm."
"Step forward, Alichino and Calcabrina,"
He began to say, "and you, Cagnazzo!
And let Barbariccia command the ten!
Libicocco should go too, and Draghignazzo,
Ciriatto with the fangs, and Graffiacane,
And Farfarello, and mad Rubicante.
Look about you in that boiling glue, and
See these two safely to the other ridge
That stretches unimpaired across the caves."
"O, master, master, what am I seeing?"
I said. "If you know the way, please let us
Go without an escort; I need none for myself.
If you are as observant as usual,
Do you not see how they gnash their teeth,
And how their brows are threatening us with grief?"
And he to me: "You need not be afraid.
Let them gnash their teeth as much as they will;
They do it only for these boiling wretches."
They now turned towards the left embankment, but, first,
They all stuck out their tongues between their teeth,
By way of signal to their leader;
And that one made a trumpet of his ass.

XXII

IO vidi già cavalier mover campo,
E cominciare stormo, e far lor mostra,
E talvolta partir per loro scampo:
Corridor vidi per la terra vostra,
O Aretini, e vidi gir gualdane,
Ferir torneamenti, e correr giostra,
Quando con trombe, e quando con campane,
Con tamburi e con cenni di castella,
E con cose nostrali e con istrane;
Nè già con sì diversa cennamella
Cavalier vidi mover, nè pedoni,
Nè nave a segno di terra o di stella.
Noi andavam con li dieci dimoni:
Ahi fiera compagnia! ma nella chiesa
Coi santi, ed in taverna coi ghiottoni.
Pure alla pegola era la mia intesa,
Per veder della bolgia ogni contegno,
E della gente ch' entro v' era incesa.
Come i delfini, quando fanno segno
Ai marinar con l' arco della schiena,
Che s' argomentin di campar lor legno;
Talor così ad alleggiar la pena
Mostrava alcun dei peccatori il dosso,
E nascondeva in men che non balena.
E come all' orlo dell' acqua d' un fosso
Stanno i ranocchi pur col muso fuori,
Sì che celano i piedi e l' altro grosso;
Sì stavan d' ogni parte i peccatori:
Ma come s' appressava Barbariccia,
Così si ritraean sotto i bollori.

22

I HAVE SEEN CAVALRYMEN breaking camp,
And falling into line for an attack;
And I have seen them fleeing for their lives.
I have seen scouting parties on your plains,
O Aretines, and foraging platoons;
I have watched clashing tournaments and jousts,
Sometimes with trumpets and sometimes with bells;
Sometimes with drums and signals from the castles,
And other things of ours and from foreign parts:
But I never saw infantry or horsemen,
Nor ship at sea by sign of shore or star,
Moved by anything like that strange instrument.
Escorted by ten devils, we resumed our way.
What dreadful company! Still, as they say,
"With saints in church, with gluttons in a tavern."
But my attention lingered on the pitch—
To see all the conditions of the chasm
And who the people burning in it were.
Much as the dolphins do when they signal
Sailors with their arching backs, to warn them
To make preparations to preserve their ship,
In such fashion, to alleviate the pain,
Some of the sinners let their backs be seen,
Then vanished faster than a flash of lightning.
The sinners were all standing everywhere
Like frogs who only put their noses out
Along the margin of a pool of water,
And keep their feet and bodies out of sight.
And just as Barbariccia was approaching,
They disappeared below the boiling surface.

Escorted by ten devils, we resumed our way.

Io vidi, ed anco il cor me n' accapriccia,
Uno aspettar così, com' egli incontra
Che una rana rimane, ed altra spiccia.
E Graffiacan, che gli era più d' incontra,
Gli arroncigliò le impegolate chiome,
E trassel su, che mi parve una lontra.
Io sapea già di tutti quanti il nome,
Sì li notai quando furono eletti,
E poi che si chiamaro, attesi come.
'O Rubicante, fa che tu gli metti
Gli unghioni addosso sì che tu lo scuoi,'
Gridavan tutti insieme i maledetti.
Ed io: 'Maestro mio, fa, se tu puoi,
Che tu sappi chi è lo sciagurato
Venuto a man degli avversari suoi.'
Lo Duca mio gli s' accostò allato,
Domandollo ond' ei fosse, e quei rispose:
'Io fui del regno di Navarra nato.
Mia madre a servo d' un signor mi pose,
Chè m' avea generato d' un ribaldo
Distruggitor di sè e di sue cose.
Poi fui famiglio del buon re Tebaldo;
Quivi mi misi a far baratteria,
Di che io rendo ragione in questo caldo.'
E Ciriatto, a cui di bocca uscia
D' ogni parte una sanna come a porco,
Gli fe' sentir come l' una sdrucia.
Tra male gatte era venuto il sorco;
Ma Barbariccia il chiuse con le braccia,
E disse: 'State in là, mentr' io lo inforco.'
Ed al Maestro mio volse la faccia:
'Domanda,' disse, 'ancor se più desii
Saper da lui, prima ch' altri il disfaccia.'
Lo Duca: 'Dunque or di' degli altri rii:
Conosci tu alcun che sia Latino
Sotto la pece?' E quegli: 'Io mi partii
Poco è da un che fu di là vicino;
Così foss' io ancor con lui coperto,
Ch' io non temerei unghia nè uncino.'

My heart still pounds in memory of one
I saw, who waited longer than the rest,
As a frog will sometimes stay when others flee;
And Graffiacan, who stood closest to him,
Plunged his pitchfork into his tarred tresses,
And fished him out looking like an otter.
I knew the names of all the fiends already,
For I made note of them when they were chosen
And later heard how they addressed each other.
"O Rubicante," those god-forsaken
Creatures all bellowed out together,
"Put your claws on him and strip his hide off!"
And I said: "O master, will you find out,
If you can, who that unfortunate is
Who fell into the clutches of his foes?"
My guide drew up close beside him
And inquired who he was; and he replied:
"My birthplace was the Kingdom of Navarre.
Having borne me of a rogue, who squandered
Both himself and everything that he possessed,
My mother sent me off to serve a lord.
Later on I served the good King Thibault;
And that was when I started to embezzle,
For which I now pay the price amid this heat."
And Ciriatto, on both sides of whose mouth
There issued fangs like those of a wild boar,
Made him feel how one of them could slash.
The mouse had come among some wicked cats.
But Barbariccia grasped him in his arms,
And said: "Stay there while I use my fork on him!"
And, turning to face my master, he said:
"If you wish to know more about him,
Ask again, before someone dismembers him."
So my guide said: "Tell me, then: among other
Criminals below the pitch, do you know
If there are some Italians, too?" And he:
"I just left one who came from that vicinity;
If only I were covered with him still,
I would have no cause to dread the claws and hooks."

E Libicocco: 'Troppo avem sofferto,'
Disse, e presegli il braccio col ronciglio,
Sì che, stracciando, ne portò un lacerto.
Draghignazzo anco i volle dar di piglio
Giuso alle gambe; onde il decurio loro
Si volse intorno intorno con mal piglio.
Quand' elli un poco rappaciati foro,
A lui che ancor mirava sua ferita,
Domandò il Duca mio senza dimoro:
'Chi fu colui, da cui mala partita
Di' che facesti per venire a proda?'
Ed ei rispose: 'Fu frate Gomita,
Quel di Gallura, vasel d' ogni froda,
Ch' ebbe i nimici di suo donno in mano,
E fe' sì lor, che ciascun se ne loda:
Denar si tolse, e lasciolli di piano,
Sì com' ei dice: e negli altri offizi anche
Barattier fu non picciol, ma soprano.
Usa con esso donno Michel Zanche
Di Logodoro: ed a dir di Sardigna
Le lingue lor non si sentono stanche.
O me! vedete l' altro che digrigna:
Io direi anco; ma io temo ch' ello
Non s' apparecchi a grattarmi la tigna.'
E il gran proposto, volto a Farfarello
Che stralunava gli occhi per ferire,
Disse: 'Fatti in costà, malvagio uccello.'
'Se voi volete vedere o udire,'
Ricominciò lo spaurato appresso,
'Toschi o Lombardi, io ne farò venire.
Ma stien le male branche un poco in cesso,
Sì ch' ei non teman delle lor vendette;
Ed io, sedendo in questo loco stesso,
Per un ch' io son, ne farò venir sette,
Quand' io sufolerò, com' è nostr' uso
Di fare allor che fuori alcun si mette.'
Cagnazzo a cotal motto levò il muso,
Crollando il capo, e disse: 'Odi malizia
Ch' egli ha pensata per gittarsi giuso.'

Saying: "We have been patient much too long!",
Libicocco jabbed him with the pitchfork,
And tore away a sinew of his arm.
Draghignazzo also wished to hook him,
Aiming at his legs, but the leader of the group
Spun quickly round and gave him a hard look.
When they had all been quieted a little,
My guide immediately inquired of him
Who was still looking at his wound:
"Who was that one whose company you say
You regretfully left to come ashore?"
And he replied: "He was Brother Gomita
Of Gallura, a vessel of all frauds who,
Having in his power his master's foes,
So treated them that they eulogized him for it.
He took money from them and set them free,
As he says. And in his other functions, too,
He was no petty grafter, but a master.
Communing with him is Don Michel Zanche
Of Logodoro, and their tongues never
Tire of talking of Sardinia.
Pity me! Look at that one baring his fangs!
I would like to say more, but I fear
He is getting ready to scratch my scurf."
And the great provost turned to Farfarello,
Whose eyes were starting from his head to strike,
And said: "Get back there, abominable bird!"
"If you wish to see or hear the Tuscans
And the Lombards, I will have them come,"
The frightened spirit started once again.
"But see that those dread claws withdraw a little,
Lest they grow fearful of their vengeance;
And I, while seated in this very place,
Though but one, shall make seven of them come,
When I start whistling—as is our practice
When any one of us pokes out his head."
Cagnazzo at these words turned up his face,
Tossed his head from side to side, and said:
"What stratagems he thinks of to duck under!"

Ond' ei ch' avea lacciuoli a gran divizia,
Rispose: 'Malizioso son io troppo,
Quand' io procuro a' miei maggior tristizia.'
Alichin non si tenne, e di rintoppo
Agli altri, disse a lui: 'Se tu ti cali,
Io non ti verrò dietro di galoppo,
Ma batterò sopra la pece l' ali:
Lascisi il collo, e sia la ripa scudo
A veder se tu sol più di noi vali.'
O tu che leggi, udirai nuovo ludo!
Ciascun dall' altra costa gli occhi volse;
Quei prima, ch' a ciò fare era più crudo.
Lo Navarrese ben suo tempo colse,
Fermò le piante a terra, ed in un punto
Saltò, e dal proposto lor si sciolse.
Di che ciascun di colpa fu compunto,
Ma quei più, che cagion fu del difetto;
Però si mosse, e gridò, 'Tu se' giunto.'
Ma poco i valse: chè l' ali al sospetto
Non potero avanzar: quegli andò sotto,
E quei drizzò, volando, suso il petto:
Non altrimenti l' anitra di botto,
Quando il falcon s' appressa, giù s' attuffa,
Ed ei ritorna su crucciato e rotto.
Irato Calcabrina della buffa,
Volando dietro gli tenne, invaghito
Che quei campasse, per aver la zuffa.
E come il barattier fu disparito,
Così volse gli artigli al suo compagno,
E fu con lui sopra il fosso ghermito.
Ma l' altro fu bene sparvier grifagno
Ad artigliar ben lui, ed ambedue
Cadder nel mezzo del bogliente stagno.
Lo caldo sghermitor subito fue:
Ma però di levarsi era niente,
Sì aveano inviscate l' ali sue.
Barbariccia, con gli altri suoi dolente,
Quattro ne fe' volar dall' altra costa
Con tutti i raffi, ed assai prestamente

And he, who had wiles in great abundance,
Replied: "I am, alas, too crafty when I
Procure still greater woes for my own kind."
Unable to restrain himself, Alichino,
Dissenting from the others, said to him:
"If you go down, I shall not come galloping
After you, but beat my wings over the pitch;
Let us leave the hill and make the bank a shield,
And see if you can beat us by yourself."
O you who read, of new games you shall hear!
Each turned his eyes now to the other slope;
The first to do so was the least inclined.
The Navarrese seized his opportunity,
Planted his feet firmly on the ground
And leaped, and thus eluded their designs.
This gave them all a guilty feeling,
Particularly the one who was to blame.
Moving swiftly, he cried: "I'll get you!"
But it was of no avail, for wings could not
Outdistance fear; that other went under,
And this one threw back his shoulders and flew up.
Not otherwise does a duck suddenly
Disappear below when a falcon nears,
And the falcon comes back balked and angry.
Maddened by the taunt, Calcabrina
Flew straight after him, eagerly welcoming
The escape as a pretext for a fight.
No sooner had the embezzler disappeared,
Than he aimed his claws at his companion
And grappled with him above the chasm.
But the other sank his claws in him like
A ravenous hawk, and the two of them
Fell in the middle of the boiling pool.
The heat separated them at once,
And, yet, try as they might, they could not rise:
Their wings had stuck together from the pitch.
Barbariccia, suffering with the others,
Made four of them fly to the other slope,
With all their hooks; and, having soon landed,

Di qua, di là, discesero alla posta:
Porser gli uncini verso gl' impaniati,
Ch' eran già cotti dentro dalla crosta:
E noi lasciammo lor così impacciati.

Some here, some there, at a given place, they reached
Their hooks out to the ones who had got glued
And who were cooked already in their crust,
And thus entangled we took our leave of them.

XXIII

TACITI, soli e senza compagnia,
N' andavam l' un dinanzi e l' altro dopo,
Come frati minor vanno per via.
Volto era in sulla favola d' Isopo
Lo mio pensier per la presente rissa,
Dov' ei parlò della rana e del topo:
Chè più non si pareggia mo ed issa,
Che l' un con l' altro fa, se ben s' accoppia
Principio e fine con la mente fissa:
E come l' un pensier dell' altro scoppia,
Così nacque di quello un altro poi,
Che la prima paura mi fe' doppia.
Io pensava così: 'Questi per noi
Sono scherniti, e con danno e con beffa
Sì fatta, ch' assai credo che lor noi.
Se l' ira sopra il mal voler s' aggueffa,
Ei ne verranno dietro più crudeli
Che 'l cane a quella lepre ch' egli acceffa.'
Già mi sentia tutti arricciar li peli
Della paura, e stava indietro intento,
Quando io dissi: 'Maestro, se non celi
Te e me tostamente, i' ho pavento
Di Malebranche: noi gli avem già dietro:
Io gl' immagino sì, che già gli sento.'
E quei: 'S' io fossi d' impiombato vetro,
L' imagine di fuor tua non trarrei
Più tosto a me, che quella d' entro impetro.
Pur mo venian li tuoi pensier tra i miei
Con simile atto e con simile faccia,
Sì che d' intrambi un sol consiglio fei:

23

SILENT, ALONE, and without any escort,
We moved along, one behind the other,
The way the friars of the minor orders do.
The altercation that had just occurred
Had brought to mind that one of Aesop's fables
In which he talks about the frog and mouse:
And *mo*[3] and *issa*[4] are not more similar
Than these two cases, provided a sharp mind
Compares the way they start and finish.
And as one thought rises from another,
So from that one there was born another,
And that one doubled my first fear.
The thought was this: "These have been ridiculed
On our account with such injuries and gibes,
That they surely must be furious with us.
If anger is entangled with their bad will,
They will pursue us more ferociously
Than does the dog that pounces on the hare."
I was peering behind me, and could already
Feel my hair standing on end from fright,
When I said: "Master, if we do not hide
Ourselves at once, I dread what the Malebranche
Will do; they are already at our heels.
The impression is so vivid I can hear them."
And he: "If I were a mirror I could not
Give a faster reflection of your body
Than the reflection of your thoughts in mine.
This very moment your thoughts, with the same
Gesture and expression, pervaded mine,
And I made a single judgment from them both.

S' egli è che sì la destra costa giaccia,
Che noi possiam nell' altra bolgia scendere,
Noi fuggirem l' immaginata caccia.'
Già non compiè di tal consiglio rendere,
Ch' io gli vidi venir con l' ali tese,
Non molto lungi, per volerne prendere.
Lo Duca mio di subito mi prese,
Come la madre ch' al romore è desta,
E vede presso a sè le fiamme accese,
Che prende il figlio e fugge e non s' arresta,
Avendo più di lui che di sè cura,
Tanto che solo una camicia vesta:
E giù dal collo della ripa dura
Supin si diede alla pendente roccia,
Che l' un dei lati all' altra bolgia tura.
Non corse mai sì tosto acqua per doccia
A volger rota di molin terragno,
Quand' ella più verso le pale approccia,
Come il Maestro mio per quel vivagno,
Portandosene me sopra il suo petto,
Come suo figlio, non come compagno.
Appena fur li piè suoi giunti al letto
Del fondo giù, ch' ei furono in sul colle
Sopresso noi: ma non gli era sospetto;
Chè l' alta provvidenza, che lor volle
Porre ministri della fossa quinta,
Poder di partirs' indi a tutti tolle.
Laggiù trovammo una gente dipinta,
Che giva intorno assai con lenti passi
Piangendo, e nel sembiante stanca e vinta.
Egli avean cappe con cappucci bassi
Dinanzi agli occhi, fatti della taglia
Che in Cologna per li monaci fassi.
Di fuor dorate son, sì ch' egli abbaglia;
Ma dentro tutte piombo, e gravi tanto,
Che Federico le mettea di paglia.
O in eterno faticoso manto!
Noi ci volgemmo ancor pure a man manca
Con loro insieme, intenti al tristo pianto:

If the right shore slopes in such a way
That we can climb down into the other chasm,
We shall elude the hunt you have imagined."
He had scarcely finished giving his advice,
When, not very far away, I saw them
Coming, with their outspread wings, to get us.
My guide immediately took hold of me,
The way a mother, roused from sleep by a noise,
Who, seeing a fire burning near her,
Picks up her child and runs, and does not stop—
Having more concern for him than for herself—
Long enough to put a single garment on.
And from the summit of that jagged bank,
He slid flat on his back down the hanging rock
That walls in one side of the other chasm.
Water never poured through a sluice so fast
To turn the wheels of a mill built on land,
When it is closest to the paddles,
As did my master down that sloping wall,
Carrying me upon his breast as if I were,
Not his companion, but his son.
His feet no sooner reached the bed of that
Ravine, than the fiends appeared above us
On the hill; but there was no more cause for fear,
For the high Providence that assigned them
To be ministers of the fifth valley
Took from all of them the right to leave it.
Down there we came upon a painted people
Who very slowly walked about in tears
And with a tired and defeated look.
They all wore capes with cowls hanging down
Over their eyes, cut in the same fashion
As those made for the monks of Cluny.
These were so gilded outwardly, they dazzled;
But they were of lead inside, and so heavy
They would make those of Frederick seem straw.
O mantle eternally wearisome!
We turned once more to our left, together
With these souls absorbed in their dismal tears.

Ma per lo peso quella gente stanca
Venia sì pian, che noi eravam nuovi
Di compagnia ad ogni mover d' anca.
Perch' io al Duca mio: 'Fa che tu trovi
Alcun ch' al fatto o al nome si conosca,
E gli occhi sì andando intorno movi.'
Ed un che intese la parola Tosca
Diretro a noi gridò: 'Tenete i piedi,
Voi che correte sì per l' aura fosca:
Forse ch' avrai da me quel che tu chiedi.'
Onde il Duca si volse e disse: 'Aspetta,
E poi secondo il suo passo procedi.'
Ristetti, e vidi due mostrar gran fretta
Dell' animo, col viso, d' esser meco;
Ma tardavagli il carco e la via stretta.
Quando fur giunti, assai con l' occhio bieco
Mi rimiraron senza far parola:
Poi si volsero in sè, e dicean seco:
'Costui par vivo all' atto della gola:
E s' ei son morti, per qual privilegio
Vanno scoperti della grave stola?'
Poi disser me: 'O Tosco, ch' al collegio
Degl' ipocriti tristi se' venuto,
Dir chi tu sei non avere in dispregio.'
Ed io a loro: 'Io fui nato e cresciuto
Sopra il bel fiume d' Arno alla gran villa,
E son col corpo ch' i' ho sempre avuto.
Ma voi chi siete, a cui tanto distilla,
Quant' io veggio, dolor giù per le guance,
E che pena è in voi che sì sfavilla?'
E l' un rispose a me: 'Le cappe rance
Son di piombo sì grosse che li pesi
Fan così cigolar le lor bilance.
Frati Godenti fummo, e Bolognesi,
Io Catalano, e questi Loderingo
Nomati, e da tua terra insieme presi,
Come suole esser tolto un uom solingo
Per conservar sua pace, e fummo tali
Ch' ancor si pare intorno dal Gardingo.'

But that wearied company moved so slowly
From the weight, that with every step we took
We found ourselves with new companions;
Which prompted me to say to my guide: "Look for
Someone whom we may know by name or deed,
And move your eyes about as we proceed."
And someone who heard and understood Tuscan
Cried out behind us: "Pause where you are,
You who go running so through this dim air!
Perhaps I can tell you what you want to know."
At which my guide turned about and said: "Wait
For him and then proceed at his own pace."
I halted, and saw two souls whose faces showed
An urgency of purpose to be with me;
But their burden and the narrow way delayed them.
When they were close, they peered sideways at me
For a long while, and never said a word;
Then they looked away and said among themselves:
"He appears alive from the way his throat acts.
But, if they are dead, by what dispensation
Do they go uncovered by the weighty capes?"
Then he said to me: "O Tuscan, who have come
To the assembly of sad hypocrites,
Do not disdain to tell us who you are!"
And I to them: "I was born and grew up
In the large city on the lovely Arno,
And I come with the body that was always mine.
But you, who are you, down whose cheeks
I see such suffering distilled; and what
Penalty is this that sparkles from you?"
And he replied to me: "Our orange capes
Are made of lead so heavy that the scales
Creak and rattle from being overweighted.
We were pleasure-loving friars of Bologna;
My name was Catalano, and his was
Loderingo, both appointed by the city,
Though only one is generally selected,
To preserve the peace; and what we were like
May still be seen around the old Gardingo."

Io cominciai: 'O frati, i vostri mali . . .'
Ma più non dissi: ch' all' occhio mi corse
Un, crocifisso in terra con tre pali.
Quando mi vide, tutto si distorse,
Soffiando nella barba coi sospiri:
E il frate Catalan ch' a ciò s' accorse,
Mi disse: 'Quel confitto che tu miri
Consigliò i Farisei, che convenia
Porre un uom per lo popolo a' martiri.
Attraversato e nudo è nella via,
Come tu vedi, ed è mestier ch' ei senta
Qualunque passa com' ei pesa pria:
Ed a tal modo il suocero si stenta
In questa fossa, e gli altri del concilio
Che fu per li Giudei mala sementa.'
Allor vid' io maravigliar Virgilio
Sopra colui ch' era disteso in croce
Tanto vilmente nell' eterno esilio.
Poscia drizzò al frate cotal voce:
'Non vi dispiaccia, se vi lece, dirci
Se alla man destra giace alcuna foce,
Onde noi ambedue possiamo uscirci
Senza costringer degli angeli neri,
Che vegnan d' esto fondo a dipartirci.'
Rispose adunque: 'Più che tu non speri
S' appressa un sasso, che dalla gran cerchia
Si move, e varca tutti i vallon feri,
Salvo ch' a questo è rotto, e nol coperchia:
Montar potrete su per la ruina,
Che giace in costa, e nel fondo soperchia.'
Lo Duca stette un poco a testa china,
Poi disse: 'Mal contava la bisogna
Colui, che i peccator di là uncina.'
E il frate: 'Io udi' già dire a Bologna
Del Diavol vizii assai, tra i quali udi'
Ch' egli è bugiardo, e padre di menzogna.'
Appresso il Duca a gran passi sen gì,
Turbato un poco d' ira nel sembiante:
Ond' io dagl' incarcati mi parti'
Dietro alle poste delle care piante.

And I began: "O friars, your misfortunes . . .",
But said no more, for there caught my eye one
Who with three sticks was crucified in earth.
When he saw me, he twisted his whole body
And breathed heavy sighs into his beard.
And Brother Catalano, who saw it all,
Said to me: "That trapped one you are looking at
Advised the Pharisees that for the people's
Sake, one man had to be put to torture.
As you can see, he lies across the road
Naked, and is condemned to feel the weight
Of everyone who happens to pass by.
And in like manner is his father-in-law
Tormented in this chasm, and others of the
Council that sowed such hardship for the Jews."
And then I noticed Virgil marveling
Over the one stretched out so despicably
Upon the cross in the eternal exile.
He then addressed these words to the friar:
"May it please you to tell us, if you are
Allowed, whether there is an opening
To our right through which we two can depart
Without compelling some of the black angels
To come and lead us out of this abyss."
To which he answered: "Much closer than you hope,
A stone ridge lies that stretches from the great
Circle and spans all the cruel chasms,
Except for this one, where it has collapsed.
You can climb up along the debris that lies
On the slope and is piled up on the bottom."
My guide lowered his head a while, then said:
"That one over there, who catches sinners
With his hook, deliberately misguided us."
And the friar: "I once heard in Bologna
Of the Devil's many vices, among them
That he lies and is the father of all lies."
After that my guide set off with long strides,
A troubled look of anger on his face.
With that I left the ones who carried loads,
And followed in the tracks of those dear feet.

XXIV

IN quella parte del giovinetto anno,
Che il sole i crin sotto l' Aquario tempra,
E già le notti al mezzodì sen vanno:
Quando la brina in sulla terra assempra
L' imagine di sua sorella bianca,
Ma poco dura alla sua penna tempra;
Lo villanello, a cui la roba manca,
Si leva e guarda, e vede la campagna
Biancheggiar tutta, ond' ei si batte l' anca:
Ritorna in casa, e qua e là si lagna,
Come il tapin che non sa che si faccia;
Poi riede, e la speranza ringavagna,
Veggendo il mondo aver cangiata faccia
In poco d' ora, e prende suo vincastro,
E fuor le pecorelle a pascer caccia:
Così mi fece sbigottir lo Mastro,
Quand' io gli vidi sì turbar la fronte,
E così tosto al mal giunse lo impiastro:
Chè come noi venimmo al guasto ponte,
Lo Duca a me si volse con quel piglio
Dolce, ch' io vidi prima a piè del monte.
Le braccia aperse, dopo alcun consiglio
Eletto seco, riguardando prima
Ben la ruina, e diedemi di piglio.
E come quei che adopera ed estima,
Che sempre par che innanzi si proveggia;
Così, levando me su ver la cima
D' un ronchion, avvisava un' altra scheggia,
Dicendo: 'Sopra quella poi t' aggrappa;
Ma tenta pria s' è tal ch' ella ti reggia.'

24

IN THAT PORTION OF THE YEAR when the sun
Refreshes its looks under Aquarius,
And the nights are lessening to half a day,
And when the frozen dew upon the ground
Duplicates its white sister's image,
Though the hardness of its pen does not last long—
The farmer who lacks adequate provisions
Gets up and looks around and sees how white
The fields have all become, and, slapping his thigh,
Goes back in the house, frets now here, now there,
Like some poor wretch completely at a loss,
Then goes outside again and finds new hope
On seeing that the world has changed its face
In that brief interval, and, taking up
His staff, drives out the little lambs to pasture.
My master similarly gave me a jolt
When I saw the trembling look upon his face;
And just as quickly the balm was on the hurt;
For, when we came to the ruined bridge,
My guide turned to me with that sweet expression
Which I first saw at the foot of the mountain.
After taking counsel with himself and
Having first surveyed the ruin carefully,
He opened wide his arms and clasped me to him.
Like one who works, and estimates his work,
And seems to be providing in advance,
So he, while lifting me to the top of
One large rock, cast his eye upon the next,
Saying: "Climb up on top of that one, but
Test it first to see if it will hold you."

Non era via da vestito di cappa,
Chè noi a pena, ei lieve, ed io sospinto,
Potevam su montar di chiappa in chiappa.
E se non fosse che da quel precinto,
Più che dall' altro, era la costa corta,
Non so di lui, ma io sarei ben vinto.
Ma perchè Malebolge in ver la porta
Del bassissimo pozzo tutta pende,
Lo sito di ciascuna valle porta
Che l' una costa surge e l' altra scende:
Noi pur venimmo alfine in sulla punta
Onde l' ultima pietra si scoscende.
La lena m' era del polmon sì munta
Quando fui su, ch' io non potea più oltre,
Anzi mi assisi nella prima giunta.
'Omai convien che tu così ti spoltre,'
Disse il Maestro, 'chè sedendo in piuma
In fama non si vien, nè sotto coltre,
Senza la qual chi sua vita consuma,
Cotal vestigio in terra di sè lascia,
Qual fummo in aer ed in acqua la schiuma:
E però leva su, vinci l' ambascia
Con l' animo che vince ogni battaglia,
Se col suo grave corpo non s' accascia.
Più lunga scala convien che si saglia:
Non basta da costoro esser partito:
Se tu m' intendi, or fa sì che ti vaglia.'
Leva' mi allor, mostrandomi fornito
Meglio di lena ch' io non mi sentia;
E dissi: 'Va, ch' io son forte ed ardito.'
Su per lo scoglio prendemmo la via,
Ch' era ronchioso, stretto e malagevole,
Ed erto più assai che quel di pria.
Parlando andava per non parer fievole,
Onde una voce uscìo dall, altro fosso,
A parole formar disconvenevole.
Non so che disse, ancor che sopra il dosso
Fossi dell' arco già che varca quivi;
Ma chi parlava ad ira parea mosso.

It was no path for those who wore the capes, for
We ourselves—he lightly, I pushed from behind—
Could barely make our way from crag to crag.
Had it not been that the slope was shorter
On that side than on the other, I surely—
I do not know about him—would have failed.
But because all of Malebolge inclines
Towards the entrance of the very lowest well,
The way each chasm is situated,
One slope rises higher than the other.
We finally reached the topmost point, where
The last stone lay that had broken off.
The breath had been emptied from my lungs, so that,
Once there, I could not take another step,
But sat down promptly on my arrival.
"You must shake off this slothfulness at once,"
My master said. "Fame is not for the man
Who lies under covers and sits on feathers;
And those who use up their lives without fame
Leave as little trace of themselves in the world,
As smoke does in the air or foam in water.
So, rise up, and master your exhaustion
With the spirit, which wins every battle,
Provided the body does not drag it down.
You must ascend a higher ladder still!
It does not suffice to have left these behind.
If you understand, act to your advantage."
I then stood up, proving to myself that I
Was better supplied with breath than I supposed,
And I said: "Lead on! I feel strong and daring!"
We continued up the cliff along a path
That was rocky, narrow, and laborious,
And more precipitous than that before.
Not to appear fatigued, I was still talking
While I walked, when from the other chasm
There came a voice unfit for shaping words.
What it said I do not know, though I stood now
Atop the arch that spans the chasm there.
But whoever spoke appeared disposed to anger.

Io era volto in giù; ma gli occhi vivi
Non potean ire al fondo per l' oscuro:
Perch' io: 'Maestro, fa che tu arrivi
Dall' altro cinghio, e dismontiam lo muro;
Chè com' i' odo quinci e non intendo,
Così giù veggio, e niente affiguro.'
'Altra risposta,' disse, 'non ti rendo,
Se non lo far: chè la domanda onesta
Si dee seguir coll' opera tacendo.'
Noi discendemmo il ponte dalla testa,
Dove s' aggiunge coll' ottava ripa,
E poi mi fu la bolgia manifesta:
E vidivi entro terribile stipa
Di serpenti, e di sì diversa mena,
Che la memoria il sangue ancor mi scipa.
Più non si vanti Libia con sua rena;
Chè, se chelidri, iaculi e faree
Produce, e cencri con amfisibena,
Nè tante pestilenzie nè sì ree
Mostrò giammai con tutta l' Etiopia,
Nè con ciò che di sopra il mar rosso ee.
Tra questa cruda e tristissima copia
Correvan genti nude e spaventate,
Senza sperar pertugio o elitropia.
Con serpi le man dietro avean legate:
Quelle ficcavan per le ren la coda
E il capo, ed eran dinanzi aggroppate.
Ed ecco ad un, ch' era da nostra proda,
S' avventò un serpente, che il trafisse
Là dove il collo alle spalle s' annoda.
Nè O sì tosto mai, nè I si scrisse,
Com' ei s' accese ed arse, e cener tutto
Convenne che cascando divenisse:
E poi che fu a terra sì distrutto,
La polver si raccolse per sè stessa,
E in quel medesmo ritornò di butto:
Così per li gran savi si confessa,
Che la Fenice more e poi rinasce,
Quando al cinquecentesimo anno appressa.

I bent down to look, but my mortal eyes
Could not discern the bottom in the dark.
I therefore said: "Master, get us to the
Other bank, and let us climb off the wall,
For I hear and cannot make out what,
And I look down and cannot see a thing."
"I shall make no reply," he said, "other
Than the action: for an honest plea
Should be followed, without a word, by what is asked."
At the end of the bridge, where it united
With the eighth embankment, we stepped down;
And then the chasm was revealed to me:
In it I saw a terrifying mass
Of serpents of such fantastic shapes,
That my blood still curdles when I think of them.
Libya can stop boasting of her sands;
And though it produces chelydri, jaculi,
Phareae, cenchres, and amphisbaena,
It never had so many dreadful plagues,
Even with all of Ethiopia
And the land that borders the Red Sea, too.
Amid this vile and miserable heap
People ran nude and frightened, without hope
Of heliotrope, or a hole to hide in.
Their hands were bound behind their backs with snakes,
Whose heads and tails protruded through their loins
And gathered into tangled coils in front.
Not far from where we stood, a serpent sprang
Upon one wretch, transfixed him at the place
Where the neck is knotted to the shoulders.
Never was "O" or "I" so quickly written
As he burst into flame, and, thus consumed,
Fell in a heap of ashes on the ground;
And after he was thoroughly demolished,
The ashes reassembled by themselves,
And in a flash he was himself again.
So—according to the great savants—
The Phoenix dies and then returns to life
As it approaches its five hundredth year;

Erba nè biado in sua vita non pasce,
Ma sol d' incenso lagrime ed amomo;
E nardo e mirra son l' ultime fasce.
E qual è quei che cade, e non sa como,
Per forza di demon ch' a terra il tira,
O d' altra oppilazion che lega l' uomo,
Quando si leva, che intorno si mira
Tutto smarrito dalla grande angoscia
Ch' egli ha sofferta, e guardando sospira;
Tal era il peccator levato poscia.
O potenzia di Dio quant' è severa,
Che cotai colpi per vendetta croscia!
Lo Duca il domandò poi chi egli era:
Perch' ei rispose: 'Io piovvi di Toscana,
Poco tempo è, in questa gola fera.
Vita bestial mi piacque, e non umana,
Sì come a mul ch' io fui: son Vanni Fucci,
Bestia, e Pistoia mi fu degna tana.'
Ed io al Duca: 'Digli che non mucci,
E domanda qual colpa quaggiù il pinse:
Ch' io il vidi uomo di sangue e di crucci.'
E il peccator, che intese, non s' infinse,
Ma drizzò verso me l' animo e il volto,
E di trista vergogna si dipinse:
Poi disse: 'Più mi duol che tu m' hai colto
Nella miseria dove tu mi vedi,
Che quando fui dell' altra vita tolto.
Io non posso negar quel che tu chiedi;
In giù son messo tanto, perch' io fui
Ladro alla sacrestia de' belli arredi;
E falsamente già fu apposto altrui.
Ma perchè di tal vista tu non godi,
Se mai sarai di fuor de' lochi bui,
Apri gli orecchi al mio annunzio, ed odi:
Pistoia in pria di Negri si dimagra,
Poi Fiorenza rinnuova genti e modi.
Tragge Marte vapor di val di Magra
Che, di torbidi nuvoli involuto,
E, con tempesta impetuosa ed agra,

Alive, it feeds on neither herb nor grain,
But only on tears of incense and balsam,
And for its final vestments nard and myrrh.
And as is he who, without knowing why, falls
Because some demon force pulls him to earth,
Or from some other hindrance that thwarts man,
And who, when he rises, looks about him
Completely unnerved by the sudden panic
He experienced, and then, while looking, sighs—
Such was the sinner who rose up again.
O how severe is the power of God
That lets such blows rain down in reprisal!
My guide then asked him who he was, to which
He answered: "From Tuscany, not long ago,
I poured down into this savage throat.
More like a mule than man, I chose a bestial,
Not a human, life; I am Vanni Fucci,
Animal; Pistoia was my worthy lair."
And I to my guide: "Tell him not to flee,
And ask him what wickedness pushed him down here,
For I knew him as a wrathful man of blood."
And the sinner, who heard without pretending,
Turned his face and his attention to me,
And looked the picture of despondent shame.
Then he said: "It gives me far more pain that
You should find me in this wretched state than did
Being whisked away from the other life.
I cannot refuse to answer what you ask:
I have been placed this far down because I stole
Some things of value from the sacristy;
For which some others were once wrongly blamed.
But that you may not find pleasure in this sight—
If you are ever outside these dark places—
Open your ears to my prophecy; listen:
Pistoia first is emptied of the Blacks;
Next Florence alters practices and people.
From the valley of the Magra, Mars draws forth
A vapor involuted with thick clouds,
And, in a storm of bitter turbulence,

Sopra Campo Picen fia combattuto:
Ond' ei repente spezzerà la nebbia,
Sì ch' ogni Bianco ne sarà feruto:
E detto l' ho, perchè doler ti debbia.'

There will be fighting on the Campo Piceno.
The vapor will suddenly burst through the mist,
And every White will be wounded by it.
I have told you this to make you suffer."

AL fine delle sue parole il ladro
Le mani alzò con ambedue le fiche,
Gridando: 'Togli, Iddio, chè a te le squadro.'
Da indi in qua mi fur le serpi amiche,
Perch' una gli s' avvolse allora al collo,
Come dicesse: 'Io non vo' che più diche:'
Ed un' altra alle braccia, e rilegollo,
Ribadendo sè stessa sì dinanzi,
Che non potea con esse dare un crollo.
Ahi Pistoia, Pistoia, chè non stanzi
D' incenerarti, sì che più non duri,
Poi che in mal far lo seme tuo avanzi?
Per tutti i cerchi dell' inferno oscuri
Non vidi spirto in Dio tanto superbo,
Non quel che cadde a Tebe giù da' muri.
Ei si fuggì, che non parlò più verbo:
Ed io vidi un Centauro pien di rabbia
Venir chiamando: 'Ov' è, ov' è l' acerbo?'
Maremma non cred' io che tante n' abbia,
Quante bisce egli avea su per la groppa,
Infin dove comincia nostra labbia.
Sopra le spalle, dietro dalla coppa,
Con l' ali aperte gli giacea un draco,
E quello affoca qualunque s' intoppa.
Lo mio Maestro disse: 'Quegli è Caco,
Che sotto il sasso di monte Aventino
Di sangue fece spesse volte laco.
Non va co' suoi fratei per un cammino,
Per lo furar che frodolente fece
Del grande armento ch' egli ebbe a vicino:

25

WHEN HE HAD FINISHED SAYING THIS, the thief
Raised his fists with both thumbs sticking through,
And cried: "Take that, God! I saved it for you!"
From that moment on the serpents were my friends,
For one entwined itself around his neck
As if to say: "Not another word from you!",
And another round his arms, retying him
And clenching itself so tightly in front,
That he could not make the slightest movement.
Oh, Pistoia, Pistoia, why not order
Your own burning, and thus put an end to life
For surpassing your seed in evil-doing?
In all the dark circles of Hell, I never
Saw a spirit so contemptuous of God,
Not even the one who fell from the walls of Thebes.
Without saying another word, he fled; and
I saw a Centaur full of rage advancing,
Who called out: "Where is he; where is that foul one?"
I doubt if Maremma has as many snakes
As he had on his lower animal part
Up to where our human features start.
Over his shoulders and in back of his head,
With open wings, a dragon lay upon him
That set on fire everyone it met.
My master said: "That one is Cacus who,
From under the rock of Mount Aventine,
Several times made a lake of blood.
He does not walk the same road as his brothers,
Because of his deceitful robbery
Of the great herd of oxen standing near him,

Onde cessar le sue opere biece
Sotto la mazza d' Ercole, che forse
Gliene diè cento, e non sentì le diece.'
Mentre che sì parlava, ed ei trascorse,
E tre spiriti venner sotto noi,
De' quai nè io nè il Duca mio s' accorse,
Se non quando gridar: 'Chi siete voi?'
Per che nostra novella si ristette,
Ed intendemmo pure ad essi poi.
Io non gli conoscea, ma ei seguette,
Come suol seguitar per alcun caso,
Che l' un nomare un altro convenette,
Dicendo: 'Cianfa dove fia rimaso?'
Perch' io, acciocchè il Duca stesse attento
Mi posi il dito su dal mento al naso.
Se tu sei or, Lettore, a creder lento
Ciò ch' io dirò, non sarà maraviglia,
Chè io che il vidi appena il mi consento.
Com' io tenea levate in lor le ciglia,
Ed un serpente con sei piè si lancia
Dinanzi all' uno, e tutto a lui s' appiglia.
Coi piè di mezzo gli avvinse la pancia,
E con gli anterior le braccia prese;
Poi gli addentò e l' una e l' altra guancia.
Gli diretani alle cosce distese,
E miseli la coda tr' ambedue,
E dietro per le ren su la ritese.
Ellera abbarbicata mai non fue
Ad arbor sì, come l' orribil fiera
Per l' altrui membra avviticchiò le sue:
Poi s' appiccar, come di calda cera
Fossero stati, e mischiar lor colore;
Nè l' un nè l' altro già parea quel ch' era:
Come procede innanzi dall' ardore
Per lo papiro suso un color bruno,
Che non è nero ancora, e il bianco more.
Gli altri due riguardavano, e ciascuno
Gridava: 'O me, Agnèl, come ti muti!
Vedi che già non sei nè due nè uno.'

His crooked ways ending under the club
Of Hercules, who gave him one hundred blows,
Perhaps, of which the first ten were not felt."
While this was said, the Centaur hurried past,
And three other spirits came below us,
Without either of us knowing they were there,
Until they all cried out: "Who are you?"
Our story having thus been interrupted,
We gave our whole attention to these three.
I did not recognize them, but, by chance,
As often happens on such occasions,
One of them mentioned someone else's name
By inquiring: "Where is Cianfa stopping?"
At which I, to draw my guide's attention,
Placed my finger on my chin up to my nose.
If you, reader, are slow to believe what
I shall tell, that will be no surprise,
For I who saw it scarcely trust myself.
While I was staring at the three of them,
A serpent with six feet darted up to
One of them and flung himself around him.
It wrapped its middle feet around his stomach,
And took hold of his arms with those in front,
And then it sank its teeth in both his cheeks.
After clamping its hind feet on his thighs,
The serpent thrust his tail between them
And curled it up in back over his loins.
Never did ivy cling so tenaciously
To a tree as that frightful monster's limbs
Entwined themselves around those of the other.
Then they fused with one another, as if made
Of melting wax, and their colors intermixed.
Neither looked any longer like himself—
The way a dark brown color, not yet black,
Moves upward on a piece of burning paper,
Just ahead of the flame: and the white dies.
The other two continued staring, and then
Both cried out: "Agnel, how you have changed!
Look at you! You are neither one nor two!"

Già eran li due capi un divenuti,
Quando n' apparver due figure miste
In una faccia, ov' eran due perduti.
Fersi le braccia due di quattro liste;
Le cosce con le gambe, il ventre e il casso
Divenner membra che non fur mai viste.
Ogni primaio aspetto ivi era casso:
Due e nessun l' imagine perversa
Parea, e tal sen gía con lento passo.
Come il ramarro, sotto la gran fersa
De' dì canicular cangiando siepe,
Folgore par, se la via attraversa:
Così parea, venendo verso l' epe
Degli altri due, un serpentello acceso,
Livido e nero come gran di pepe.
E quella parte, donde prima è preso
Nostro alimento, all' un di lor trafisse;
Poi cadde giuso innanzi lui disteso.
Lo trafitto il mirò, ma nulla disse:
Anzi coi piè fermati sbadigliava,
Pur come sonno o febbre l' assalisse.
Egli il serpente, e quei lui riguardava:
L' un per la piaga, e l' altro per la bocca
Fumavan forte, e il fummo si scontrava.
Taccia Lucano omai, là dove tocca
Del misero Sabello e di Nassidio,
Ed attenda ad udir quel ch' or si scocca.
Taccia di Cadmo e d' Aretusa Ovidio:
Chè se quello in serpente, e quella in fonte
Converte poetando, io non l' invidio:
Chè due nature mai a fronte a fronte
Non trasmutò, sì ch' ambedue le forme
A cambiar lor materia fosser pronte.
Insieme si risposero a tai norme,
Che il serpente la coda in forca fesse,
E il feruto ristrinse insieme l' orme.
Le gambe con le cosce seco stesse
S' appiccar sì, che in poco la giuntura
Non facea segno alcun che si paresse.

Both heads had already become one,
As two figures before our eyes mingled
In one face in which two had disappeared.
Two arms were made of what had been four limbs;
The thighs and legs, the stomach and the chest,
Became members such as no one ever saw.
His whole earlier appearance was effaced:
The perverse image seemed both two and none;
And in that form it slowly went away.
As a lizard changing hedges,
Under the heavy lash of the dog days,
Looks like lightning when it darts across the path;
So a vicious little reptile appeared,
Livid and black like a grain of pepper,
And headed for the bellies of those two.
It pierced that part of one of them
Through which our first nourishment is taken,
Then fell and lay upon the ground before him.
The one, transfixed, looked at it, and said nothing;
But, rather, with his feet rendered motionless,
Yawned as if overcome by sleep or fever.
The reptile looked at him, and he at it.
From the wound of one and from the other's mouth
Smoke poured heavily, and intermingled.
Let Lucan be still where he treats of Sabellus
And Nassidius, and listen carefully
To what comes next; and let Ovid be silent
About Cadmus, and Arethusa, too:
I do not envy him if, as a poet,
He turned them into snake and fountain;
For he never changed two beings, front to front,
In such a way that both forms readily
Exchanged one substance for the other.
Their effect on one another was now such,
That the serpent split his tail in two,
And the maimed one squeezed his two feet into one.
His legs and thighs had coalesced so fully
With each other, that there was scarcely any
Sign of where the joint between them had once been.

Togliea la coda fessa la figura
Che si perdeva là, e la sua pelle
Si facea molle, e quella di là dura.
Io vidi entrar le braccia per l' ascelle,
E i due piè della fiera, ch' eran corti,
Tanto allungar quanto accorciavan quelle.
Poscia li piè diretro, insieme attorti,
Diventaron lo membro che l' uom cela,
E il misero del suo n' avea due porti.
Mentre che il fummo l' uno e l' altro vela
Di color nuovo, e genera il pel suso
Per l' una parte, e dall' altra il dipela,
L' un si levò, e l' altro cadde giuso,
Non torcendo però le lucerne empie,
Sotto le quai ciascun cambiava muso.
Quel ch' era dritto, il trasse ver le tempie,
E di troppa materia che in là venne,
Uscir gli orecchi delle gote scempie:
Ciò che non corse in dietro e si ritenne,
Di quel soperchio fe' naso alla faccia,
E le labbra ingrossò quanto convenne.
Quel che giacea, il muso innanzi caccia,
E gli orecchi ritira per la testa,
Come face le corna la lumaccia:
E la lingua, che avea unita e presta
Prima a parlar, si fende, e la forcuta
Nell' altro si richiude, e il fummo resta.
L' anima ch' era fiera divenuta
Si fuggì sufolando per la valle,
E l' altro dietro a lui parlando sputa.
Poscia gli volse le novelle spalle,
E disse all' altro: 'Io vo' che Buoso corra,
Com' ho fatt' io, carpon, per questo calle.'
Così vid' io la settima zavorra
Mutare e trasmutare; e qui mi scusi
La novità, se fior la penna abborra.
Ed avvegnachè gli occhi miei confusi
Fossero alquanto, e l' animo smagato,
Non poter quei fuggirsi tanto chiusi,

The fissured tail took the appearance
Of what the other lost; the skin was soft,
Whereas that of the other had grown hard.
I saw the forearms enter at the armpits,
And the two feet of the monster, which were short,
Become as long as the two arms now were short.
As for the hind feet, they twisted into one,
And thus became the member that man hides,
While two had sprouted from the wretch's own.
While the vapor veiled one and the other
In a new color, and made hair grow
On one part, and removed it from another,
One fell down as the other straightened up,
Without shifting in the least their impious eyes,
Under which the two were changing faces.
The one standing pulled his towards the temples,
And from the excess tissue gathered there
The ears protruded from the hollow cheeks.
From the surplus of that part of it
That stayed in front, a nose formed on the face,
And the lips were widened in proportion.
The one on the ground thrust his face forward,
And pulled both ears back into his head,
Exactly as a snail does with his horns.
The tongue was split that had before been whole
And swift for speech, and like a fork was lodged
Within the other. Just then the fumes subsided.
Having thus been turned into a monster,
The soul fled hissing through the valley,
The other at its heels, spitting while it talked.
Presently he spun his strange new shoulders round,
Saying to the other: "I want Buoso to run
On hands and feet, as I have, on this road."
This was how I used to see the seventh ballast
Changing and rechanging, and if my pen errs,
Let the strangeness of it all be my excuse.
And even though my eyes were to some degree
Confused, and my mind tired to distraction,
Those souls could not make off so furtively

Ch' io non scorgessi ben Puccio Sciancato:
Ed era quei che sol, de' tre compagni
Che venner prima, non era mutato:
L' altro era quel che tu, Gaville, piagni.

That I failed to recognize Puccio Sciancato;
And, of the three companions who first approached,
He was the only one unchanged; the other,
O Gaville, was the one who makes you weep.

XXVI

GODI, Fiorenza, poi che sei sì grande
Che per mare e per terra batti l' ali,
E per l' inferno il tuo nome si spande.
Tra li ladron trovai cinque cotali
Tuoi cittadini, onde mi vien vergogna,
E tu in grande onranza non ne sali.
Ma se presso al mattin del ver si sogna,
Tu sentirai di qua da picciol tempo
Di quel che Prato, non ch' altri, t' agogna.
E se già fosse, non saria per tempo.
Così foss' ei, da che pure esser dee;
Chè più mi graverà, com' più m' attempo.
Noi ci partimmo, e su per le scalee,
Che n' avean fatte i borni a scender pria,
Rimontò il mio Maestro, e trasse mee.
E proseguendo la solinga via
Tra le schegge e tra' rocchi dello scoglio,
Lo piè senza la man non si spedia.
Allor mi dolsi, ed ora mi ridoglio,
Quand' io drizzo la mente a ciò ch' io vidi;
E più lo ingegno affreno ch' io non soglio,
Perchè non corra che virtù nol guidi;
Sì che se stella buona, o miglior cosa
M' ha dato il ben, ch' io stesso nol m' invidi.
Quante il villan, ch' al poggio si riposa,
Nel tempo che colui che il mondo schiara
La faccia sua a noi tien meno ascosa,
Come la mosca cede alla zenzara,
Vede lucciole giù per la vallea,
Forse colà dove vendemmia ed ara:

26

BE HAPPY, FLORENCE, that you are so great,
That you beat your wings over land and sea,
And that your name has spread all over Hell.
Among the thieves I found five who had been
Citizens of yours, a fact that gives me shame,
And does not elevate you to great honor.
But if what we dream near morning is the truth,
You shall experience shortly what Prato,
Not to mention others, has in store for you.
If it came now, it would not be too soon;
Since come it must, the earlier the better,
For the older I grow the more it weighs on me.
We now moved on, and up the crags, which had served
As stairs when we descended earlier,
My guide climbed once more, and pulled me after him;
And as we went our solitary way
Among the precipice's jagged stones,
Our feet could scarcely move without our hands.
I now began to grieve, and I still grieve
Whenever I recall what I then saw,
And rein my fancy in more than usual,
Lest it run without virtue to direct it,
And thus belittle those advantages
Which my good star, or something better, gave me.
Perhaps a farmer, resting on a hillside,
At the hour that he who lights the world
Keeps his face least concealed from us,
And at the time the fly yields to the gnat,
Sees as many fireflies in the valley
Below, even where he ploughs and tends the vine,

Di tante fiamme tutta risplendea
L' ottava bolgia, sì com' io m' accorsi
Tosto ch' io fui là 've il fondo parea.
E qual colui che si vengiò con gli orsi
Vide il carro d' Elia al dipartire,
Quando i cavalli al cielo erti levorsi;
Chè nol potea sì con gli occhi seguire
Ch' ei vedesse altro che la fiamma sola,
Sì come nuvoletta, in su salire:
Tal si movea ciascuna per la gola
Del fosso, chè nessuna mostra il furto,
Ed ogni fiamma un peccatore invola.
Io stava sopra il ponte a veder surto,
Sì che, s' io non avessi un ronchion preso,
Caduto sarei giù senza esser urto.
E il Duca, che mi vide tanto atteso,
Disse: 'Dentro da' fochi son gli spirti:
Ciascun si fascia di quel ch' egli è inceso.'
'Maestro mio,' rispos' io, 'per udirti
Son io più certo; ma già m' era avviso
Che così fusse, e già voleva dirti:
Chi è in quel foco, che vien sì diviso
Di sopra, che par surger della pira,
Ov' Eteócle col fratel fu miso?'
Risposemi: 'Là entro si martira
Ulisse e Diomede, e così insieme
Alla vendetta vanno come all' ira:
E dentro dalla lor fiamma si geme
L' aguato del caval che fe' la porta
Ond' uscì de' Romani il gentil seme.
Piangevisi entro l' arte per che morta
Deidamìa ancor si duol d' Achille,
E del Palladio pena vi si porta.'
'S' ei posson dentro da quelle faville
Parlar,' diss' io, 'Maestro, assai ten prego
E riprego, che il prego vaglia mille,
Che non mi facci dell' attender nego,
Finchè la fiamma cornuta qua vegna:
Vedi che del disio ver lei mi piego.'

As there were flames illuminating all
Of the eighth chasm, as I suddenly was
Aware when I came where the bottom could be seen.
As it was with him whom the bears avenged
When he saw Elijah's chariot take off,
And the horses stood up facing Heaven,
But could not follow it with his eyes,
And saw nothing but that solitary flame
Rising up as if it were a little cloud—
Thus each flame moved within the gullet of that
Abyss, and though none gave outward signs of theft,
Each fire had abducted one wrongdoer.
As I was standing on the bridge, I rose to look
In such a way that, if I had not grasped a rock,
I would have dropped below without a push.
And my guide, who saw me thus absorbed,
Said: "The spirits are within those fires;
Each clothes himself in what is burning him."
To which I answered: "Master, to hear you
Reassures me; but I had already
Noticed it myself, and was about to ask:
Who is in that fire which divides so
At the top that it seems to rise from the pyre
Where Eteocles was placed beside his brother?
He answered me: "Ulysses and Diomed
Are being tortured in it; together
They go in punishment, as they went in wrath.
And there, inside their flame, both lament
The ambush of the horse—the door from which
Issued the noble founder of the Romans.
And they repent, inside, the ruse by which the dead
Deïdamia still grieves for Achilles,
And bear punishment for the Palladium."
And I said: "If they, from within those sparks,
Can speak, master, I beg you, and beg again,
And may my plea be worth a thousand pleas:
Do not deny me your permission
To wait until the horn-shaped flame approaches.
See with what eagerness I bend towards it!"

Ed egli a me: 'La tua preghiera è degna
Di molta lode, ed io però l' accetto;
Ma fa che la tua lingua si sostegna.
Lascia parlare a me: ch' io ho concetto
Ciò che tu vuoi: ch' ei sarebbero schivi,
Perch' ei fur Greci, forse del tuo detto.'
Poichè la fiamma fu venuta quivi,
Dove parve al mio Duca tempo e loco,
In questa forma lui parlare audivi:
'O voi, che siete due dentro ad un foco,
S' io meritai di voi mentre ch' io vissi,
S' io meritai di voi assai o poco,
Quando nel mondo gli alti versi scrissi,
Non vi movete; ma l' un di voi dica
Dove per lui perduto a morir gissi.'
Lo maggior corno della fiamma antica
Cominciò a crollarsi mormorando,
Pur come quella cui vento affatica.
Indi la cima qua e là menando,
Come fosse la lingua che parlasse,
Gittò voce di fuori, e disse: 'Quando
Mi diparti' da Circe, che sottrasse
Me più d' un anno là presso a Gaeta,
Prima che sì Enea la nominasse;
Nè dolcezza di figlio, nè la pieta
Del vecchio padre, nè il debito amore,
Lo qual dovea Penelope far lieta,
Vincer poter dentro da me l' ardore
Ch' i' ebbi a divenir del mondo esperto,
E degli vizii umani e del valore:
Ma misi me per l' alto mare aperto
Sol con un legno e con quella compagna
Picciola, dalla qual non fui deserto.
L' un lito e l' altro vidi infin la Spagna,
Fin nel Morrocco, e l' isola de' Sardi,
E l' altre che quel mare intorno bagna.
Io e i compagni eravam vecchi e tardi,
Quando venimmo a quella foce stretta
Ov' Ercole segnò li suoi riguardi,

And he to me: "Your plea is worthy of
Great praise, and for that reason I accede;
But see to it that you control your tongue.
Let me do the talking; for I can imagine
What you wish to know; besides, being Greek,
They might be embarrassed by the way you speak."
When the flame had finally reached a point
That seemed appropriate to my guide in time
And place, I heard him speak to it as follows:
"O you who are two inside one fire,
If I deserved something of you while I lived—
Whether that something was much or little—
When I wrote my lofty verses in the world,
Do not move on, but one of you tell me
Where, when you were lost, you went to die?"
The larger of the horns of the antique flame
Now began to quiver as it murmured,
The way a flame will flutter in the wind.
The tip of it went flickering back and forth,
As if it were a real tongue that was speaking,
And from it came a voice that said:
"When I left Circe, who for a year and more
Diverted me not far from Gaeta,
Long before Aeneas named it that,
Nothing—not sweetness of son, not piety
To an aging father, not the promised love
That would have brought joy to Penelope—
Could overcome in me a burning wish
To experience the entire world
And learn of human vices and of worth.
So I sailed out into the deep open sea
With a single ship, and with that little
Company of men that never left me.
I saw one shore and the other as far as Spain
And Morocco; and the island of Sardinia,
And other islands, which that sea washes round.
I and my companions were already old
And feeble when we came to that narrow mouth
Where Hercules implanted his insignia,

Acciocchè l' uom più oltre non si metta:
Dalla man destra mi lasciai Sibilia,
Dall' altra già m' avea lasciata Setta.
"O frati, dissi, che per cento milia
Perigli siete giunti all' occidente,
A questa tanto picciola vigilia
De' nostri sensi ch' è del rimanente,
Non vogliate negar l' esperienza,
Diretro al sol, del mondo senza gente.
Considerate la vostra semenza:
Fatti non foste a viver come bruti,
Ma per seguir virtute e conoscenza."
Li miei compagni fec' io sì acuti,
Con questa orazion picciola, al cammino,
Che appena poscia gli avrei ritenuti.
E volta nostra poppa nel mattino,
De' remi facemmo ali al folle volo,
Sempre acquistando dal lato mancino.
Tutte le stelle già dell' altro polo
Vedea la notte, e il nostro tanto basso,
Che non surgeva fuor del marin suolo.
Cinque volte racceso, e tante casso
Lo lume era di sotto dalla luna,
Poi ch' entrati eravam nell' alto passo,
Quando n' apparve una montagna bruna
Per la distanza, e parvemi alta tanto
Quanto veduta non n' aveva alcuna.
Noi ci allegrammo, e tosto tornò in pianto;
Chè dalla nuova terra un turbo nacque,
E percosse del legno il primo canto.
Tre volte il fe' girar con tutte l' acque,
All quarta levar la poppa in suso,
E la prora ire in giù, com' altrui piacque,
Infin che il mar fu sopra noi richiuso.'

So that no man should ever go beyond.
On my right I left Seville, and I had
Already left Ceuta on the other.
'O brothers,' I said, 'who through a hundred thousand
Perils have reached the Occident at last,
Do not forbid your senses, in this
So brief vigil that remains to you,
The adventure of the world without
Human beings that lies beyond the sun.
Consider the nature of your origin.
You were not made to live like beasts, but for
The pursuit of virtue and of knowledge.'
With this short address I made my companions
So enthusiastic for the journey, that
I would scarcely have been able to restrain them.
And, having turned our stern around at morning,
We made wings of our oars for that wild flight,
And continued making headway towards the left.
Already the night beheld all the stars
Of the other pole, while ours was so low
That it did not rise above the ocean floor.
Under the moon the light had burned again
Five times, and just as many times gone out,
Since we had penetrated that deep strait,
When a mountain, dark and blurred by distance,
Came into sight that seemed to me
The highest mountain I had ever seen.
We were overjoyed, but that soon turned to tears,
For a great whirlwind sprang up from the new land
And started battering the vessel's prow.
Three times, with all the waves, it made the ship
Spin round; the fourth time it lifted up the stern,
And sent the prow down—as Another willed—
Until the ocean had closed over us."

XXVII

GIA' era dritta in su la fiamma e queta,
Per non dir più, e già da noi sen gía
Con la licenza del dolce Poeta;
Quando un' altra, che dietro a lei venia,
Ne fece volger gli occhi alla sua cima,
Per un confuso suon che fuor n' uscia.
Come il bue Cicilian che mugghiò prima
Col pianto di colui (e ciò fu dritto)
Che l' avea temperato con sua lima,
Mugghiava con la voce dell' afflitto,
Sì che, con tutto ch' ei fosse di rame,
Pure e' pareva dal dolor trafitto:
Così per non aver via nè forame
Dal principio nel foco in suo linguaggio
Si convertivan le parole grame.
Ma poscia ch' ebber colto lor viaggio
Su per la punta, dandole quel guizzo
Che dato avea la lingua in lor passaggio,
Udimmo dire: 'O tu, a cui io drizzo
La voce, e che parlavi mo Lombardo,
Dicendo: "issa ten va, più non t' adizzo:"
Perch' io sia giunto forse alquanto tardo,
Non t' incresca restare a parlar meco:
Vedi che non incresce a me, ed ardo.
Se tu pur mo in questo mondo cieco
Caduto sei di quella dolce terra
Latina ond' io mia colpa tutta reco,
Dimmi se i Romagnuoli han pace o guerra;
Ch' io fui de' monti là intra Urbino
E il giogo di che 'l Tever si disserra.'

27

HAVING NOTHING MORE TO SAY, the flame stood still
And straight, and was already leaving us—
With the permission of the gentle poet—
When another flame, which came in back of us,
Made us turn our eyes to where its tip was,
Because of the strange sound that came from it.
Just as the Sicilian bull—which first lowed
With the agonies of him (and that was
Only right) whose file had so created it—
Bellowed with the tortured victim's voice
In such a way that, although made of brass,
It seemed pervaded through and through with pain;
So, here, because at first they had no passage
And no outlet in the flame, their bleak words
Were transmuted into the speech of fire.
But once they had forced their way up to the tip
Of the flame, imparting to it the vibrations
Given to them in their passage by the tongue,
We heard this said: "O you to whom I direct
My voice, and who spoke just now in Lombardese,
Saying, 'You may go now; I urge no more of you,'
Though I have come perhaps a little late,
Do not let it irk you to stay and talk;
See how it does not irk me, and yet I burn.
If you have this very moment fallen
Into this blind world from that sweet Latian land
From which I carried all my guilt, tell me
If the Romagnoles are fighting or at peace.
For I come from those mountains between Urbino
And the chain from which the Tiber frees itself."

Io era ingiuso ancora attento e chino,
Quando il mio Duca mi tentò di costa,
Dicendo: 'Parla tu, questi è Latino.'
Ed io ch' avea già pronta la risposta,
Senza indugio a parlare incominciai:
'O anima, che se' laggiù nascosta,
Romagna tua non è, e non fu mai,
Senza guerra ne' cor de' suoi tiranni;
Ma 'n palese nessuna or vi lasciai,
Ravenna sta come stata è molti anni:
L' aquila da Polenta la si cova,
Sì che Cervia ricopre co' suoi vanni.
La terra che fe' già la lunga prova,
E di Franceschi sanguinoso mucchio,
Sotto le branche verdi si ritrova.
Il Mastin vecchio, e il nuovo da Verrucchio,
Che fecer di Montagna il mal governo,
Là dove soglion, fan de' denti succhio.
Le città di Lamone e di Santerno
Conduce il leoncel dal nido bianco,
Che muta parte dalla state al verno;
E quella a cui il Savio bagna il fianco,
Così com' ella sie' tra il piano e il monte,
Tra tirannia si vive e stato franco.
Ora chi sei ti prego che ne conte:
Non esser duro più ch' altri sia stato,
Se il nome tuo nel mondo tegna fronte.'
Poscia che il foco alquanto ebbe rugghiato
Al modo suo, l' acuta punta mosse
Di qua, di là, e poi diè cotal fiato:
'S' io credessi che mia risposta fosse
A persona che mai tornasse al mondo,
Questa fiamma staria senza più scosse:
Ma perocchè giammai di questo fondo
Non tornò vivo alcun, s' i' odo il vero,
Senza tema d' infamia ti rispondo.
Io fui uom d' arme, e poi fui cordelliero,
Credendomi, sì cinto, fare ammenda:
E certo il creder mio veniva intero,

I was still bending down attentively,
When my leader nudged me in the side
And said: "Speak up! He is an Italian."
And I, who already had an answer,
Started speaking without hesitation:
"O soul who are hidden there below,
Your Romagna is not, and never was,
Without war in the hearts of her tyrants;
But there was no open warfare when I left.
Ravenna stands, as it has for many years,
Brooded over by the eagle of Polenta
That covers even Cervia with its wings.
The city which underwent such a long siege,
With its sanguinary mound of Frenchmen,
Finds itself once more under the green claws.
The old mastiff of Verrucchio, and the new,
Who disposed so brutally of Montagna,
Still use their teeth to gore where they are wont.
The little lion of the white den guides
The cities of Lamone and Santerno,
And changes parties with the change of weather;
And the one whose side the Savio River bathes,
Lying between the mountain and the plain,
Lives on between tyranny and freedom.
I beg you now to tell us who you are.
And if your name is to mean something in the world,
Do not be more stubborn than the others."
The fire having roared a while the way
Fires do, the sharp point now began to move
Back and forth, and then breathed out the following:
"If I thought I were answering someone
Who would ever again go back to the world,
This flame would stop flickering altogether.
But since no one ever got out of this
Abyss alive, if what I hear is true,
I can answer without risk of infamy.
I was a man of arms, then a Franciscan,
Thinking, thus corded round, to make atonement;
And my hope surely would have been fulfilled

Se non fosse il gran Prete, a cui mal prenda,
Che mi rimise nelle prime colpe;
E come e quare voglio che m' intenda.
Mentre ch' io forma fui d' ossa e di polpe,
Che la madre mi diè, l' opere mie
Non furon leonine, ma di volpe.
Gli accorgimenti e le coperte vie
Io seppi tutte; e sì menai lor arte,
Ch' al fine della terra il suono uscie.
Quando mi vidi giunto in quella parte
Di mia etade, ove ciascun dovrebbe
Calar le vele e raccoglier le sarte,
Ciò che pria mi piaceva, allor m' increbbe,
E pentuto e confesso mi rendei;
Ahi miser lasso! e giovato sarebbe.
Lo Principe de' nuovi Farisei,
Avendo guerra presso a Laterano,
E non con Saracin, nè con Giudei;
Chè ciascun suo nimico era Cristiano,
E nessuno era stato a vincer Acri,
Nè mercatante in terra di Soldano:
Nè sommo offizio, nè ordini sacri
Guardò in sè, nè in me quel capestro
Che solea far li suoi cinti più macri.
Ma come Constantin chiese Silvestro
Dentro Siratti a guarir della lebbre,
Così mi chiese questi per maestro
A guarir della sua superba febbre:
Domandommi consiglio, ed io tacetti,
Perchè le sue parole parver ebbre.
E poi mi disse: "Tuo cor non sospetti:
Finor t' assolvo, e tu m' insegna fare
Sì come Penestrino in terra getti.
Lo ciel poss' io serrare e disserrare,
Come tu sai; però son due le chiavi,
Che il mio antecessor non ebbe care."
Allor mi pinser gli argomenti gravi
Là 've il tacer mi fu avviso il peggio,
E dissi: "Padre, da che tu mi lavi

But for that great priest—may evil seize him!—
Who forced me back to my first sinful ways.
I want you to hear how and why it was.
When I was still made of the flesh and bones
That my mother gave me, my actions
Were more those of a fox than of a lion.
I knew all the tricks and undercover ways,
And practiced them so artfully that
The sound reached all corners of the earth.
When I realized I had come to that portion
Of my life in which everyone should
Lower his sails and gather in the ropes,
What once had given me pleasure wearied me.
Repentant and confessed, I gave myself to God.
Unlucky me! How it could have saved me!
The prince of the new Pharisees,
Having brought war so close to the Lateran—
Not with the Saracens or Jews, however,
For everyone of his foes was a Christian,
Not one of whom had helped to conquer Acre,
Or been a merchant in the Sultan's land—
Respected neither high office nor holy
Orders in himself, nor in me that cord
Which once used to make its wearers thinner.
But just as Constantine asked Sylvester
On Soracte to cure him of leprosy,
So this man sought me as a specialist
To cure him of the fever of his pride.
He demanded my advice; I said nothing,
Because his language sounded drunken to me;
Then he resumed: 'Have no misgivings;
I absolve you in advance. Instruct me how
I can hurl Penestrino to the ground.
As you already know, I can close or
Unclose Heaven; there are, therefore, two keys,
For which my predecessor had no love.'
The force of such weighty reasoning
Compelled me to think silence ill-advised,
And I said: 'Father, since you purge my soul

Di quel peccato, ov' io mo cader deggio,
Lunga promessa con l' attender corto
Ti farà trionfar nell' alto seggio."
Francesco venne poi, com' io fui morto,
Per me; ma un de' neri Cherubini
Gli disse: "Non portar; non mi far torto.
Venir se ne dee giù tra' miei meschini,
Perchè diede il consiglio frodolente,
Dal quale in qua stato gli sono a' crini;
Ch' assolver non si può chi non si pente,
Nè pentere e volere insieme puossi,
Per la contradizion che nol consente."
O me dolente! come mi riscossi,
Quando mi prese, dicendomi: "Forse
Tu non pensavi ch' io loico fossi!"
A Minos mi portò: e quegli attorse
Otto volte la coda al dosso duro,
E, poi che per gran rabbia la si morse,
Disse: "Questi è de' rei del foco furo":
Perch' io là dove vedi son perduto,
E sì vestito andando mi rancuro.'
Quand' egli ebbe il suo dir così compiuto,
La fiamma dolorando si partio,
Torcendo e dibattendo il corno acuto.
Noi passammo oltre, ed io e il Duca mio,
Su per lo scoglio infino in sull' altr' arco
Che copre il fosso, in che si paga il fio
A quei che scommettendo acquistan carco.

Of that sin into which I must now fall,
A long promise and a short fulfillment
Will bring you victory in the High Seat."
Later, when I was dead, St. Francis came
For me, but one of the black cherubim
Said to him: 'Do not insult me by taking him.
He belongs down there among my rabble
For having given fraudulent advice,
From which time to now I have been at his hair.
For none can be absolved who do not repent,
Nor can one repent and want at the same time.
The very contradiction disallows it.'
Miserable me! How I shook with fear
When he grasped me, saying to me: 'Perhaps
You did not think that I was a logician.'
He carried me to Minos, who eight times
Around his hardened back entwined his tail,
And, after biting it ferociously,
Said: 'This one belongs among the blazing thieves.'
Thus was I doomed to where you see me now,
And thus appareled I go about and grieve."
When he had said what he had to say,
The flame departed in great affliction,
Twisting and fluttering its pointed horn.
We continued on our way, my guide and I,
Up the precipice as far as the arch
That covers the chasm where the fee is paid
To those who, causing rifts, incur their weight of guilt.

XXVIII

CHI poria mai pur con parole sciolte
Dicer del sangue e delle piaghe appieno,
Ch' i' ora vidi, per narrar più volte?
Ogni lingua per certo verria meno
Per lo nostro sermone e per la mente,
Ch' hanno a tanto comprender poco seno.
S' ei s' adunasse ancor tutta la gente
Che già in sulla fortunata terra
Di Puglia fu del suo sangue dolente
Per li Troiani, e per la lunga guerra
Che dell' anella fe' sì alte spoglie,
Come Livio scrive, che non erra:
Con quella che sentì di colpi doglie
Per contrastare a Roberto Guiscardo,
E l' altra, il cui ossame ancor s' accoglie
A Ceperan, là dove fu bugiardo
Ciascun Pugliese, e là da Tagliacozzo
Ove senz' arme vinse il vecchio Alardo:
E qual forato suo membro, e qual mozzo
Mostrasse, da equar sarebbe nulla
Al modo della nona bolgia sozzo.
Già veggia per mezzul perdere o lulla,
Com' io vidi un, così non si pertugia,
Rotto dal mento infin dove si trulla:
Tra le gambe pendevan le minugia;
La corata pareva, e il tristo sacco
Che merda fa di quel che si trangugia.
Mentre che tutto in lui veder m' attacco,
Guardommi, e con le man s' aperse il petto,
Dicendo: 'Or vedi come io mi dilacco:

28

WHO COULD EVER TELL, even in straight prose,
The full story of the blood and of the wounds
That I now saw, often though it be told?
Certainly every tongue would falter, for
Neither our speech nor our intellect
Is capable of encompassing so much.
If all the people were brought together
Who, in that fortunate land of Apulia,
Mourned the blood they shed there because
The Trojans came; then in that lengthy war
When rings alone made such a mighty booty,
As Livy, who never makes an error, writes;
Adding those who knew the throes of battle
When they stood up against Robert Guiscard;
And the others, whose bones are still collected
At Ceperano, where every Apulian
Proved a liar; and those at Tagliacozzo,
Where, unarmed, the old Alardo triumphed:
And though the limbs of some were gored and others
Severed—all this was nothing in comparison
With the mutilations of the ninth abyss.
Even a barrel, with its mid- or side stave
Missing, never gaped so wide as one I saw
Split from the chin to where the farting's done.
The entrails dangled there between the legs;
Liver, lungs, and heart were seen, and the bleak sack
Which turns whatever is engorged to shit.
While I was thus absorbed with watching him,
He looked at me and opened his breast with his hands,
Saying: "See how I tear myself apart;

Vedi come storpiato è Maometto.
Dinanzi a me sen va piangendo Alì
Fesso nel volto dal mento al ciuffetto:
E tutti gli altri che tu vedi qui,
Seminator di scandalo e di scisma
Fur vivi; e però son fessi così.
Un diavolo è qua dietro che n' accisma
Sì crudelmente, al taglio della spada
Rimettendo ciascun di questa risma,
Quando avem volta la dolente strada;
Perocchè le ferite son richiuse
Prima ch' altri dinanzi gli rivada.
Ma tu chi se' che in sullo scoglio muse,
Forse per indugiar d' ire alla pena,
Ch' è giudicata in sulle tue accuse?'
'Nè morte il giunse ancor, nè colpa il mena,'
Rispose il mio Maestro, 'a tormentarlo;
Ma per dar lui esperienza piena,
A me, che morto son, convien menarlo
Per lo inferno quaggiù di giro in giro:
E questo è ver così com' io ti parlo.'
Più fur di cento che, quando l' udiro,
S' arrestaron nel fosso a riguardarmi,
Per maraviglia obbliando il martiro.
'Or di' a Fra Dolcin dunque che s' armi,
Tu che forse vedrai lo sole in breve,
S' egli non vuol qui tosto seguitarmi,
Sì di vivanda che stretta di neve
Non rechi la vittoria al Noarese,
Ch' altrimenti acquistar non saria lieve.'
Poi che l' un piè per girsene sospese,
Maometto mi disse esta parola,
Indi a partirsi in terra lo distese.
Un altro, che forata avea la gola
E tronco il naso infin sotto le ciglia,
E non avea ma' ch' un' orecchia sola,
Restato a riguardar per maraviglia
Con gli altri, innanzi agli altri aprì la canna
Ch' era di fuor d' ogni parte vermiglia;

See how mutilated Mahomet is.
Ahead of me Ali walks lamenting;
His face is split from chin to forelock.
And all the others whom you see here were
Scandalmongers and schismatics when they
Were alive; for that they have been cut in two.
A devil standing here in back tailors us
Thus cruelly, and then subjects the lot of us
To still another sword-cut each time
We make the journey round the dismal path,
Because the wounds have all closed by the time
Anyone is back again before him.
But who are you who brood upon the cliff,
Perhaps to put off going to your doom,
Which is determined by your own admission?"
"Death has not yet come to him, nor has guilt
Brought him to be tortured here," said my master,
"But to give him a complete experience.
It has devolved on me, who am dead, to lead him
From ring to ring down here through Hell.
And this is as true as my talking to you."
When they heard him speak, more than a hundred
Stopped walking in the chasm to look at me,
And, marveling, forgot their sufferings.
"Tell Fra Dolcin, then—you who soon, perhaps,
Shall see the sun—that, unless he wishes
To follow me here soon, he must fortify himself
With such provisions that the barrier of snow
Deny the victory to the Novarese,
Which could not otherwise be lightly won."
Mahomet had already raised one foot
To go, before he spoke these words to me;
Then he brought it down and started on his way.
Another, who had an opening in his throat,
And whose nose had been lopped off up to
The eyebrows, and who only had one ear,
Remaining to watch in wonder with the rest,
In front of all the others opened his gullet,
Which was all of crimson on the outside,

E disse: 'O tu, cui colpa non condanna,
E cui io vidi su in terra Latina,
Se troppa simiglianza non m' inganna,
Rimembriti di Pier da Medicina,
Se mai torni a veder lo dolce piano,
Che da Vercelli a Marcabò dichina.
E fa saper ai due miglior di Fano,
A messer Guido ed anco ad Angiolello
Che, se l' antiveder qui non è vano,
Gittati saran fuor di lor vasello,
E mazzerati presso alla Cattolica,
Per tradimento d' un tiranno fello.
Tra l' isola di Cipri e di Maiolica
Non vide mai sì gran fallo Nettuno,
Non da pirati, non da gente Argolica.
Quel traditor che vede pur con l' uno,
E tien la terra, che tal è qui meco
Vorrebbe di vedere esser digiuno,
Farà venirli a parlamento seco;
Poi farà sì che al vento di Focara
Non farà lor mestier voto nè preco.'
Ed io a lui: 'Dimostrami e dichiara,
Se vuoi ch' io porti su di te novella,
Chi è colui dalla veduta amara.'
Allor pose la mano alla mascella
D'un suo compagno, e la bocca gli aperse
Gridando: 'Questi è desso, e non favella:
Questi, scacciato, il dubitar sommerse
In Cesare, affermando che il fornito
Sempre con danno l' attender sofferse.'
O quanto mi pareva sbigottito
Con la lingua tagliata nella strozza,
Curio, ch' a dire fu così ardito!
Ed un ch' avea l' una e l' altra man mozza,
Levando i moncherin per l' aura fosca,
Sì che il sangue facea la faccia sozza,
Gridò: 'Ricordera' ti anche del Mosca,
Che dissi, lasso! "Capo ha cosa fatta,"
Che fu il mal seme per la gente tosca.'

And said: "You whom guilt does not condemn,
And whom I saw above on Italian soil—
If I am not deceived by over-likeness—
Remember Pier da Medicina,
If you should ever see again the sweet plain
That from Vercelli slopes to Marcabo.
And let the two best citizens of Fano,
Messer Guido and Angiolello, know
That, unless prophesying here is vain,
Both shall be thrown overboard from their own ship
And drowned, not far from the Cattolica,
By the treachery of a loathsome tyrant.
Neptune never saw a worse crime done,
Between the islands of Cyprus and Majorca,
Whether by pirates or the Argive people.
That traitor, who sees with only one eye
And rules the land which someone here with me
Wishes he had never seen at all,
Will make them come to have a talk with him;
And what he will then do will make all vows
And prayers to Focara's winds unneeded."
And I to him: "Show me and explain,
If you wish me to bear news of you above,
Who was he to whom that sight was bitter?"
Placing his hand on the jaw of one of his
Companions, he pried his mouth open,
Shouting: "This is he, and he does not speak;
He it was who put an end to doubt in
Caesar, by stating that a man prepared
To act invariably suffers if he waits."
How completely terrified he seemed to me,
With his tongue divided in his throat—
Curio, who once spoke up so boldly!
Another, whose hands had both been severed,
Lifted the two stumps in the putrid air,
In such wise that the blood besmeared his face,
And cried: "You will remember Mosca, too,
Who said, poor wretch, 'Once done, a thing is finished,'
Which was the bad seed of the Tuscan people."

Ed io gli aggiunsi: 'E morte di tua schiatta;'
Perch' egli accumulando duol con duolo
Sen gío come persona trista e matta.
Ma io rimasi a riguardar lo stuolo,
E vidi cosa ch' io avrei paura,
Senza più prova, di contarla solo;
Se non che coscienza mi assicura,
La buona compagnia che l' uom francheggia
Sotto l' osbergo del sentirsi pura.
Io vidi certo, ed ancor par ch' io 'l veggia,
Un busto senza capo andar, sì come
Andavan gli altri della trista greggia.
E il capo tronco tenea per le chiome,
Pesol con mano a guisa di lanterna,
E quel mirava noi, e dicea: 'O me!'
Di sè faceva a sè stesso lucerna,
Ed eran due in uno, ed uno in due;
Com' esser può, Quei sa che sì governa.
Quando diritto al piè del ponte fue,
Levò il braccio alto con tutta la testa
Per appressarne le parole sue,
Che furo: 'Or vedi la pena molesta
Tu che, spirando, vai veggendo i morti:
Vedi se alcuna è grande come questa;
E perchè tu di me novella porti,
Sappi ch' io son Bertram dal Bornio, quelli
Che diedi al re giovane i mai conforti.
Io feci il padre e il figlio in sè ribelli:
Achitofel non fe' più d' Ansalone
E di David co' malvagi pungelli.
Perch' io partii così giunte persone,
Partito porto il mio cerebro, lasso!
Dal suo principio ch' è in questo troncone.
Così s' osserva in me lo contrapasso.'

"And the death of your relatives," I added;
At which, accumulating pain on pain,
He went away like someone mad with grief.
But I remained to watch the company,
And I saw something that I would fear to tell
About alone, without further evidence,
Except that my conscience reassures me—
That good companion, which emboldens man
With the coat of armor of its purity.
I distinctly saw, and still seem to see,
A figure without a head walking about
The way the others of that sad herd were.
His hand held the severed head by the hair,
Swinging it as if it were a lantern;
And it looked at us and said: "Pity me!"
It made itself a lamp out of itself,
And they were two in one, and one in two;
How this could be, only He knows who so rules.
When he was at the foot of the bridge
He lifted high his arm, with head and all,
In order to bring nearer what he said,
Which was: "Gaze at this fearful punishment,
You who, breathing, go looking at the dead;
And see if any is as great as this.
And, that you may have news of me to tell,
Know that I am that same Bertram de Born
Who gave the young king scoundrelly advice.
I turned the father and the son against each other.
Achitophel, with his malicious prodding,
Did not do more with Absalom and David.
For separating people so closely bound,
I now, alas, carry my brain about
Separated from its base, which is this trunk.
Thus you see in me how retribution works."

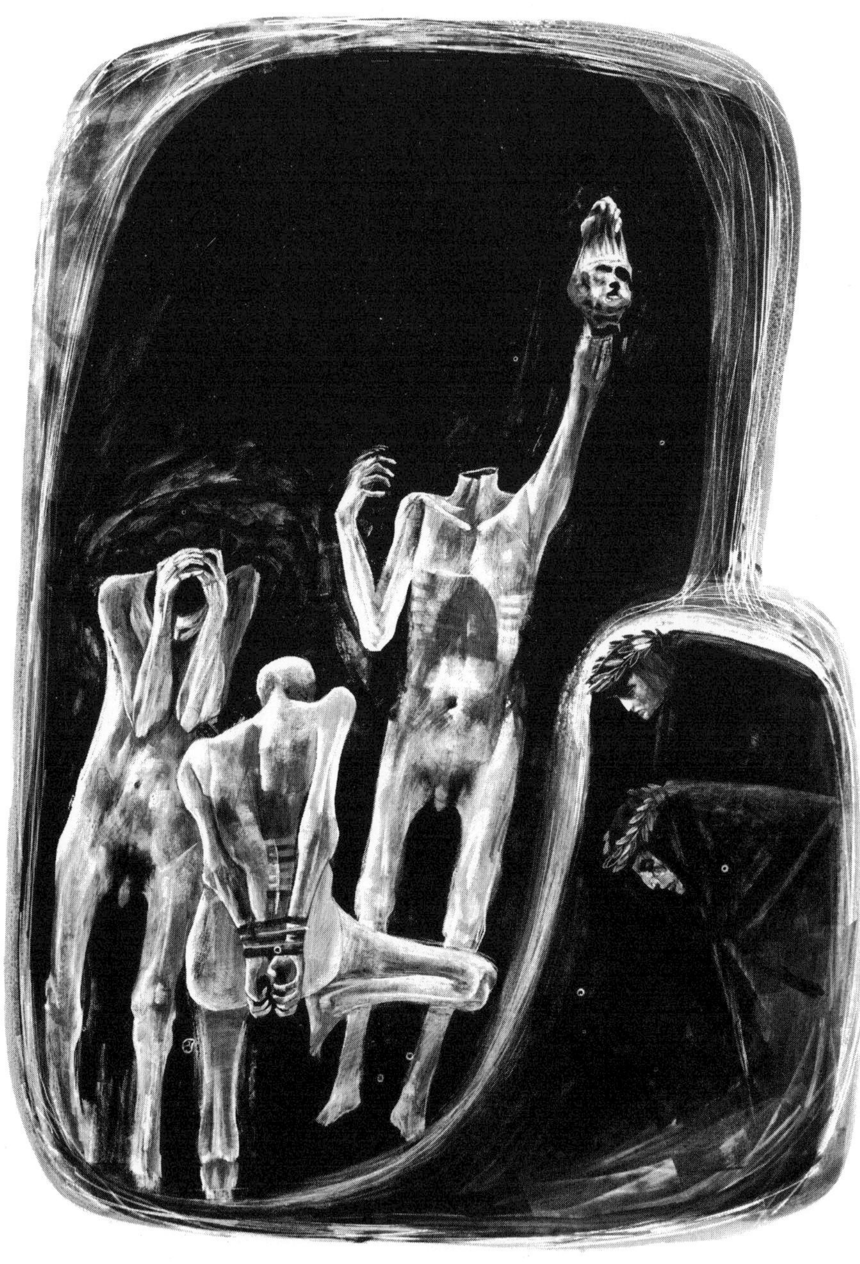

I distinctly saw, and still seem to see,
A figure without a head walking about

LA molta gente e le diverse piaghe
Avean le luci mie sì inebriate,
Che dello stare e piangere eran vaghe;
Ma Virgilio mi disse: 'Che pur guate?
Perchè la vista tua pur si soffolge
Laggiù tra l' ombre triste smozzicate?
Tu non hai fatto sì all' altre bolge:
Pensa, se tu annoverar le credi,
Che miglia ventidue la valle volge;
E già la luna è sotto i nostri piedi:
Lo tempo è poco omai che n' è concesso,
Ed altro è da veder che tu non vedi.'
'Se tu avessi,' rispos' io appresso,
'Atteso alla cagion perch' io guardava,
Forse m' avresti ancor lo star dimesso.'
Parte sen gía, ed io retro gli andava,
Lo Duca, già facendo la risposta,
E soggiungendo: 'Dentro a quella cava
Dov' io teneva or gli occhi sì a posta,
Credo che un spirto del mio sangue pianga
La colpa che laggiù cotanto costa.'
Allor disse il Maestro: 'Non si franga
Lo tuo pensier da qui innanzi sopr' ello:
Attendi ad altro, ed ei là si rimanga;
Ch' io vidi lui a piè del ponticello
Mostrarti, e minacciar forte col dito,
Ed udî 'l nominar Geri del Bello.
Tu eri allor sì del tutto impedito
Sopra colui che già tenne Altaforte,
Che non guardasti in là; sì fu partito.'

29

THE MANY PEOPLE and the varied wounds
Had brought my eyes to such a drunken state,
They wanted only to remain and weep.
But Virgil said to me: "Are you still gaping?
Why do your eyes still linger among
The sad dismembered shadows there below?
You never did so in the other chasms.
If you think of taking count, remember
That the valley is twenty-two miles round;
And the moon is already beneath our feet.
The time that still remains to us is little,
And there are other things for you to see."
I replied at once: "If you had understood
The reason why I continued looking,
You might have permitted me to stay."
Meanwhile my guide walked on, and I behind,
Already formulating my reply
And then continuing: "Inside that cavern
On which my eyes were fixed just now,
I think a spirit of my blood laments
The wrong he did that costs so much down there."
Then the master said: "Do not squander any
Thoughts upon him from this moment on. Think
Of something else; let him stay where he is.
For I saw him pointing to you at the foot
Of the little bridge, threatening with his finger,
And I heard him called Geri del Bello.
At the time, you were so deeply involved
With him who once held Altaforte
That you never looked that way, and so he left."

'O Duca mio, la violenta morte
Che non gli è vendicata ancor,' diss' io,
'Per alcun che dell' onta sia consorte,
Fece lui disdegnoso; ond' ei sen gío
Senza parlarmi, sì com' io stimo;
Ed in ciò m' ha e' fatto a sè più pio.'
Così parlammo infino al loco primo
Che dello scoglio l' altra valle mostra,
Se più lume vi fosse, tutto ad imo.
Quando noi fummo in sull' ultima chiostra
Di Malebolge, sì che i suoi conversi
Potean parere alla veduta nostra,
Lamenti saettaron me diversi,
Che di pietà ferrati avean gli strali:
Ond' io gli orecchi colle man copersi.
Qual dolor fora, se degli spedali
Di Valdichiana tra il luglio e il settembre,
E di Maremma e di Sardigna i mali
Fossero in una fossa tutti insembre;
Tal era quivi, e tal puzzo n' usciva,
Qual suol venir delle marcite membre.
Noi discendemmo in sull' ultima riva
Del lungo scoglio, pur da man sinistra,
Ed allor fu la mia vista più viva
Giù ver lo fondo, là 've la ministra
Dell' alto Sire, infallibil giustizia,
Punisce i falsator che qui registra.
Non credo che a veder maggior tristizia
Fosse in Egina il popol tutto infermo,
Quando fu l' aer sì pien di malizia,
Che gli animali infino al picciol vermo
Cascaron tutti, e poi le genti antiche,
Secondo che i poeti hanno per fermo,
Si ristorar di seme di formiche;
Ch' era a veder per quella oscura valle
Languir gli spirti per diverse biche.
Qual sopra il ventre, e qual sopra le spalle
L' un dell' altro giacea, e qual carpone
Si trasmutava per lo tristo calle.

"O my guide," I said, "his violent death,
That to this day has never been avenged
By anyone related to his shame,
Made him disdainful, which is why, I think,
He went away without a word to me.
I feel more pity for him on that account."
We talked till we reached the first place of the cliff
From which the chasm, if there had been more light,
Would have been visible down to the bottom.
When we were standing over the last cloister
Of Malebolge, and its lay brothers
Were well within our range of vision,
Strange lamentations went through me like arrows
Whose shafts had pity for their arrowheads.
I had to cover my ears with my hands.
Such would be the pain, if all the ills between
July and September, of all the hospitals
Of Valdichiana, of Maremma, and of
Sardinia, were gathered in one pit,
As there was here; and such a stench there was
As only issues from decaying limbs.
We descended to the remaining bank
Of the long ridge, continuing to the left,
And only then could I see clearly down
Into the bottom where the ministress
Of the Great Sire—unerring Justice—
Punishes the cheats who are enrolled there.
It was no greater cause for sorrow to see
The population of Aegina stricken—
When the air was so infested with disease
That even animals, down to the smallest worm,
Were overcome, and that ancient people,
According to the poets who affirm it,
Were brought back to life from the seeds of ants—
Than it was to see those souls, in strange heaps,
Withering away in that dark valley.
This one on the stomach of another lay;
That one, on the shoulders; and some proceeded
On all fours along that melancholy route.

Passo passo andavam senza sermone,
Guardando ed ascoltando gli ammalati,
Che non potean levar le lor persone.
Io vidi due sedere a sè poggiati,
Come a scaldar si poggia tegghia a tegghia,
Dal capo al piè di schianze maculati:
E non vidi giammai menare stregghia
Da ragazzo aspettato dal signorso,
Nè da colui che mal volentier vegghia;
Come ciascun menava spesso il morso
Dell' unghie sopra sè per la gran rabbia
Del pizzicor, che non ha più soccorso.
E sì traevan giù l' unghie la scabbia,
Come coltel di scardova le scaglie,
O d' altro pesce che più larghe l' abbia.
'O tu che colle dita ti dismaglie,'
Cominciò il Duca mio all' un di loro,
'E che fai d' esse tal volta tanaglie,
Dinne s' alcun Latino è tra costoro
Che son quinc' entro, se l' unghia ti basti
Eternalmente a cotesto lavoro.'
'Latin sem noi, che tu vedi sì guasti
Qui ambedue,' rispose l'un piangendo:
'Ma tu chi se', che di noi domandasti?'
E il Duca disse: 'Io son un che discendo
Con questo vivo giù di balzo in balzo,
E di mostrar l' inferno a lui intendo.'
Allor si ruppe lo comun rincalzo;
E tremando ciascuno a me si volse
Con altri che l' udiron di rimbalzo.
Lo buon Maestro a me tutto s' accolse,
Dicendo: 'Di' a lor ciò che tu vuoli.'
Ed io incominciai, poscia ch' ei volse:
'Se la vostra memoria non s' imboli
Nel primo mondo dall' umane menti,
Ma s' ella viva sotto molti soli,
Ditemi chi voi siete e di che genti:
La vostra sconcia e fastidiosa pena
Di palesarvi a me non vi spaventi.'

Step by step, without a word, we walked on,
Watching and giving heed to the afflicted,
Who were not strong enough to raise themselves.
I saw two leaning against each other, seated—
Looking like pans placed together for heating—
Each one covered with scales from head to foot.
I never saw a stable-boy apply
The currycomb while his master waited,
Or because he hated to be kept awake,
The way each one of these applied his biting
Nails to himself in the ferocity
Of itching—for which that is the sole relief.
And their fingernails scraped off the scabs
The way a knife removes the scales of carp,
Or of a fish that has them even larger.
"You who remove your armor with your fingers,"
Began my guide, addressing one of them,
"And who make pincers of them now and then,
Tell us if among those here is one
From Italy; then may your nails suffice
For such a job as yours unto eternity."
"Italians are we, both of us, whom you see
All shriveled here," one answered, weeping.
"But who are you who wish to know about us?"
And my guide said: "I am one who descends
With this live mortal, from ledge to ledge, and
I intend to show him all there is of Hell."
The bond that held them suddenly came apart;
And, trembling, they turned their faces to me,
As did some others who had heard the echo.
The good teacher drew up close to me
And said: "Tell them what it is you wish to know."
And, since he so desired, I began:
"That your memory may never vanish
From human minds, above in the first world,
But continue living under many suns,
Tell me who you are and of what people.
Fear not to disclose your names to me because
Of your vile and toilsome punishment."

'Io fui d' Arezzo, ed Albero da Siena,'
Rispose l' un, 'mi fe' mettere al foco;
Ma quel perch' io mori' qui non mi mena.
Ver è ch' io dissi a lui, parlando a gioco,
Io mi saprei levar per l' aere a volo:
E quei, che avea vaghezza e senno poco,
Volle ch' io gli mostrassi l' arte; e solo
Perch' io nol feci Dedalo, mi fece
Ardere a tal, che l' avea per figliuolo.
Ma nell' ultima bolgia delle diece
Me per alchimia che nel mondo usai
Dannò Minos, a cui fallar non lece.'
Ed io dissi al Poeta: 'Or fu giammai
Gente sì vana come la sanese?
Certo non la francesca sì d' assai.'
Onde l' altro lebbroso che m' intese
Rispose al detto mio: 'Trammene Stricca,
Che seppe far le temperate spese;
E Niccolò, che la costuma ricca
Del garofano prima discoperse
Nell' orto dove tal seme s' appicca;
E tranne la brigata in che disperse
Caccia d' Ascian la vigna e la gran fronda,
E l' Abbagliato suo senno proferse.
Ma perchè sappi chi sì ti seconda
Contra i Sanesi, aguzza ver me l' occhio
Sì che la faccia mia ben ti risponda;
Sì vedrai ch' io son l' ombra di Capocchio,
Che falsai li metalli con alchimia,
E ti dei ricordar, se ben t' adocchio,
Com' io fui di natura buona scimia.'

One replied: "I was from Arezzo, and
Albero da Siena consigned me to the flame.
But why I died was not what brought me here.
The truth is: I once said to him, in jest,
That I could rise up in the air and fly,
And he, an inquisitive man of little sense,
Insisted that I show him, and, because
I could not make a Daedalus of him,
He had me burned by one to whom he was a son.
But Minos, who cannot make an error,
Condemned me to the last of the ten chasms
For practicing alchemy in the world."
And I said to the poet: "Was there ever
A people as arrogant as Siena's?
Surely not the French, even approximately."
At this, the other leper, who was listening,
Replied to my question: "All except Stricca,
Who knew how to keep his spending temperate;
And Niccolo, the man who introduced
The expensive custom of the clove
Into that orchard where its seed still propagates;
And except for that brigade in which Caccia
D'Asciano frittered away his vines and woods,
And Abbagliato proffered his good sense.
That you may know who seconds you against
The Sienese, look sharply at me:
My face will give you the reply you seek.
You will see I am the shade of Capocchio,
Who counterfeited metals by alchemy,
And, if I recognize you clearly, you must
Recall how good an ape I was of nature."

NEL tempo che Junone era crucciata
Per Semelè contra il sangue tebano,
Come mostrò una ed altra fiata,
Atamante divenne tanto insano,
Che veggendo la moglie con due figli
Andar carcata da ciascuna mano,
Gridò: 'Tendiam le reti, sì ch' io pigli
La leonessa e i leoncini al varco:'
E poi distese i dispietati artigli,
Prendendo l' un che avea nome Learco,
E rotollo, e percosselo ad un sasso;
E quella s' annegò con l' altro carco.
E quando la fortuna volse in basso
L' altezza de' Troian che tutto ardiva,
Sì che insieme col regno il re fu casso;
Ecuba trista misera e cattiva,
Poscia che vide Polissena morta,
E del suo Polidoro in sulla riva
Del mar si fu la dolorosa accorta,
Forsennata latrò sì come cane;
Tanto il dolor le fe' la mente torta.
Ma nè di Tebe furie nè Troiane
Si vider mai in alcun tanto crude,
Non punger bestie, non che membra umane,
Quant' io vidi in due ombre smorte e nude
Che mordendo correvan di quel modo
Che il porco quando del porcil si schiude.
L' una giunse a Capocchio, ed in sul nodo
Del collo l' assannò sì che tirando
Grattar gli fece il ventre al fondo sodo.

30

AT THE TIME that Juno was raging against
The Theban blood because of Semele—
As she demonstrated time and time again—
Athamas so completely lost his mind that,
Seeing his wife walking with a son in each hand,
He cried: "Stretch out the nets! I want to catch
The lioness and little lions at the pass!"
And then, extending his unpitying claws,
Snatched up the son whose name was Learchus,
And swung him round and crushed him on a stone;
And she, the other in her arms, drowned herself.
And when Fortune brought down the arrogance
Of Troy, that was audacious in all matters,
Overwhelming king and kingdom in the crash,
Sad, miserable, and captive Hecuba,
Who, after seeing Polyxena dead,
And, grieving, come upon the body of
Her Polydorus lying on the seashore,
Lost her reason and started barking like a dog—
So distorted was her mind from pain.
But neither Theban Furies nor Trojan were
Ever seen to be so cruel to anyone—
Goring not animals, but human limbs—
As were the two pale and naked shades I now saw,
Who ran about biting, the way pigs do
When they have been locked out of their pen.
No sooner had one reached Capocchio
Than he gored him in the neck, then dragged him
Till the rugged ground tore at his stomach.
And the Aretine, who stood there trembling,

E l' Aretin, che rimase tremando,
Mi disse: 'Quel folletto è Gianni Schicchi,
E va rabbioso altrui così conciando.'
'O,' diss' io lui, 'se l' altro non ti ficchi
Li denti addosso, non ti sia fatica
A dir chi è, pria che di qui si spicchi.'
Ed egli a me: 'Quell' è l' anima antica
Di Mirra scellerata, che divenne
Al padre, fuor del dritto amore, amica.
Questa a peccar con esso così venne,
Falsificando sè in altrui forma,
Come l' altro che là sen va sostenne,
Per guadagnar la donna della torma,
Falsificare in sè Buoso Donati,
Testando, e dando al testamento norma.'
E poi che i due rabbiosi fur passati,
Sopra cu' io avea l' occhio tenuto,
Rivolsilo a guardar gli altri mal nati.
Io vidi un fatto a guisa di liuto,
Pur ch' egli avesse avuta l' anguinaia
Tronca dall' altro che l' uomo ha forcuto
La grave idropisì, che sì dispaia
Le membra con l' umor che mal converte,
Che il viso non risponde alla ventraia,
Faceva a lui tener le labbra aperte,
Come l' etico fa, che per le sete
L' un verso il mento e l' altro in su riverte.
'O voi, che senza alcuna pena siete
(E non so io perchè) nel mondo gramo,'
Diss' egli a noi, 'guardate ed attendete
Alla miseria del maestro Adamo;
Io ebbi vivo assai di quel ch' io volli,
Ed ora, lasso! un gocciol d' acqua bramo.
Li ruscelletti che dei verdi colli
Del Casentin discendon giuso in Arno,
Facendo i lor canali freddi e molli,
Sempre mi stanno innanzi, e non indarno;
Chè l' imagine lor vie più m' asciuga,
Che il male ond' io nel volto mi discarno.

Said to me: "That imp is Gianni Schicchi,
And he races round in wrath, clawing others."
And I said: "If the other does not threaten
To sink its teeth in you, and if it be no hardship,
Tell us who that is, before it hurries off."
And he to me: "That is the ancient spirit
Of the despicable Myrrha, who was in love,
Beyond the rightful love, with her father.
To sin with him she came masquerading
As another person—exactly
As that other, moving off, once did, who,
To win the prize mare of the stable,
Disguised himself as Buoso Donati,
Dictated a will, and made it legal."
When the two rabid creatures had departed
On whom my eyes had been fixed, I turned
To look at some other misbegotten souls.
I saw one who would have looked more like a lute,
If he had been truncated at the hip,
Where the division of man's body starts.
The weighty dropsy—which so unbalances
The limbs with unassimilated fluid
That the face is out of all proportion
To the stomach—made him keep his lips open,
As a consumptive does, who, thirsting,
Turns one lip up, the other to the chin.
"O you who without punishment go about
In this desolate world—why, I do not know,"
He said to me, "observe and consider
The wretchedness of one named Master Adamo.
Alive, I had enough of what I wanted;
Now, alas, all I crave is a drop of water.
The smallest streams descending from the green hills
Of Casentino down to the Arno,
Making their little channels cold and soft,
Are forever before me; and not for nothing;
For the image of them leaves me drier
Than does the malady gnawing at my face.
Unbending Justice, who ransacks me,

. . . That is the ancient spirit
Of the despicable Myrrha, who was in love,
Beyond the rightful love, with her father.

La rigida giustizia che mi fruga,
Tragge cagion del loco ov' io peccai,
A metter più li miei sospiri in fuga.
Ivi è Romena, là dov' io falsai
La lega suggellata del Batista,
Perch' io il corpo su arso lasciai.
Ma s' io vedessi qui l' anima trista
Di Guido, o d' Alessandro, o di lor frate,
Per fonte Branda non darei la vista.
Dentro c' è l' una già, se l' arrabbiate
Ombre che van dintorno dicon vero:
Ma che mi val, ch' ho le membra legate?
S' io fossi pur di tanto ancor leggiero
Ch' io potessi in cent' anni andare un' oncia,
Io sarei messo già per lo sentiero,
Cercando lui tra questa gente sconcia,
Con tutto ch' ella volge undici miglia,
E men d' un mezzo di traverso non ci ha.
Io son per lor tra sì fatta famiglia:
Ei m' indussero a battere i fiorini,
Che avevan tre carati di mondiglia.'
Ed io a lui: 'Chi son li due tapini
Che fuman come man bagnate il verno,
Giacendo stretti a' tuoi destri confini?'
'Qui li trovai, e poi volta non dierno,'
Rispose, 'quand' io piovvi in questo greppo,
E non credo che dieno in sempiterno.
L' una è la falsa che accusò Joseppo;
L' altro è il falso Sinon greco da Troia:
Per febbre acuta gittan tanto leppo.'
E l' un di lor, che si recò a noia
Forse d' esser nomato sì oscuro,
Col pugno gli percosse l' epa croia:
Quella sonò come fosse un tamburo:
E mastro Adamo gli percosse il volto
Col braccio suo che non parve men duro,
Dicendo a lui: 'Ancor che mi sia tolto
Lo mover, per le membra che son gravi,
Ho io il braccio a tal mestiere sciolto.'

Finds, even in the place I sinned, a means
Of putting my sighs to still swifter flight.
That is where Romena is; there I debased
The coined alloy with the Baptist's seal,
For which I left my body burning there.
And if I were to see the vile soul here
Of Guido, Alessandro, or their brother,
I would not trade that sight for Branda's fountain.
If those infuriated shades that go round
And round speak the truth, one is here already.
But what good is it to me, since my legs are tied?
If I were only light enough that I could
In a hundred years advance an inch,
I would have been already on my way,
Looking for him among this hideous people,
Even though the road is eleven miles around,
And nowhere less than half of that across.
I am in this family because of them.
It was they who inveigled me to mint
The florins with three carats of base metal."
And I to him: "Who are those two wretches
Lying up against the border to your right,
Who give off smoke like hands washed in winter?"
"I found them here," he answered, "when I rained down
Upon this rocky bank; they have not turned once,
Nor will they, I think, through all eternity.
One is the woman who falsely accused Joseph,
The other is false Sinon, the Greek of Troy.
The high fever makes them give off that stench."
One of them, who may have been insulted
Because of the sinister description,
Struck him a blow in the hard belly,
And it resounded just as if it were a drum;
And Master Adamo, striking back, hit him
In the face with an arm that was just as hard,
Saying to him: "Even though I am denied
All movement because of my heavy limbs,
I have an arm that is free for such a need."
The other replied: "When you were going

Ond' ei rispose: 'Quando tu andavi
Al foco non l' avei tu così presto;
Ma sì e più l' avei quando coniavi.'
E l' idropico: 'Tu di' ver di questo;
Ma tu non fosti sì ver testimonio,
Là 've del ver a Troia fosti richiesto.'
'S' io dissi 'l falso, e tu falsasti il conio,'
Disse Sinone, 'e son qui per un fallo,
E tu per più che alcun altro demonio.'
'Ricorditi, spergiuro, del cavallo,'
Rispose quel ch' avea enfiata l' epa;
'E siati reo che tutto il mondo sallo.'
'E te sia rea la sete onde ti crepa,'
Disse il Greco, 'la lingua, e l' acqua marcia
Che il ventre innanzi a gli occhi sì t' assiepa.'
Allora il monetier: 'Così si squarcia
La bocca tua per suo mal come suole;
Chè s' i' ho sete ed umor mi rinfarcia,
Tu hai l' arsura e il capo che ti duole,
E per leccar lo specchio di Narcisso,
Non vorresti a invitar molte parole.'
Ad ascoltarli er' io del tutto fisso,
Quando il Maestro mi disse: 'Or pur mira,
Che per poco è che teco non mi risso.'
Quand' io 'l senti' a me parlar con ira,
Volsimi verso lui con tal vergogna,
Ch' ancor per la memoria mi si gira.
E quale è quei che suo dannaggio sogna,
Che sognando desidera sognare.
Sì che quel ch' è, come non fosse, agogna;
Tal mi fec' io, non potendo parlare,
Che desiava scusarmi, e scusava
Me tuttavia, e nol mi credea fare.
'Maggior difetto men vergogna lava,'
Disse il Maestro, 'che il tuo non è stato;
Però d' ogni tristizia ti disgrava:
E fa ragion ch' io ti sia sempre allato,
Se più avvien che fortuna t' accoglia
Ove sien genti in simigliante piato;
Chè voler ciò udire è bassa voglia.'

To be burnt, you did not have it quite so ready;
You did, though, and more, when you minted coins."
And the one with dropsy: "What you say is true;
But you were not such an honest witness
When they sought the truth from you at Troy."
"I testified falsely, and you falsified coins,"
Said Sinon. "I am here for but one crime;
You, for more than any of the demons'."
"Remind yourself, you liar, of the horse!"
Replied the one with the inflated stomach,
"And may it plague you that the whole world knows!"
"And may the thirst plague you that cracks your tongue!"
Said the Greek, "and the water be polluted that
Before your eyes makes a hedge of your belly!"
Then the coin-maker: "Your mouth is wide open
For the bad things you always have to say;
And if I am thirsty, yet stuffed with water,
You have the headache and the inflammation,
And to lick the mirror of Narcissus
You would not need a wordy invitation."
I was wholly engrossed in listening to them,
When I heard my master say: "Keep on staring!
I am very close to quarreling with you."
Hearing him address me angrily,
I turned to him with such great shame that even now
I suffer at the memory of it.
And as a man who dreams of something bad,
And while dreaming wishes to be dreaming,
So that what is he longs for not to be,
Such I became, incapable of speech,
Desiring to apologize, and yet
Apologizing, and thinking I had not.
"Less shame," said the master, "would wash away
A greater dereliction than was yours.
So, unburden yourself of any sorrow.
Keep in mind that I am always at your side,
If by any chance you find yourself again
Where people are engaged in such bickering.
To want to hear them is a vulgar craving."

UNA medesma lingua pria mi morse,
Sì che mi tinse l' una e l' altra guancia,
E poi la medicina mi riporse.
Così od' io che soleva la lancia
D' Achille e del suo padre esser cagione
Prima di trista e poi di buona mancia.
Noi demmo il dosso al misero vallone
Su per la ripa che il cinge dintorno,
Attraversando senza alcun sermone.
Quivi era men che notte e men che giorno,
Sì che il viso m' andava innanzi poco:
Ma io senti' sonare un alto corno,
Tanto ch' avrebbe ogni tuon fatto fioco,
Che, contra sè la sua via seguitando,
Dirizzò gli occhi miei tutti ad un loco:
Dopo la dolorosa rotta, quando
Carlo Magno perdè la santa gesta,
Non sonò sì terribilmente Orlando.
Poco portai in là volta la testa,
Che mi parve veder molte alte torri;
Ond' io: 'Maestro, di', che terra è questa?'
Ed egli a me: 'Però che tu trascorri
Per le tenebre troppo dalla lungi,
Avvien che poi nel 'maginare aborri.
Tu vedrai ben, se tu là ti congiungi,
Quanto il senso s' inganna di lontano:
Però alquanto più te stesso pungi.'
Poi caramente mi prese per mano,
E disse: 'Pria che noi siam più avanti,
Acciocchè il fatto men ti paia strano,

31

THE SAME TONGUE, which at first had cut me so
That both my cheeks were reddened by it,
Also administered the remedy to me.
In like manner, I have heard, was Achilles'
And his father's lance the single instrument
Of a cruel, then of a kindly, gift.
We now turned our backs to the joyless valley,
High upon the bank that circles it around,
Saying nothing to each other as we crossed.
There, it was less than night and less than day,
So that I saw only a little way ahead.
But I heard the sound of a horn that was so loud
It would have made any thunder feeble.
Following the path of that sound in reverse,
My eyes were thus directed to its source.
After the tragic rout of Charlemagne,
When he lost that holy undertaking,
Even Roland did not blow so powerfully.
My head was turned that way for but a while,
When I thought I saw several high towers.
I therefore asked: "Master, what city is this?"
And he to me: "Because you have been
Traveling in the darkness far too long,
Your imagination has begun to stray.
You will see for yourself, if you get there,
How our senses are deceived by distance.
Give yourself a greater push meanwhile."
Then he took me gently by the hand
And said: "Before we proceed any further,
In order that the fact may seem less strange,

Sappi che non son torri, ma giganti,
E son nel pozzo intorno dalla ripa
Dall' umbilico in giuso tutti quanti.'
Come, quando la nebbia si dissipa,
Lo sguardo a poco a poco raffigura
Ciò che cela il vapor che l' aere stipa:
Così forando l' aura grossa e scura,
Più e più appressando in ver la sponda,
Fuggíemi errore, e cresce'mi paura.
Perocchè come in sulla cerchia tonda
Montereggion di torri si corona;
Così la proda che il pozzo circonda
Torreggiavan di mezza la persona
Gli orribili giganti, cui minaccia
Giove del cielo ancora quando tuona.
Ed io scorgeva già d' alcun la faccia,
Le spalle e il petto, e del ventre gran parte,
E per le coste giù ambo le braccia.
Natura certo, quando lasciò l' arte
Di sì fatti animali, assai fe' bene,
Per torre tali esecutori a Marte:
E s' ella d' elefanti e di balene
Non si pente, chi guarda sottilmente
Più giusta e più discreta la ne tiene:
Chè dove l' argomento della mente
S' aggiunge al mal volere ed alla possa,
Nessun riparo vi può far la gente.
La faccia sua mi parea lunga e grossa
Come la pina di san Pietro a Roma;
Ed a sua proporzione eran l' altr' ossa:
Sì che la ripa, ch' era perizoma
Dal mezzo in giù, ne mostrava ben tanto
Di sopra, che di giungere alla chioma
Tre Frison s' averian dato mal vanto:
Perocch' io ne vedea trenta gran palmi
Dal loco in giù, dov' uomo affibbia il manto.
'Rafel mai amech zabi almi,'
Cominciò a gridar la fiera bocca,
Cui non si convenian più dolci salmi.

Know that they are giants, and not castles,
And that all of them are standing in the well
Up to their navels, all around the bank."
As, when the mist has started to disperse,
The vision gradually distinguishes
Things that the vapor in the air had hidden;
So, groping through the dark and heavy air
And coming closer and closer to the edge,
As fast as my error fled, my fear grew.
And as Montereggione crowns itself
With turrets on the wall encircling it,
So those horrible giants, whom Jove
Still menaces from Heaven whenever
There is thunder, towered by half their bodies
Above the bank that goes around the well.
Already I could make out the face of one,
His shoulders, chest, much of his stomach,
And, hanging at his sides, both his arms.
Nature surely did an excellent thing
When she stopped creating monsters of this kind
And so deprived Mars of such executioners.
And if she shows no remorse for elephants
And whales, whoever studies this with care
Will hold her wiser and more just on that account:
For where the apparatus of the mind
Allies itself with power and ill will,
People are without defense against it.
The giant's face seemed as long and broad to me
As the pine cone of St. Peter's that is in Rome,
And his other bones were in proportion,
So that the bank, which served as apron
From the middle down, still revealed so much
That three Frisians, standing on each other,
Could not have boasted to have reached his hair.
I estimated it was thirty palm-spans
Down from the place where people clasp their mantles.
"Rafel mai amech zabi almi":
The shouting started from that beastly mouth,
For which no sweeter psalmody was suited.

E il Duca mio ver lui: 'Anima sciocca,
Tienti col corno, e con quel ti disfoga,
Quand' ira o altra passion ti tocca.
Cercati al collo, e troverai la soga
Che il tien legato, o anima confusa,
E vedi lui che il gran petto ti doga.'
Poi disse a me: 'Egli stesso s' accusa;
Questi è Nembrotto, per lo cui mal coto
Pure un linguaggio nel mondo non s' usa.
Lasciamlo stare, e non parliamo a voto:
Chè così è a lui ciascun linguaggio,
Come il suo ad altrui ch' a nullo è noto.
Facemmo adunque più lungo viaggio
Volti a sinistra; ed al trar d' un balestro
Trovammo l' altro assai più fiero e maggio.
A cinger lui, qual che fosse il maestro
Non so io dir, ma ei tenea succinto
Dinanzi l' altro, e dietro il braccio destro
D' una catena, che il teneva avvinto
Dal collo in giù, sì che in sullo scoperto
Si ravvolgeva infino al giro quinto.
'Questo superbo voll' esser esperto
Di sua potenza contra il sommo Giove,'
Disse il mio Duca, 'ond' egli ha cotal merto.
Fialte ha nome; e' fece le gran prove,
Quando i giganti fer paura ai Dei:
Le braccia ch' ei menò giammai non move.'
Ed io a lui: 'S' esser puote, io vorrei
Che dello ismisurato Briareo
Esperienza avesser gli occhi miei.'
Ond' ei rispose: 'Tu vedrai Anteo
Presso di qui, che parla, ed è disciolto,
Che ne porrà nel fondo d' ogni reo.
Quel che tu vuoi veder più là è molto,
Ed è legato e fatto come questo,
Salvo che più feroce par nel volto.'
Non fu tremoto già tanto rubesto
Che scotesse una torre così forte,
Come Fialte a scotersi fu presto.

And my guide said to him: "You imbecile soul,
Take your horn and use it, if you must relieve
Your anger or any other passion.
Search around your neck, O confused soul,
And you will find the rope that holds it fast.
The horn lies curved across your massive chest."
Then he said to me: "He betrays himself;
That is Nimrod, because of whose designs
The world does not use one language only.
Let us ignore him, and not waste any words;
For all languages are as unknown to him
As his own language is unknown to others."
Having then turned to the left, we covered
Much more ground, and at a bow-shot's distance
We found another, even larger and more savage.
Who was the master that so entwined him
I cannot say, but both his arms were bound,
The right behind him, the other in front,
With a chain that wound about him
From the neck down, over the part of him
That was uncovered, to the fifth time round.
"This haughty creature desired to test
His power against that of mighty Jove,"
Said my guide, "for which he was thus rewarded.
Named Ephialtes, he made the great attempt
When the giants brought fear unto the gods.
The arms he once shook he now never moves."
And I to him: "If it is possible,
I would like to see with my own eyes
The immeasurable Briareus."
To which he answered: "You shall see Antaeus,
Not far from here, who speaks and is unchained.
He will bear us to the lowest depths of guilt.
The one you want to see is much further on,
And he is bound and made the same as this one,
Except that he looks even more ferocious."
There never was an earthquake
That shook a tower more violently
Than Ephialtes suddenly shook himself.

Allor temett' io più che mai la morte,
E non v' era mestier più che la dotta,
S' io non avessi viste le ritorte.
Noi procedemmo più avanti allotta,
E venimmo ad Anteo, che ben cinqu' alle,
Senza la testa, uscía fuor della grotta.
'O tu, che nella fortunata valle
Che fece Scipion di gloria ereda,
Quando Annibal co' suoi diede le spalle,
Recasti già mille leon per preda,
E che, se fossi stato all' alta guerra
De' tuoi fratelli, ancor par ch' e' si creda,
Che avrebber vinto i figli della terra;
Mettine giù (e non ten venga schifo)
Dove Cocito la freddura serra.
Non ci far ire a Tizio nè a Tifo:
Questi può dar di quel che qui si brama:
Però ti china, e non torcer lo grifo.
Ancor ti può nel mondo render fama;
Ch' ei vive, e lunga vita ancor aspetta,
Se innanzi tempo grazia a sè nol chiama.'
Così disse il Maestro: e quegli in fretta
Le man distese, e prese il Duca mio,
Ond' Ercole sentì già grande stretta.
Virgilio, quando prender si sentio,
Disse a me: 'Fatti in qua, sì ch' io ti prenda:'
Poi fece sì, che un fascio er' egli ed io.
Qual pare a riguardar la Carisenda
Sotto il chinato, quando un nuvol vada
Sopr' essa sì, che ella incontro penda;
Tal parve Anteo a me che stava a bada
Di vederlo chinare, e fu tal ora
Ch' io avrei volut' ir per altra strada:
Ma lievemente al fondo che divora
Lucifero con Giuda ci sposò;
Nè sì chinato lì fece dimora,
E come albero in nave si levò.

I never in my life was so afraid of death,
And fright alone would easily have done it,
If I had not already seen his chains.
After moving forward somewhat more, we came
To Antaeus, of whom five ells at least,
Not counting the head, stuck out from the grotto.
"O you, who in the fortunate valley
That made Scipio an heir of glory—
When Hannibal and all his men had turned their backs—
Once carried off as prey a thousand lions;
And who, if you had taken part in that great war
Of your brothers, many still seem to think
That the sons of earth would have won it;
Put us down there—and have no qualms about it—
Where Cocytus is locked up in the cold.
Would you have us go to Tityus or Typhon?
This man can give what you all wish for here;
So, bend down now, and stop your sneering.
He can still make you famous in the world,
For he lives and expects to live much longer,
Unless called earlier by the grace of God."
So said the master; and the other at once
Stretched out his hands—which once had given
Hercules a mighty squeeze—and took my guide.
When he felt himself being grasped, Virgil
Said to me: "Come close, that I may hold you,"
And made a bundle of the two of us.
As the Carisenda seems, to someone
Looking up its slanted side, to be falling
Towards him, when a cloud passes over it,
So seemed Antaeus to me as I stood
Watching him bend forward; at that moment
I would have preferred to take another road.
But he put us down lightly on the bottom,
Which devours Lucifer and Judas;
Nor did he remain there stooping,
But pulled himself up straight, like a ship's mast.

XXXII

S' io avessi le rime aspre e chiocce,
Come si converrebbe al tristo buco,
Sopra il qual pontan tutte l' altre rocce,
Io premerei di mio concetto il suco
Più pienamente; ma perch' io non l' abbo,
Non senza tema a dicer mi conduco.
Chè non è impresa da pigliare a gabbo,
Descriver fondo a tutto l' universo,
Nè da lingua che chiami mamma e babbo.
Ma quelle Donne aiutino il mio verso,
Ch' aiutaro Amfion a chiuder Tebe,
Sì che dal fatto il dir non sia diverso.
O sopra tutte mal creata plebe,
Che stai nel loco onde 'l parlare è duro,
Me' foste state qui pecore o zebe.
Come noi fummo giù nel pozzo scuro
Sotto i piè del gigante, assai più bassi,
Ed io mirava ancora all' alto muro,
Dicere udimmi: 'Guarda, come passi;
Va sì che tu non calchi con le piante
Le teste de' fratei miseri lassi.'
Perch' io mi volsi, e vidimi davante
E sotto i piedi un lago, che per gelo
Avea di vetro e non d' acqua sembiante.
Non fece al corso suo sì grosso velo
D' inverno la Danoia in Osteric,
Nè Tanai là sotto il freddo cielo,
Com' era quivi: chè, se Tambernic
Vi fosse su caduto, o Pietrapana,
Non avria pur dal' orlo fatto cric.

32

IF I HAD RHYMES that were rough and hoarse,
Such as would suit that melancholy pit
Over which the precipices met,
I would more fully squeeze the juice from my
Conceptions; but, since I do not have them,
Not without fear do I undertake to speak.
For to describe the bottom of the universe
Is not a matter to be taken lightly,
Nor one for a tongue that calls "Mama" and "Papa."
That the telling may not differ from the facts,
Let those ladies aid my poetry who
Assisted Amphion in closing Thebes.
O most ill-created of all people,
Inhabiting a place so hard to speak of,
Better for you had you been sheep or goats!
While we were there below in the dark well,
Far down underneath the giants' feet,
And I was staring still at the high wall,
I heard someone say to me: "Watch where you walk,
Lest you trample underfoot the heads
Of your miserable and weary brothers."
That made me turn; and I saw, before me
And beneath my feet, a lake that, being frozen,
Appeared to be of glass and not of water.
Not the Danube in Austria, nor the Don
There under the cold sky, ever fashioned
So large a veil for its winter current
As did that one there: for if Mount Tamberni
Had fallen on it, or Pietrapana,
There would not have been a creak along its edge.

E come a gracidar si sta la rana
   Col muso fuor dell' acqua, quando sogna
   Di spigolar sovente la villana:
Livide insin là dove appar vergogna
   Eran l' ombre dolenti nella ghiaccia,
   Mettendo i denti in nota di cicogna.
Ognuna in giù tenea volta la faccia:
   Da bocca il freddo, e dagli occhi il cor tristo
   Tra lor testimonianza si procaccia.
Quand' io ebbi d' intorno alquanto visto,
   Volsimi a' piedi, e vidi due sì stretti
   Che il pel del capo avieno insieme misto.
'Ditemi voi, che sì stringete i petti,'
   Diss' io, 'chi siete.' E quei piegaro i colli;
   E poi ch' ebber li visi a me eretti,
Gli occhi lor, ch' eran pria pur dentro molli,
   Gocciar su per le labbra, e il gielo strinse
   Le lagrime tra essi, e riserrolli:
Con legno legno mai spranga non cinse
   Forte così; ond' ei, come due becchi,
   Cozzaro insieme: tant' ira li vinse.
Ed un ch' avea perduti ambo gli orecchi
   Per la freddura, pur col viso in giue
   Disse: 'Perchè cotanto in noi ti specchi?
Se vuoi saper chi son cotesti due,
   La valle onde Bisenzio si dichina,
   Del padre loro Alberto e di lor fue.
D' un corpo usciro: e tutta la Caina
   Potrai cercare, e non troverai ombra
   Degna più d' esser fitta in gelatina:
Non quelli a cui fu rotto il petto e l' ombra
   Con esso un colpo per la man d' Artù:
   Non Focaccia: non questi che m' ingombra
Col capo sì ch' io non veggio oltre più,
   E fu nomato Sassol Mascheroni:
   Se Tosco se', ben sa' omai chi fu.
E perchè non mi metti in più sermoni,
   Sappi ch' io fui il Camicion de' Pazzi,
   Ed aspetto Carlin che mi scagioni.'

Just as the frog, when he croaks, puts his snout
Out of the water, at that time of year
When farmers' wives often dream of gleaning,
So those doleful shades stood livid in the ice
Up to that place where shame is shown,
Their teeth making sounds such as the stork makes.
Every one of them kept his face turned down.
Among themselves their mouths gave testimony
Of the cold, and their eyes, of their sad hearts.
Having looked about me for a while,
I lowered my gaze to my feet and saw two shades
So squeezed in one that their hair was intertwined.
"You whose bosoms press so close together,
Who are you?" I said; and they bent their necks.
And when again they raised their faces to me,
Their eyes, which up till then were only wet inside,
Watered at the lids; but these closed again
As the frost laid hold of the tears between them.
No clamp ever fastened wood to wood
So firmly round. They were so overcome with rage,
They butted one another like two goats.
Another among them, who had lost both ears
From the cold, said, with his face still lowered:
"Why do you keep staring at us?
If you wish to know who those two are,
The valley into which the Bisenzo flows
Belonged to their father Albert, and to them.
They issued from one body, and you can search
All Caina and not find a single shade
Who deserves more to be locked in this ice:
Certainly not him whose breast and shadow
Were broken by one thrust of Arthur's hand;
Not Focaccia; nor this one, whose head
So blocks my view I cannot see beyond it,
And whose name was Sassol Mascheroni:
If you are a Tuscan, you know all about him.
And, lest you draw me into further talk,
Know that I was Camicion de' Pazzi;
And I await Carlino to make me guiltless."

Poscia vid' io mille visi, cagnazzi
Fatti per freddo: onde mi vien riprezzo,
E verrà sempre, de' gelati guazzi.
E mentre che andavamo in ver lo mezzo,
Al quale ogni gravezza si raduna,
Ed io tremava nell' eterno rezzo:
Se voler fu, o destino, o fortuna,
Non so: ma passeggiando tra le teste,
Forte percossi il piè nel viso ad una.
Piangendo mi sgridò: 'Perchè mi peste?
Se tu non vieni a crescer la vendetta
Di Mont' Aperti, perchè mi moleste?'
Ed io: 'Maestro mio, or qui m' aspetta,
Sì ch' io esca d' un dubbio per costui:
Poi mi farai, quantunque vorrai, fretta.'
Lo Duca stette; ed io dissi a colui
Che bestemmiava duramente ancora:
'Qual se' tu, che così rampogni altrui?'
'Or tu chi se', che vai per l' Antenora
Percotendo,' rispose, 'altrui le gote
Sì che, se fossi vivo, troppo fora?'
'Vivo son io, e caro esser ti puote,'
Fu mia risposta, 'se domandi fama,
Ch' io metta il nome tuo tra l' altre note.'
Ed egli a me: 'Del contrario ho io brama:
Levati quinci, e non mi dar più lagna:
Chè mal sai lusingar per questa lama.'
Allor lo presi per la cuticagna,
E dissi: 'E' converrà che tu ti nomi,
O che capel qui su non ti rimagna.'
Ond' egli a me: 'Perchè tu mi dischiomi,
Nè ti dirò ch' io sia, nè mostrerolti,
Se mille fiate in sul capo mi tomi.'
Io avea già i capelli in mano avvolti,
E tratti glien' avea più d' una ciocca,
Latrando lui con gli occhi in giù raccolti;
Quando un altro gridò: 'Che hai tu, Bocca?
Non ti basta sonar con le mascelle,
Se tu non latri? qual diavol ti tocca?'

Then I saw a thousand faces, which the cold
Made so doglike, I shiver, and always shall,
At the thought of them and of that icy pond.
And while we were advancing towards the center,
Which is the place where all weight is collected,
And I was trembling in the eternal shade,
Whether it was by my wish, or fate, or chance,
I struck the face of one so hard with my foot,
He screamed at me, in tears: "Why do you kick me?
Unless you come to wreak more vengeance for
Montaperti, why must you molest me?"
And I said to my master: "Wait here for me,
While I free myself of doubt concerning him;
Then you can make me move as fast as you wish."
The leader halted where he was, and I said
To him who was still cursing bitterly:
"Which one are you, who thus revile the others?"
"And who may you be," he replied, "who go through
Antenora kicking others in the cheek, so
That if you were alive it would be too much?"
"I am alive, and can be useful to you,
If fame is what you want," was my reply.
"I can put your name among my other notes."
And he: "What I want is just the opposite.
Stop bothering me, and get out of here.
You are a poor flatterer in this meadow."
At that I grabbed him by the scalp, and said
To him: "Either you tell me what your name is,
Or not a hair will be left standing here!"
And he said: "Even if you leave me hairless,
I shall not tell or indicate who I am,
Though you pounce on my head a thousand times."
I had already wrapped his hair around
My hand and pulled away more than one tuft,
The while he barked and kept his eyes turned down,
When another cried: "What's wrong with you, Bocca?
Must you bark besides performing with your jaws?
What devil is possessing you now?"
"I do not care to hear you speak," I said;

'Omai,' diss' io, 'non vo' che tu favelle,
Malvagio traditor, chè alla tua onta
Io porterò di te vere novelle.'
'Va via,' rispose, 'e ciò che tu vuoi, conta;
Ma non tacer, se tu di qua entr' eschi,
Di quei ch' ebbe or così la lingua pronta.
Ei piange qui l' argento de' Franceschi:
Io vidi, potrai dir, quel da Duera
Là dove i peccatori stanno freschi.
Se fossi domandato, altri chi v' era,
Tu hai da lato quel di Beccheria,
Di cui segò Fiorenza la gorgiera.
Gianni de' Soldanier credo che sia
Più là con Ganellone e Tribaldello,
Ch' aprì Faenza quando si dormia.'
Noi eravam partiti già da ello,
Ch' io vidi due ghiacciati in una buca
Sì che l' un capo all' altro era cappello;
E come il pan per fame si manduca,
Così il sopran li denti all' altro pose
Là 've il cervel s' aggiunge colla nuca.
Non altrimenti Tideo si rose
Le tempie a Menalippo per disdegno,
Che quei faceva il teschio e l' altre cose.
O tu che mostri per sì bestial segno
Odio sopra colui che tu ti mangi,
Dimmi il perchè,' diss' io, 'per tal convegno,
Che se tu a ragion di lui ti piangi,
Sappiendo chi voi siete e la sua pecca,
Nel mondo suso ancor io te ne cangi,
Se quella con ch' io parlo non si secca.'

"And to your lasting shame, you monstrous traitor,
I shall carry back a true account of you."
"Go away!" he answered. "Report what you please!
But say something, if you get out of here,
About him who just now showed a ready tongue.
Here he repents the money of the French.
'I saw,' you might say, 'the man of Duera
Where all the sinners are kept nice and cool.'
If anyone should ask who else was there,
There at your side is that Beccheria
Whose throat the city of Florence sawed in two.
Gianni de' Soldanier is over there,
I think, with Ganellone and Tribaldello,
Who left Faenza open while it slept."
We had already gone away from him,
When I saw two others frozen in one hole
In such a way that one head was the other's hat.
The one above put his teeth into the other
Where the back of the neck and brain are joined,
The way a hungry man devours bread.
Not otherwise did Tydeus, out of scorn,
Chew on the temples of Menalippus,
Than did this one on that skull and other things.
"O you who show, by such a bestial act,
Hatred for the one that you are eating,
Tell me the reason why," I said, "on the promise
That, if you have cause for deploring him,
Knowing who you are and his wrong-doing,
I shall yet redeem you in the world above—
If that with which I speak does not dry up."

XXXIII

LA bocca sollevò dal fiero pasto
Quel peccator, forbendola ai capelli
Del capo ch' egli avea diretro guasto.
Poi cominciò: 'Tu vuoi ch' io rinnovelli
Disperato dolor che il cor mi preme,
Già pur pensando, pria ch' io ne favelli.
Ma se le mie parole esser den seme
Che frutti infamia al traditor ch' io rodo,
Parlare e lagrimar vedrai insieme.
I' non so chi tu sei, nè per che modo
Venuto se' quaggiù; ma Fiorentino
Mi sembri veramente quand' io t' odo.
Tu dei saper ch' io fui Conte Ugolino,
E questi l' Arcivescovo Ruggieri:
Or ti dirò perch' io son tal vicino.
Che per l' effetto de' suo' ma' pensieri,
Fidandomi di lui, io fossi preso
E poscia morto, dir non è mestieri.
Però quel che non puoi avere inteso,
Ciò è come la morte mia fu cruda,
Udirai, e saprai se m' ha offeso.
Breve pertugio dentro dalla muda
La qual per me ha il titol della fame,
E in che conviene ancor ch' altri si chiuda,
M' avea mostrato per lo suo forame
Più lune già, quand io feci il mal sonno
Che del futuro mi squarciò il velame.
Questi pareva a me maestro e donno,
Cacciando il lupo e i lupicini al monte
Per che i Pisan veder Lucca non ponno.

33

FROM THAT SAVAGE MEAL the sinner raised
His mouth and wiped it with the hair of the head
The back of which he had been ravaging.
Then he began: "You ask me to make new
Again a desperate pain, the thought of which
Weighs on my heart before I speak of it.
But if my words will be a seed the fruit
Of which is infamy for the traitor whom I gnaw,
You shall see how one can speak and weep together.
I do not know who you are, nor how you
Came down here, but when I hear you speak
You appear to be a real Florentine.
You should know that I was Count Ugolino,
And this one is the Archbishop Ruggieri.
I shall tell you why I am such a neighbor.
That, as a result of his evil designs,
And while I trusted him, I was seized
And later killed, there is no need to say.
However, what you could not have heard—that is,
How cruel was the manner of my death—
You shall hear, and know whether he wronged me.
A small opening in that molting-place—
Which on my account now bears the name of Hunger,
And in which others are fated to be walled—
Had already shown me many moons,
When I dreamed an evil dream that tore away
The veil that hid the future from me.
In my dream this man seemed lord and master,
Hunting the wolf and whelps on that mountain
Because of which no Pisan can see Lucca.

Con cagne magre, studiose e conte,
Gualandi con Sismondi e con Lanfranchi
S' avea messi dinanzi dalla fronte.
In picciol corso mi pareano stanchi
Lo padre e i figli, e con l' acute scane
Mi parea lor veder fender li fianchi.
Quando fui desto innanzi la dimane,
Pianger senti' fra il sonno i miei figliuoli
Ch' eran con meco, e domandar del pane.
Ben se' crudel, se tu già non ti duoli,
Pensando ciò ch' il mio cor s' annunziava:
E se non piangi, di che pianger suoli?
Già eran desti, e l' ora s' appressava
Che il cibo ne soleva essere addotto,
E per suo sogno ciascun dubitava:
Ed io sentii chiavar l' uscio di sotto
All' orribile torre; ond' io guardai
Nel viso a' miei figliuoi senza far motto.
Io non piangeva; sì dentro impietrai:
Piangevan elli; ed Anselmuccio mio
Disse: "Tu guardi sì, padre: che hai?"
Perciò non lagrimai, nè rispos' io
Tutto quel giorno, nè la notte appresso,
Infin che l' altro sol nel mondo uscìo.
Come un poco di raggio si fu messo
Nel doloroso carcere, ed io scorsi
Per quattro visi il mio aspetto stesso;
Ambo le man per lo dolor mi morsi.
Ed ei, pensando ch' io 'l fessi per voglia
Di manicar, di subito levorsi,
E disser: "Padre, assai ci fia men doglia
Se tu mangi di noi: tu ne vestisti
Queste misere carni, e tu le spoglia."
Queta' mi allor per non farli più tristi:
Lo dì e l' altro stemmo tutti muti:
Ahi dura terra, perchè non t' apristi?
Posciachè fummo al quarto dì venuti,
Gaddo mi si gittò disteso a' piedi,
Dicendo: "Padre mio, chè non m' aiuti?"

Up ahead, in front of him, he had placed
Gualandi, Sismondi, and Lanfranchi,
With keen and well-trained hounds for the hunt.
After a short run, the father and his sons
Appeared to me exhausted, and I thought I saw
Deep gashes in their sides from the sharp fangs.
When I awoke, before daybreak,
I heard my little boys, who were with me,
Crying in their sleep and asking for bread.
You must be cold-blooded, if you feel no pain
At the thought of what my heart was being told.
And if you are not crying now, when do you cry?
By now they were awake, and the time was near
When food was ordinarily brought to us,
And each of them was frightened by his dream.
I heard them below, bolting up the door
Of that dreadful tower. Without a word
I looked into the faces of my sons.
I was like stone inside and could not weep. But they
Were weeping, and my Anselmuccio said:
'Father, why do you look at us that way?'
And still I did not weep, nor once reply
That entire day, nor the following night,
Till another sun had come up in the world.
As a small ray of light fell into
That miserable prison, and I could see
In those four faces what was on my own,
Out of pain I bit both my hands;
And they, thinking I did so from wanting
To eat, rose suddenly to their feet and said:
'Father, we would suffer much less
If you would eat us instead; you clothed us
In this wretched flesh; take it from us now.'
Not to make them sadder still, I calmed myself.
None of us said a word that day, nor the next.
Ah, hard, hard earth, why did you not open?
When we finally came to the fourth day,
Gaddo flung himself flat at my feet,
Saying: 'Father, why do you not help me?'

Quivi morì: e come tu mi vedi,
Vid' io cascar li tre ad uno ad uno
Tra il quinto dì e il sesto: ond' io mi diedi
Già cieco a brancolar sopra ciascuno,
E due dì li chiamai poi che fur morti:
Poscia, più che il dolor, potè il digiuno.'
Quand' ebbe detto ciò, con gli occhi torti
Riprese il teschio misero coi denti,
Che furo all' osso, come d' un can, forti.
Ahi Pisa, vituperio delle genti
Del bel paese là, dove il sì suona;
Poi che i vicini a te punir son lenti,
Movasi la Caprara e la Gorgona,
E faccian siepe ad Arno in sulla foce,
Sì ch' egli anneghi in te ogni persona.
Chè se il Conte Ugolino aveva voce
D' aver tradita te delle castella,
Non dovei tu i figliuoi porre a tal croce.
Innocenti facea l' età novella,
Novella Tebe, Uguccione e il Brigata,
E gli altri due che il canto suso appella.
Noi passamm' oltre, là 've la gelata
Ruvidamente un' altra gente fascia,
Non volta in giù, ma tutta riversata.
Lo pianto stesso lì pianger non lascia,
E il duol, che trova in sugli occhi rintoppo,
Si volve in entro a far crescer l' ambascia:
Chè le lagrime prime fanno groppo,
E, sì come visiere di cristallo,
Riempion sotto il ciglio tutto il coppo.
Ed avvegna che, sì come d' un callo,
Per la freddura ciascun sentimento
Cessato avesse del mio viso stallo,
Già mi parea sentire alquanto vento;
Perch' io: 'Maestro mio, questo chi move?
Non è quaggiù ogni vapore spento?'
Ond' egli a me: 'Avaccio sarai dove
Di ciò ti farà l' occhio la risposta,
Veggendo la cagion che il fiato piove.'

With that he died; and, just as you now see me,
I saw the other three drop one by one
Between the fifth and sixth day, when, blind by now,
I began to stumble over all of them.
For two days after they died I called their names;
In the end starvation did what grief could not."
Having said this, and with a wild look in his eyes,
He seized the hateful skull again with his teeth,
Which, like a dog's, were strongest at the bone.
Ah, Pisa, anathema to the people
Of the fair land where the sound of *sì* is heard!
Because your neighbors are slow to punish you,
May the isles of Capraia and Gorgona
Move, and like a hedge dam up the Arno's mouth,
And drown every one of your inhabitants!
Even if Count Ugolino was reported
To have defrauded you of fortresses,
You had no right to put his children to such torture.
Their tender age, O newest Thebes, made Brigata
And Uguccione, and the other two
Named in my song above, all innocent."
We journeyed further on to where the ice
Roughly swaddled still another people.
These were not bowed down, but lay upon their backs.
Their very tears would not let them weep,
For sorrow, which found no outlet through their eyes,
Recoiled and heightened the distress within.
The tears would form at first into a cluster,
Then, as if they were a vizor made of crystal,
Fill up the hollows underneath the brows.
And it happened that, although the cold
Had banished every trace of feeling from
My face, exactly as a callus might,
I now began to feel a little wind
And so I said: "Master, where does this blow from?
Is not everything that blows extinguished here?"
To which he replied to me: "Presently
You shall be where your eyes will give the answer
And know the reason why this breath pours down."

Ed un de' tristi della fredda crosta
Gridò a noi: 'O anime crudeli
Tanto, che data v' è l' ultima posta,
Levatemi dal viso i duri veli,
Sì ch' io sfoghi il dolor che il cor m' impregna,
Un poco, pria che il pianto si raggeli.'
Perch' io a lui: 'Se vuoi ch' io ti sovvegna,
Dimmi chi sei, e s' io non ti disbrigo,
Al fondo della ghiaccia ir mi convegna.'
Rispose adunque: 'Io son Frate Alberigo,
Io son quel delle frutta del mal orto,
Che qui riprendo dattero per figo.'
'O,' diss' io lui: 'Or sei tu ancor morto?'
Ed egli a me: 'Come il mio corpo stea
Nel mondo su, nulla scienza porto.
Cotal vantaggio ha questa Tolomea,
Che spesse volte l' anima ci cade
Innanzi ch' Atropòs mossa le dea.
E perchè tu più volentier mi rade
Le invetriate lagrime dal volto,
Sappi che tosto che l' anima trade,
Come fec' io, il corpo suo l' è tolto
Da un demonio, che poscia il governa
Mentre che il tempo suo tutto sia volto.
Ella ruina in sì fatta cisterna;
E forse pare ancor lo corpo suso
Dell' ombra che di qua retro mi verna.
Tu il dei saper, se tu vien pur mo giuso:
Egli è Ser Branca d' Oria, e son più anni
Poscia passati ch' ei fu sì racchiuso.'
'Io credo,' diss' io lui, 'che tu m' inganni;
Chè Branca d' Oria non morì unquanche,
E mangia e bee e dorme e veste panni.'
'Nel fosso su,' diss' ei, 'di Malebranche,
Là dove bolle la tenace pece,
Non era giunto ancora Michel Zanche,
Che questi lasciò un diavolo in sua vece
Nel corpo suo, ed un suo prossimano
Che il tradimento insieme con lui fece.

And one of the sad souls on that cold crust
Cried out to us: "You spirits, so cruel
That the last place has been given to you,
Lift from my face these hardened veils,
That the pain which crowds my heart may find some small
Relief before the tears are ice again!"
To which I answered: "If you want my help,
Tell me who you are, and if I fail to help,
May the bottom of the ice be my fate."
He answered: "I am Brother Alberigo,
He of the fruits of that bad orchard
Who for my figs have been repaid with dates."
"O," I said to him, "are you dead already?"
And he: "What the condition of my body
In the world is, I have no way of knowing.
Such advantage has this Ptolomaea
That often a soul plunges into it
Long before Atropos gives it a push.
And, that you may more readily erase
From my face the tears that are like glass,
Know that the moment any soul betrays,
As I did, its body is snatched from it
By a demon, who then dominates it
Till its allotted time has run out
And it tumbles down into this cistern.
Perhaps the body of this shade wintering
Here behind me is still to be seen above.
You must know, if you have just come down,
That he is Ser Branca d'Oria, and
Many years have passed since he was thus confined."
"I think you are deceiving me," I said,
Because Branca d'Oria has not died,
But eats and drinks and sleeps and still wears clothes."
"In the abyss above Malebranche,"
He said, "where the clinging pitch is seething,
Michel Zanche had not as yet arrived,
When this one left a devil in his place
In his own body, and a relative's,
Who committed that betrayal with him.

Ma distendi oramai in qua la mano,
Aprimi gli occhi:' ed io non gliele apersi,
E cortesia fu in lui esser villano.
Ahi Genovesi, uomini diversi
D' ogni costume, e pien d' ogni magagna,
Perchè non siete voi del mondo spersi?
Chè col peggiore spirto di Romagna
Trovai di voi un tal, che per sua opra
In anima in Cocito già si bagna,
Ed in corpo par vivo ancor di sopra.

Now stretch out your hand to me and open up
My eyes." But I did not open them for him:
To be mean to him was courtesy itself.
Ah, you Genoese, you men without morals
And full of every kind of rottenness,
Why have you not been exiled from the world?
For with the vilest spirit of Romagna
I found a certain one of you whose soul,
For what he did, already bathes in Cocytus,
Though his body in the world still seems alive.

XXXIV

'VEXILLA Regis prodeunt inferni
Verso di noi: però dinanzi mira,'
Disse il Maestro mio, 'se tu il discerni.'
Come quando una grossa nebbia spira,
O quando l' emisperio nostro annotta,
Par da lungi un molin che il vento gira;
Veder mi parve un tal 'dificio allotta:
Poi per lo vento mi ristrinsi retro
Al Duca mio; chè non gli era altra grotta.
Già era (e con paura il metto in metro)
Là dove l' ombre eran tutte coperte,
E trasparean come festuca in vetro.
Altre sono a giacere, altre stanno erte,
Quella col capo, e quella con le piante;
Altra, com' arco, il volto a' piedi inverte.
Quando noi fummo fatti tanto avante,
Ch' al mio Maestro piacque di mostrarmi
La creatura ch' ebbe il bel sembiante,
Dinanzi mi si tolse, e fe' restarmi,
'Ecco Dite,' dicendo, 'ed ecco il loco,
Ove convien che di fortezza t' armi.'
Com' io divenni allor gelato e fioco,
Nol domandar, Lettor, ch' io non lo scrivo,
Però ch' ogni parlar sarebbe poco.
Io non morii, e non rimasi vivo:
Pensa oramai per te, s' hai fior d' ingegno,
Qual io divenni, d' uno e d' altro privo.
Lo imperador del doloroso regno
Da mezzo il petto uscia fuor della ghiaccia;
E più con un gigante io mi convegno,

34

"THE BANNERS OF THE KING OF HELL are moving
Towards us," my master said to me.
"Look straight ahead and maybe you will see him."
Sometimes, when a heavy mist blows away
Or when night overtakes our hemisphere,
In the distance a windmill starts to turn:
Such was the structure that I thought I saw,
And, since there was no shelter from the wind
In that place, I fell back against my guide.
I now was where—and with fear I put it down
In meter—the shades were covered, and yet
Were all as visible as straw in glass.
Some lay on their backs; some were standing up,
That one on his head, another on his feet.
One looked like a bow, his face bent to his feet.
When we had gone far enough ahead,
It pleased my master to point out to me
The creature that had once been beautiful.
As he moved to one side in front of me,
He stopped me, saying: "Here is Dis, the place
Where you must arm yourself with strength and courage."
Reader, do not inquire how frozen stiff
And faint I became; I shall not write it down;
Whatever might be said would be too little.
I did not die, nor was I still alive!
If you have any imagination, think
What I was, being neither this nor that.
The emperor of the woeful kingdom
Was standing in the ice up to his breast;
And I am closer to a giant in size

The emperor of the woeful kingdom
Was standing in the ice up to his breast

Che i giganti non fan con le sue braccia:
Vedi oramai quant' esser dee quel tutto
Ch' a così fatta parte si confaccia.
S' ei fu sì bel com' egli è ora brutto,
E contra il suo Fattore alzò le ciglia,
Ben dee da lui procedere ogni lutto.
O quanto parve a me gran maraviglia,
Quando vidi tre facce alla sua testa!
L' una dinanzi, e quella era vermiglia;
L' altre eran due, che s' aggiungieno a questa
Sopr' esso il mezzo di ciascuna spalla,
E si giungieno al loco della cresta;
E la destra parea tra bianca e gialla;
La sinistra a vedere era tal, quali
Vengon di là, onde il Nilo s' avvalla.
Sotto ciascuna uscivan due grandi ali,
Quanto si convenia a tanto uccello;
Vele di mar non vid' io mai cotali.
Non avean penne, ma di vipistrello
Era lor modo; e quelle svolazzava,
Sì che tre venti si movean da ello.
Quindi Cocito tutto s' aggelava:
Con sei occhi piangeva, e per tre menti
Gocciava il pianto e sanguinosa bava.
Da ogni bocca dirompea coi denti
Un peccatore, a guisa di maciulla,
Sì che tre ne facea così dolenti.
A quel dinanzi il mordere era nulla
Verso il graffiar, che tal volta la schiena
Rimanea della pelle tutta brulla.
'Quell' anima lassù che ha maggior pena,'
Disse il Maestro, 'è Giuda Scariotto,
Che il capo ha dentro, e fuor le gambe mena.
Degli altri due ch' hanno il capo di sotto,
Quei che pende dal nero ceffo è Bruto:
Vedi come si storce, e non fa motto:
E l' altro è Cassio, che par sì membruto.
Ma la notte risurge; ed oramai
E' da partir, che tutto avem veduto.'

Than giants themselves are to his arms.
You see how large the whole of him must be,
If it is in proportion to that part.
If he was as fair as he is ugly now,
And yet raised his brows against his Maker,
Every sorrow must indeed come from him.
What a fantastic thing it seemed to me
When I saw there were three faces to his head!
The color of the one in front was red.
Just over the middle of each shoulder
The two other faces were attached to this,
And all three joined together at the head.
The right one seemed between white and yellow,
While the left one, to look at, was the hue
Of those who come from where the Nile descends.
Two huge wings issued from under each of them,
Of the right magnitude for such a bird.
Sails of the sea I never saw like these.
They had no feathers on them, but were fashioned
Like a bat's, and he kept flapping them
In such a way that three winds blew from him.
That was why all Cocytus was frozen.
With his six eyes he wept, and down three chins
There dribbled tears and bloody slobbering.
From every mouth he slashed a sinner
With his teeth, as if they were a hackle,
Thus keeping three suffering at a time.
To the one in front, the biting was nothing
Compared to the rending, for sometimes the skin
Was ripped away completely from his back.
"That soul up there in greatest torment, who has
His head inside and outside shakes his legs,"
My master said, "is Judas Iscariot.
Of the other two, who have their heads below,
The one swinging from the black face is Brutus;
Look how he twists and turns and yet says nothing.
The other is Cassius, of sturdy limb.
But night is coming up again; the time
Has come to leave. We have seen all there is."

Com' a lui piacque, il collo gli avvinghiai;
Ed ei prese di tempo e loco poste:
E quando l' ali furo aperte assai,
Appigliò sè alle vellute coste:
Di vello in vello giù discese poscia
Tra il folto pelo e le gelate croste.
Quando noi fummo là dove la coscia
Si volge appunto in sul grosso dell' anche,
Lo Duca con fatica a con angoscia
Volse la testa ov' egli avea le zanche,
Ed aggrappossi al pel come uom che sale,
Sì che in inferno io credea tornar anche.
'Attienti ben, chè per sì fatte scale,'
Disse il Maestro, ansando com' uom lasso,
'Conviensi dipartir da tanto male.'
Poi uscì fuor per lo foro d' un sasso,
E pose me in sull' orlo a sedere:
Appresso porse a me l' accorto passo.
Io levai gli occhi, e credetti vedere
Lucifero com' io l' avea lasciato,
E vidili le gambe in su tenere.
E s' io divenni allora travagliato,
La gente grossa il pensi, che non vede
Qual è quel punto ch' io avea passato.
'Levati su,' disse il Maestro, 'in piede:
La via è lunga e il cammino è malvagio,
E già il sole a mezza terza riede.'
Non era camminata di palagio
Là 'v' eravam, ma natural burella
Ch' avea mal suolo e di lume disagio.
'Prima ch' io dell' abisso mi divella,
Maestro mio,' diss' io quando fui dritto,
'A trarmi d' erro un poco mi favella.
Ov' è la ghiaccia? e questi com' è fitto
Sì sottosopra? e come in sì poc' ora
Da sera a mane ha fatto il sol tragitto?'
Ed egli a me: 'Tu immagini ancora
D' esser di là dal centro, ov' io mi presi
Al pel del vermo reo che il mondo fora.

At his wish, I clasped my arms about his neck,
And he, choosing the right place and moment,
When all the wings were spread wide apart,
Fastened himself upon the shaggy flanks
And started climbing down from tuft to tuft,
Between the thick hair and the frozen scabs.
When at length we came to the place
Where the thigh turns upon the bulging hip,
My guide, with effort and concern, reversed
His head to where his feet had been
And gripped the hair like someone climbing, so that
I thought that we were going back to Hell.
"Take hold firmly," said my master to me,
Panting like a man exhausted. "By way of
These stairs shall we leave all this woe behind."
He went out through an opening in a rock
And, stepping with great caution for my sake,
He then set me down on the edge of it.
I raised my eyes, believing I would see
Lucifer exactly as I had left him,
But saw him with his legs turned up instead.
Let all crude people, who do not realize
What the juncture was that I had reached,
Imagine how bewildered I became.
"Get on your feet," my master said to me.
"The way is long, and the traveling will be hard,
And the sun has come back to the middle third."
It was no palatial promenade, the place
Where we were standing, but a natural dungeon
With an evil floor and no light at all.
"Before I uproot myself from this abyss,
O master," I said, when I had risen,
"Say a few words to rid me of some doubts.
Where is the ice? And how does this one happen
To be standing on his head? And how has the sun
Made its trip so fast from night to morning."
And he to me: "You still seem to think that
You are on that side of the center where I grasped
The hair of the vile worm that perforates the world.

Di là fosti cotanto quant' io scesi:
Quando mi volsi, tu passasti il punto
Al qual si traggon d' ogni parte i pesi:
E se' or sotto l' emisperio giunto
Ch' è contrapposto a quel che la gran secca
Coperchia, e sotto il cui colmo consunto
Fu l' uom che nacque e visse senza pecca:
Tu hai li piedi in su picciola spera
Che l' altra faccia fa della Giudecca.
Qui è da man quando di là è sera:
E questi che ne fe' scala col pelo,
Fitto è ancora, sì come prim' era.
Da questa parte cadde giù dal cielo:
E la terra che pria di qua si sporse
Per paura di lui fe' del mar velo,
E venne all' emisperio nostro; a forse
Per fuggir lui lasciò qui il loco voto
Quella che appar di qua, e su ricorse.'
Loco è laggiù da Belzebù remoto
Tanto, quanto la tomba si distende,
Che non per vista, ma per suono è noto
D' un ruscelletto che quivi discende
Per la buca d' un sasso, ch' egli ha roso
Col corso ch' egli avvolge, e poco pende.
Lo Duca ed io per quel cammino ascoso
Entrammo a ritornar nel chiaro mondo:
E senza cura aver d' alcun riposo
Salimmo suso, ei primo ed io secondo,
Tanto ch' io vidi delle cose belle
Che porta il ciel, per un pertugio tondo;
E quindi uscimmo a riveder le stelle.

You were on that side, but only coming down.
When I reversed myself, you passed the point
Towards which, from every side, all weights are pulled.
You have now arrived below the hemisphere
Which is directly opposite to that which
Covers the great dryness, and beneath whose top
Was slain He who was born and lived without sin.
Your feet are resting on a little disc
Which is the other face of Giudecca.
It is morning here, when it is evening there,
And this one, who made a ladder for us
Of his hair, is still stuck as he was before.
It was in this place that he fell from Heaven;
And the land, which up to then extended out,
Made a veil of the sea out of fear of him
And moved to our hemisphere. And, perhaps
To escape him, the land we see from here
Left behind this hollow and sped upwards."
There is a place below, as distant from
Beelzebub as the full length of his tomb,
Known not by sight but only by the sound
Of a small rivulet flowing down along
The crevice of a stone eroded
By its winding course that slopes but little.
Along that secret path, my guide and I
Began our journey back to the bright world;
And, without thought of pausing for a rest,
We kept climbing up, he first, I second,
Until, through a round opening, I glimpsed
Some of the beautiful things the sky carries:
And then we came out to see the stars again.

Notes

1. Meant, possibly, to be Hebrew: "Here Satan, here Satan rules."
2. Old Bolognese for later form, *sia*, "yes."
3 and 4. Both mean "now" *issa* being Lucchese.